Culture, Power and Difference: Discourse analysis in South Africa

Culture, Power and Difference:
Discourse analysis in South Africa

edited by

Ann Levett, Amanda Kottler,
Erica Burman and Ian Parker

Zed Books Ltd
LONDON & NEW JERSEY

University of Cape Town Press
CAPE TOWN

Culture, Power and Difference: Discourse analysis in South Africa
was first published by Zed Books Ltd, 7 Cynthia Street,
London N1 9JF, UK, and 165 First Avenue, Atlantic
Highlands, New Jersey 07716, USA in 1997.

Published in Southern Africa by University of Cape Town
Press (Pty) Ltd, Private Bag, Rondebosch 7700, South Africa.

Cover designed by Andrew Corbett
Set in Monotype Garamond by Ewan Smith
Printed and bound in the United Kingdom
by Biddles Ltd, Guildford and King's Lynn

A catalogue record for this book is available from the British
Library

Library of Congress Cataloging-in-Publication Data

Culture, power, and difference : discourse analysis in South
   Africa / edited by Ann Levett ... [et al.]
         p.   cm.
   Based on papers originally presented at a discourse
analysis workshop.
   Includes bibliographical references and index.
   ISBN 1-85649-471-3 (hb). — ISBN 1-85649-472-1 (pb)
   1. Discourse analysis—Social aspects—South Africa.
   2. South Africa—Social conditions—1961–   I. Levett, Ann,
   1935–   .
   P302.84.C85   1997
   401'.41'0968–dc20   96–28127
                                                          CIP

ISBN 1 85649 471 3 cased
ISBN 1 85649 472 1 limp
ISBN 1 919713 08 5 Southern Africa

Contents

Notes on contributors

Jane Foress Bennett obtained her Ed.D. from Columbia University, and has taught linguistics, literature and women's studies at universities in New York and in South Africa. She is currently programme director at the African Gender Institute of the University of Cape Town, where her research and action focuses on the prevention of sexual harassment and sexual violence in Southern Africa.

Jocelyn Blumberg studied psychology at the University of Cape Town. After her studies she worked for the Independent Electoral Commission, helping to organize the first democratic election in South Africa. She then furthered her education travelling through Eastern Europe and India, and now lives in London, where she works for a marketing company.

Erica Burman is a senior lecturer in psychology in the Discourse Unit at Manchester Metropolitan University, and has written about connections between discourse analysis and feminism. She is editor of *Feminists and Psychological Practice* (Sage, 1990), co-editor of *Discourse Analytic Research* (Routledge, 1993), author of *Deconstructing Developmental Psychology* (Routledge, 1994) and co-author of *Qualitative Methods in Psychology* (Open University Press, 1994).

Anthony Collins is a critical theorist and performance artist. Having taught psychology at Rhodes University and the University of Witwatersrand, he is now a Fulbright Scholar in the history of consciousness Ph.D. programme at the University of California, Santa Cruz. His current work includes post-structuralist readings of psychology and a critical social psychology of violence in South Africa.

Cheryl de la Rey, at the time of the Discourse Analysis Workshop, was a member of the Psychology Department, University of Durban-Westville. In 1995 she joined the Psychology Department, University of Cape Town. Her areas of academic interest are race, racism and gender studies. She has a history of activism in feminist politics, and she is a member of the editorial collective of *Agenda: A Journal about Women and Gender*.

John Dixon is a lecturer in psychology at the Worcester College of Higher Education, UK, and before that, at the time of the Discourse Analysis Workshop, was a lecturer in psychology at the University of Cape Town.

He has published research on the psychology of intergroup relations and the analysis of racist discourse. His Ph.D. work concerns the social construction of place and identity within discourse about South Africa's 'squatter crisis'.

Kevin Durrheim has lectured on courses in social psychology and discourse analysis in the Department of Psychology at the University of Cape Town and now teaches at the University of Natal, Pietermaritzburg. He is interested in political rhetoric and his particular bugbear is the neo-conservative elements in 'peace psychology'.

Kevin Kelly is a clinical psychologist and senior lecturer in the Department of Psychology at Rhodes University, Grahamstown, South Africa. His principal interests are psychology in public health, research methodology and community clinical psychology.

Amanda Kottler is a lecturer and clinical psychologist in the Department of Psychology and a founding member of the Discourse Unit in this Department at the University of Cape Town. She has written about the dilemmas facing progressive psychologists working within the multiple and contradictory discourses of race and identity in apartheid South Africa, and is currently involved in innovative multidisciplinary action research on sexual harassment in institutional settings. She is co-editor of the 1995 special issue of the *South African Journal of Psychology* on 'Postmodernism and Psychology'.

Natalie Leon was a lay counsellor with Rape Crisis, Cape Town. She studied at the Universities of the Western Cape and Cape Town, where she received an MA (Clin.Psych.) in 1991. She has since worked at the Avalon Treatment Centre for substance abuse and at the local state psychiatric hospital, Valkenberg. She is now a community clinical psychologist with Valkenberg and maintains her interest in research on gender violence.

Ann Levett is a clinical psychologist and discourse analytic researcher whose main occupation currently is as a psychotherapist. She came to discourse analysis through the bewildering uncharted seas of experience in recent South African social history, as a white and middle-class lesbian feminist. She retired from the University of Cape Town in 1996 to enter full-time therapy practice.

Carol Long studied psychology at the University of Cape Town, graduating in 1994. She has worked as a tutor in the department of psychology for a number of years. She has also been actively involved in Rape Crisis, Cape Town. She is currently in training as a clinical psychologist at the University of Cape Town.

Pindile Mabena grew up and attended school in Soweto and came to the

University of Cape Town for further studies. Awarded an MA in 1994 for work on the educational experiences of black South African students at a white university, she is now working in the business world. She lives in Johannesburg.

Trevor Mulder lives in Cape Town, where he works as a business analyst. His activities include lobbying government to retain equal rights for lesbians and gay men in the new Constitution, working with men's encounter groups and writing film music.

Nomsa Ngqakayi-Motaung conducts educational research for the Academic Development Programme at the University of Witwatersrand. She was previously attached to the Department of Psychology at the University of Cape Town, where she worked in the area of health research. She has an MA (Clin.Psych.) from UCT.

Ian Parker is professor of psychology in the Discourse Unit at Bolton Institute, and has written about theories of discourse and subjectivity. He is author of *The Crisis in Modern Social Psychology* (Routledge, 1989) and *Discourse Dynamics* (Routledge, 1992), co-author of *Qualitative Methods in Psychology* (Open University Press, 1994) and *Carrying out Investigations in Psychology* (British Psychological Society, 1995).

Judith Soal studied psychology at the University of Cape Town, after working for a number of years as a computer programmer. She then joined the Medical Research Council, evaluating services available to people living with HIV and Aids. She now works as a journalist at a Cape Town daily newspaper.

Anna Strebel is a senior lecturer in the Psychology Department at the University of the Western Cape. She is involved in the training of clinical and research psychology students and also teaches in a women and gender studies post-graduate programme. Her current interests are in women's mental health and abuse, AIDS prevention, gender and research methodology.

Martin Terre Blanche is a lecturer in the Department of Psychology at the University of South Africa. He has been involved in a variety of community projects and has co-authored a number of papers on postmodernity, qualitative methods, oral history, psychiatry and community psychology.

Hilda van Vlaenderen is a research psychologist and lecturer in the Department of Psychology, Rhodes University, Grahamstown, South Africa. She has a particular interest in participatory research methodology, psychological issues relating to community development in rural contexts, and in organizational development in non-governmental and community-based organizations.

Nomfundo Walaza received an MA (Clin.Psych.) degree at the University of Cape Town in 1991. She currently is coordinator of the Urban Violence Project at the Trauma Centre for Victims of Violence and Torture, Cape Town. This work is geared toward establishing community partnership programmes that will assist victims of violence in urban settings. Her current research interests concern the effects of violence on women and children and the presentation of post-traumatic stress disorder within an African context.

Lindy Wilbraham is a lecturer in social psychology at the University of Durban-Westville in KwaZulu-Natal. Combining interests in postmodernism, feminism and community empowerment, her current research is concerned with talking with women from varieties of racial, class and cultural backgrounds about their bodies, their 'selves' and their relationships; and in collaboratively workshopping sex educational programmes for black adolescents in semi-rural schools in KwaZulu-Natal.

CHAPTER I

Power and discourse: culture and change in South Africa

Erica Burman, Amanda Kottler,
Ann Levett and Ian Parker

This book brings together a set of critical discussions about discourse in a South Africa on the brink of transition from the regime of apartheid towards black majority democratic rule. The papers that form the basis of this book were originally presented at a Discourse Analysis workshop organized by Ann Levett and Amanda Kottler from the Department of Psychology, University of Cape Town in 1994. Erica Burman and Ian Parker were participants in this workshop. The discourse workshop was timed also to coincide with the Psychology and Social Transformation conference, a historic occasion designed to mark the end of PASA (Psychological Association of South Africa), the old psychology organization which was complicit with apartheid, and the beginning of something better. It is fitting, therefore, to open this book by con-textualizing debates about the relevance of discourse to social relations, and in particular the specific 'take' on these issues warranted by the South African context.

Discourse and power

Across the social and human sciences, and across a range of political, geographical and intellectual arenas, discourse perspectives have emerged as a means of addressing the structuring effects of language, and of connecting institutional power relations with talk. The turn to the text, the concern with the textually mediated character of experience and action, have been associated with a range of political and academic positions. In this book, discourse perspectives have been taken up to connect analyses of practice – whether research, policy, politics, mass media or everyday talk – with the cultural-political contexts that produce them. While we acknowledge the political ambiguities of some varieties of discourse work, and the way these may either encourage a focus on the reproduction of global relations of power in local practices or simply allow new forms of colonialism to spread within the rhetoric of 'postmodernity' or 'postcoloniality', this book indicates how such work can provide a facilitating framework for *critical* intervention and *radical* political engagement.

While informed by a variety of perspectives, and associated with a range of different theorists, what the works that fall within the rubric of 'discourse' have in common is a deconstruction of the opposition between ideology and subjectivity, of the workings of power as if they were external and incomprehensible to the deluded, falsely conscious, individual. Rather than positing an autonomous sphere of either genuine or misguided human experience and relations nestling beneath a conspiring state apparatus, discourse work departs from such a static, structural account to explore how acts of power are *performed*, and the *conditions* which allow these acts to work. The critique here is double edged: first, there is no safe retreat into authentic experience to escape the insidious regimes of truth that institutions construct; but, second, such institutions and their powers of regulation and evaluation are no longer accorded so absolute a determination of our action as to make resistance hopeless. If, as Foucault (1980) suggests, power is *productive* rather than only repressive, then it becomes an urgent political project to document and theorize the field of action and modes of resistance possible within prevailing social arrangements. For it is by attending to these things that change becomes possible.

Most of the contributors to this book directly use, or are influenced by, approaches in discourse analysis that draw upon the work of Michel Foucault. Foucault's analysis of modern culture is invaluable for analysing discourse, and it is peculiarly appropriate for the analysis of discourse in psychology. South African apartheid culture often prided itself on being independent, but it was, at the same time, a particularly vicious manifestation of Western *modern* culture. Foucauldian discourse analytic approaches allow us to connect directly with issues of power and subjectification. These approaches help us to address how we are made into selves that speak, how we *experience* the self as if it were an individual enclosed thing, and the way in which modes of disciplinary apparatus govern us. They are also particularly useful for examining the circulation of psychological talk through culture. Foucault provides an analysis of discipline (how we are observed and regulated) and confession (how we are compelled to reveal ourselves) as the double operation that holds and mobilizes us as subjects in this society (Foucault, 1975, 1976). When this is combined with the description of the 'psy-complex' that has been elaborated by writers using his work (Ingleby, 1985; Rose, 1985), it makes for a critical version of discourse analysis in qualitative research.

By the 'psy-complex' we mean the network of psychological discourses and practices that regulates us as subjects and incites us to look deep within to find a truth. Psychology in South Africa has been deeply complicit with this apparatus, in the apartheid psychology associations and in the activities of psychologists trying to persuade the subjects of apartheid of the 'truth' of their racial differences. There is, in this complex, a web of accounts of subjectivity that we must experience in the depths of our selves as true before we can be accorded rights within its institutions. Those rights may either be accorded to us as subjects of the psychological gaze when we are 'users' of psychology services, or as agents within the institution when we work as researchers and teachers. In either case, Foucault reminds us that it is not enough simply to speak the right language, to participate in the appropriate discourses. We must also find the *truth* of psychological statements within ourselves. Many of the chapters in this book illustrate the way racial and sexual categories are not simply imposed, but are lived out by their subjects as 'true' for them. Some of the discourses that comprise the psy-complex are powerful in encouraging us to participate as actors and subjects *in* psychology, and our contributors trace the way some of these discourses work in the course of the book.

Power, as Foucault (1980) was quick to remind us, is not the exercise of some dramatic force emanating from a single point at the apex of the state. The power of apartheid was relayed through millions of channels of communication, from the government-controlled media through to everyday conversation. Power is, rather, a function of a multiplicity of discursive practices that fabricates and positions subjects. We have taken some care in this book to focus on the different varieties of oppression that together locked people into systems of power under apartheid, and that still function in the 'new' South Africa.

When we use Foucauldian discourse analysis as psychologists – and it is worth remembering that Foucault himself was a psychologist (Parker, 1995) – we also need to turn around and reflect upon the discursive practices that lock psychology into the wider psy-complex. Foucault's account of the development of modernity, and of a type of subject fit to drive it, is in many ways *anti-psychological* in the sense that we would usually understand psychology within the discipline. He talks of the way in which language and identity are historically given, fragmented and performative, arguing, for example that 'we are difference, that our reason is the difference of discourses, our history the difference of times, our selves the difference of masks' (Foucault, 1969: 131). Foucauldian discourse analysis, then, unravels notions of identity that we normally take for granted, and it opens texts up in three kinds of ways: first to analyse how they construct images of the self as if it were something coherent; second to explore how those images function to reproduce certain experiences consistent with a coherent self; and third to highlight how texts themselves are riven by variation. The Foucauldian tradition of discourse analysis is conceptually powerful because it allows us to hold on to the way in which each of the three aspects of discourse identified in recent work in psychology – those of construction, function and variation (Potter and Wetherell,

1987) – is linked with *power*. The forms of discourse analysis that have drawn on Foucault's work (Burman and Parker, 1993; Parker, 1992) make that link with power, and some of the most interesting analyses of racism in discourse have addressed the way power and ideology work in everyday talk (Wetherell and Potter, 1992).

A Foucauldian view of subjectivity is of a self torn in different directions by competing discourses, and of a fragmented discursive space which sabotages the hope of internal coherence at the very moment that it attempts to grasp it. This conception of the subject as 'difference' is not, however, a simple or universal philosophical puzzle. Rather, it emerges from an historical account of the intermeshing of discourses with power. For Foucault (1980), power is not only coercive, but also productive of kinds of relationship and experience. Our own investment in the discourses is emphasized when we consider who would promote and who would oppose these discourses. Foucault's histories of surveillance and confession do not necessarily lead to the view that psychological and psycho-therapeutic forms of discourse are bad, but a historical reflection does help us to locate the images of the self that those modern discourses carry with them. With these general considerations in mind, we should briefly enter a note of caution. It is true that discourse analysis applied to any text threatens to naturalize patterns of language just as efficiently as, for example, therapeutic discourses (Parker and Burman, 1993), and it is worth keeping in mind its role as a strategic intervention in the politics of the psy-complex rather than as the revelation of truth. However, psychological discourses thread their way through culture, and Foucauldian theory does help us throw them into question. By such means it is possible to reflect upon our own commitment to individual, psychological dis-courses and the way they operate both as empowering stories and as prisons of subjectivity.

Power in South Africa

The chapters in this book address the hold that apartheid and its corollaries have exercised in a wide range of arenas, and they document some of the consequences of dismantling it. You will read, for example, about the prevalence of racialized descriptions in mental health records, and the complexities of the process of developing a policy against racial harass-ment in which the institutional imperative works to impose precisely those closures over issues of definition and identification that the policy-makers aimed to avoid. The chapters range from a consideration of issues of trust and accountability in community development, to the subtleties of translation and culturally specific meanings in understandings of sexual abuse. But more than this, the chapters highlight something of the over-whelming, far-reaching ways in which the apartheid regime defined the array of possible meanings and relationships. All social categories have functioned in its grim shadow.

This book therefore provides a unique and specific window onto a moment of great significance in South Africa. It also demonstrates how sets of meanings that maintain oppression are under contest and in flux within a changing political context. As such, these chapters provide a vital inspirational document of a society in transition, and explore issues that are also of general significance to researchers concerned with the way in which language reproduces culture and power.

The power relations that were institutionalized through government and civil society in South Africa over the course of the last 350 years remain in residual forms even today, although since 1994 (when the first democratic elections took place in South Africa) there have been some beginnings of change. The domination of local communities and groups by colonialist and expansionist enterprise, which originated in Holland and England, was characterized by the so-called Enlightenment systems of knowledge. These were associated with the technical developments of Europe (and, later, the USA) which depended in part on the use of raw and processed natural resources, unskilled and semi-skilled labour, and an increasing emphasis on the individual. With the consequent accumulation of wealth to a small number of individuals and groups of merchants, dominant systems of knowledge focused increasingly on technology and control. The control of wealth rapidly evolved through expanding specializations which became branches of the sciences, and later the social sciences. Boundary and population control became very important, to ensure bureaucracies of entitlement to certain natural resources and to pools of cheap labour. It is not surprising to reflect that, against this background, peoples of Southern Africa and other subjugated parts of the world were regarded as 'lesser' in various ways than the wealthy, modernity-skilled and literate colonizing forces. Certain ways of thinking about everyday life, work, relationships and aspirations have become hegemonic in the sense that they dominate our lives. Until recently, racist discrimination was justified through statutory legislation in South Africa as part of a particular set of colonialist discourses, but the pervasive notions of self, Other and legitimacy that saturate racist ideas and behaviour will long outlive the dismantling of apartheid. In this respect South Africa has represented what is perhaps an extreme case of colonialist exploitation. For the critical social scientist (attentive to issues of power and to the conflicts and contradictions of subjectivity), daily life is shot through with constant sharp reminders of past and continuing unequal access to resources.

However, certain points require discussion and emphasis because they are so contradictory in contemporary South Africa, where a significant agenda is racial reconciliation. In debates over the last decade arguments have been presented for the importance and value of 'indigenous knowledges' and the 'Africanization' of theory and practice in the health professions. In the 'global village' the accumulation of cultural and material wealth is facilitated by literacy, communication via Euro-American languages, and styles of business and interpersonal practice. In order to participate successfully in the national and international arena it seemed to be common sense to adapt to these hegemonic discourses that dominate world markets. These include the academic and intellectual markets. The production and reproduction of internationally 'acceptable' theory and practice are closely linked with the globalization of modern forms of knowledge. On the other hand, in contemporary South Africa 'experience on the ground' is what counts: and if you are 'white – [you'll] never get it right'. A local journalist, Mark Gevisser, following up on a recent major confrontation at the University of Witwatersrand, profiled a number of the 'new South African elite'. He comments:

> It was sobering, though, to hear how central race was to their work, whether they saw themselves as Africanists, humanists, communists, conciliators or any combination thereof. Most of the non-African people I interviewed – progressive or otherwise – made it clear that race (the 'national question' as the ANC called it when still in exile) was still the major issue they needed to confront. Minorities and majorities respectively, both were, in part, talking to their own interests. In contrast to the 'we're all the same under our skin' universalism rooted in both the dogma of hard lefties and the sentimentality of soft liberals – there is a centrality of race-identity to the new African elite. Their fundamental rationalisation of power is the organic one, an obvious one: the assertion that because they – unlike minority intellectuals – hail from impoverished black communities, they know what's best for these communities ... New Director of Health Olive Shisana responded with appropriate indignation to the oft-repeated allegation that she was not up to the job: 'Wait a minute! Where do I come from? I come from the very people I'm trying to help! It's not academic or theoretical for me! I'm talking about my brother, my sister, my mother, my neighbour; I'm talking about the people I grew up with in Mamelodi, in Makotopong. Why do I have to prove anything beyond that? (*Weekly Mail and Guardian*, 22 December 1995: 9).

In most instances we are unaware of the ways in which our subjectivities have been formed and are maintained within contexts of familiarity. The discourses that constitute our unquestioned perceptions, languages and practices may become visible when they are disrupted by a challenge or a contradiction, or when we notice the way the workings of power play out a scenario of subjugation in the life or lives of others, or in our own.

These systems of invisible imperialism are similarly played out in academic and intellectual life. Certain ways of understanding and approaching things have been established through global hegemonies of knowledge. For example, it is well understood that research which is based on frequency counts and comparisons, and which lends itself to the identification of cause–effect links, tends to dominate the social sciences in South Africa as it does elsewhere in the world. This is because it is readily accessible to policy-shapers and easily represented in the media, where (often oversimplified) it achieves goals of comprehensibility and influences the general public. There is a limited tolerance for more complex, more self-reflexive approaches that often do not end in answering a question or clarifying a position. As academics we are expected to meet the expectations of 'providing answers' rather than expanding the list of questions. As intellectuals, then, if we wish to 'succeed' in our academic careers, we are likely to be caught up in the hegemonic discourses of positivist empiricism: in other words we are subjugated to the global tendency to support the status quo.

It has been a small group of progressive social scientists who have challenged the status quo in South Africa. An even smaller number have engaged with discourse analysis as a result of personal experience of the daily contradictions of South African life and the political violence that have been with us, around issues of 'race', class and gender, all our lives.

Discourse and psychology in South Africa

We have already mentioned how discourse perspectives portray individual experience as socially constructed. It is this resistance to individualism and humanism that makes this body of work so attractive to critical psychologists. Psychology has traditionally celebrated the freedom and autonomy of the individual, disembodied psyche as if it were separate from social relations. As such, the subject of psychology has seemed to float free of prevailing social categories and identities. Apparently devoid of race, gender, class or sexuality, psychology's subject has maintained a fiction of a subjectivity subsisting outside these categories and identities. Further, by its very ignorance of these contemporary axes of experience, it all the more subtly and effectively *re-inscribes* traditional systems of racial, cultural, gender and sexual privilege. Unless marked otherwise, the subject of psychology is assumed to be male, white, middle-class and heterosexual. Psychology's abstractions have been both historical and geographical, with its findings formulated from restricted Anglo-European and North American English-speaking samples that presume to hold good everywhere, every time.

It is therefore striking that discourse work has emerged as one of the tools in the struggle within, and for, a deeply divided discipline. In one sense discourse work inside and outside South Africa refuses the traditional distinction made between individual and society: language constitutes who we are, constructs the positions we occupy, is the medium by which we interact with other people and understand ourselves. Discourse here therefore refers to language-in-action, to sets of social practices that are linguistic, but more than 'merely' linguistic. We take discourse to mean frameworks of meaning that are realized in language but produced by institutional and ideological structures and relations. While claims vary about whether there is a 'real world' outside language, and whether it is possible to access it if there is (Parker, in press), the purpose of discourse work is to address how those institutional power relations are both reproduced and contested within more 'low-level', everyday contexts of talk and action.

It is important to comment on the existence of distinct groupings of psychologists in South Africa, separated by the apparatus of apartheid and the historical role psychological research (as a positivist enterprise) has played in supporting and maintaining the apartheid system of oppression. For example, there is a long history of research on race and its link to IQ which been challenged by critical psychologists. Attempts to counter this approach have been made by a range of progressive social scientists positioned on the other side of the apartheid divide. Various progressive psychologists drew on the work of Tajfel, and more recently on Social Identity Theory (e.g. Foster and Louw-Potgieter, 1991).

With the gradual acceptance of the need for richness and the rejection of 'value-free' scientific research, through growing political sophistication, significant methodological shifts were initiated. In one strand of this, there has been a recent and flourishing turn towards discourse analysis, particularly in Cape Town, which has a history of liberalism and a strong representation of progressive academics. Undergraduate and postgraduate courses have long had a Marxist flavour and a distinctly anti-apartheid thrust at the University of Cape Town and the University of Western Cape, as well as at various other South African universities. Discourse analysis was introduced in the late 1980s and various studies using this method were completed. The first Discourse Analysis workshop was organized in 1994 in Cape Town, and in 1995 a conference at the University of the Witwatersrand was devoted to qualitative and alternative research. Clearly these provide useful vehicles for politically informed research within psychology in South Africa. It is also noteworthy that recent issues of the *South African Journal of Psychology* have contained articles that draw on discourse analysis or examine the complexities of subjectivity. Levett and Kottler (in press) point out, however, that issues of gender have had only a nominal place in published South African research, taking a second place to the political and intellectual struggles around apartheid. Now that there is some space for this, since the official end to apartheid, one might hope for more work on gender-related issues. However, given the realities of the 'rainbow nation', issues related to ethnic difference and poverty are likely to predominate.

Some problems associated with the use of discourse analysis pose particularly exciting and potentially fruitful challenges that are not peculiar to South Africa. This approach was developed in monolinguistic contexts (in the UK, for example) where the intersection between discourse and other forms of research, such as cross-cultural work, has not been attempted. For those steeped in positivistic methods there are major problems involved in translating or transplanting this kind of research. The influence of positivist empiricism on undergraduate-level texts and understanding of psychology is related to a need for scientific certainty, authoritarian approaches to learning and beliefs in the validity of unitary subjects, objectivity and fundamental truths.

Against this background, discourse analysis is often considered to be an élitist European import. It is seen as something only white academics with privileged access to power and knowledge can do, and there is some hostility towards discourse analysis because although it addresses issues of power, it is not easily learned and understood, nor can it be readily co-opted to serve one set of interests – those of political activists, for example. Hardline political activists want and need answers to hardline questions and, indeed, often find them through straightforward positivist empiricism. It requires an investment of intellectual energy and time to get on top of discourse analysis, because it is out of line with mainstream methods. Academics in South Africa are increasingly under pressure to teach large classes, and politicians and policy-makers are under pressure to 'deliver the goods' promised in the Reconstruction and Development Programme set out before the first democratic elections. This makes the confrontation of contradictions and elaboration of understanding increasingly difficult.

It is frequently repeated that South African academics visiting other countries find the way that issues are presented, both in the media and in research, bland and unchallenging. This is not because there is no conflict or contradiction elsewhere. However, experience of violence and blatant discrimination has sensitized South Africa intellectuals. We continue to be challenged in this period of major change. Although South Africa is not a comfortable space to be in, it is fruitful for debate and research. However, we do not think South Africa is unique in these respects and expect that this book will help to inform intellectual political debates elsewhere.

Overview of the book

Having outlined the contexts and rationale for this book, we now present an overview of its key themes, with some specific comments about each chapter. The book is organized into four sections. Part One focuses on discursive expressions of the process of dismantling the apartheid regime. Part Two addresses issues of gender and sexuality in popular culture, everyday talk, counselling practice and preventative health policy. These are issues historically framed within racialized discourses, but also now asserting some autonomy from them. Part Three is concerned with particular methodological applications and problems arising from discourse analysis work in South Africa. Part Four both looks back over the chapters and reflects on the wider contexts in which they function to consider the potential of, and challenges for, this kind of work in supporting the process of change in South Africa.

The chapters in Part One explore three diverse forms of oral and written texts produced in relation to the changing landscape of racial oppression in South Africa. Apartheid is a doctrine and practice of racial segregation. Discourses about space and its ownership and occupation are therefore profoundly racialized, but the changing political context makes the markers of such racialization correspondingly shift to become coded in different ways. In Chapter 1 John Dixon discusses a corpus of text concerned with the government of space. He analyses letters published in local newspapers protesting against the development of a black 'squatter' community in one of the white villages near Cape Town. From these he identifies not only how the arguments proffered are fundamentally contradictory, but also how the ecological discourses put forward work to justify the continuing racist division of space.

Chapter 2 concerns the emergence and proliferation of 'peace talk' in politics and in the mass media during the period prior to the 1994 elections in South Africa. Adopting a Foucauldian perspective, Kevin Durrheim suggests that the peace movement functioned as a form of pastoral power, producing peace-loving subjects through dividing practices of confession and surveillance. This chapter draws links between resistance and the effects of power associated with knowledges (including psychological knowledges) of peace. Rather than being antithetical to the state of violence, Durrheim highlights the intimate relationship between peace and violence.

Moving from the analysis of media and cultural texts to their production, in Chapter 3 Amanda Kottler and Carol Long discuss the process of attempting to arrive at policies and structures for dealing with individual and institutional racism at the University of Cape Town. There is a double layering of analysis in this chapter, since it both analyses discussions held at a one-day 'racism workshop' designed to inform the policy and includes discussion of that text and of those issues by the delegates at the first Discourse Analysis workshop held at the University of Cape Town in 1994. Both sets of material are drawn upon to illustrate how well-intentioned efforts to institutionalize equal opportunities can founder by virtue of the very group and institutional processes that demanded the policies in the first place. This chapter not only indicates the reflexive nature of discourse analysis such that every analysis can be treated as material for further analysis, but also shows how this treatment may provide important resources for training and policy development.

Discourses of 'race' have formed the primary social divide in South

Africa, and other power relations, such as gender and sexuality have been structured according to this. Racialized identities are also articulated through representations of gender. A vital intervention of this book is to situate the overriding focus on race in South Africa within consideration of its connections with other forms of oppression. The material analysed in Part Two of the book graphically highlights the complexities of South Africa as a country that is both colonizer and colonized. The fact that three of the four chapters in this part concern representations of gendered subjectivities and sexuality as espoused by white women, one of whom was not even South African, is indicative of the position of feminist work. Apart from the wider problems of the ethics of the gaze (in terms of subjecting historically subordinated peoples to the scrutiny of the dominant group), it is also an accurate reflection of the circulation of Western narratives of femininity in South Africa. Here, as elsewhere in this book, it is the dominant discourses that are analysed, in the spirit of questioning and contest.

In Chapter 5, Lindy Wilbraham explores discourses of monogamy and relationship maintenance within an advice column of a magazine produced for, and by, white women. She uses these to illustrate the ways in which women are exhorted to 'work' to effect normalization in the 'crisis' of a male partner's infidelity. Thus psychologized technologies and practices produce rewards of power for subjection, and these powers are critically discussed in terms of various strategies for women's empowerment and resistance.

Spaces of resistance form the theme for Chapter 6, in Jocelyn Blumberg and Judith Soal's analysis of discussions of a group of women who identify themselves as bisexual. Within the modern era issues around sexuality and sexual practice have shifted markedly towards the social and political domains, leading to the emergence of a wide range of discourses relating to sex. The academic interest in 'sex-talk' that forms the focus of this chapter was prompted by an awareness of the authors' mutual ambivalence around the operation and effect of discourses of sexual liberation in our personal lives and their promise of social transformation. This chapter explores the dynamics of liberation and regulation in the talk of a group of women who identify themselves as bisexual and who, by forming a 'bisexual women's group', explicitly created a 'confessional' framework in which to discuss their sexuality.

While postmodernists and their fellow travellers celebrate the social construction of individual and collective histories, questions of the status of women's accounts have recently been imported into the courtroom. Efforts to legislate on the viability of recovering memories of sexual abuse in adulthood have brought feminists and false-memory supporters into conflict over radically divergent models of memory and memory-making. Jane Foress Bennett's analysis of the range of discursive and identificatory positions assumed within the narration of a personal account of sexual assault in childhood in Chapter 7 offers a valuable alternative both to the fundamentalism of memory as reflection of reality and the radical constructionism of memory as wilful, unreliable deception.

Chapter 8, by Anna Strebel, moves from a legal to health context to describe the application of a discourse analytic approach to AIDS prevention in South Africa. As elsewhere, discourses about AIDS have both ignored women and positioned them as responsible. Strebel's analyses were motivated by a commitment to work towards effective and concrete AIDS interventions. She analyses the varieties of discourses around AIDS intervention and discusses issues raised by the research process. In this we see analyses of discourse harnessed towards practical ends, in informing the development of policy and practice.

The four chapters in Part Three reflect on the challenges to the approach and the process of applying discourse analysis. Whether exploring the complexities of linguistic and cultural definitions of sexual abuse, of psychiatric description, of community development, or of homosexuality, the specific forms of these debates, and the moral-political issues encountered in addressing them form the focus.

In Chapter 9, Ann Levett, Amanda Kottler and their co-authors (Pindi Mabena, Nomfundo Walaza, Natalie Leon and Nomsa Ngqakayi) use brief vignettes of common situations of child sexual abuse as a focusing device. The interviews were conducted with indigenous language-speaking, working-class (minimally educated) South African women, in their home languages, to elicit 'local knowledge' about child sexual abuse. The audio-taped interviews (in Xhosa, Zulu, Sotho and Afrikaans) were conducted by home-language speakers who were all psychologists. The tapes were translated into English by the original interviewers in a further interview situation where the process of interpretation was examined and problems documented. In this chapter, popular ideas of child sexual abuse produced by these women are outlined. These are compared to discourses within which English-speaking, white and black middle-class South African women placed themselves and sexually abused children, largely reflecting the professional literature. The chapter concludes with a more general discussion of the problems of research that uses translation/interpretation without attention to shifts in discursive positioning.

Martin Terre Blanche in Chapter 10 critiques two very different discourses – those of institutional psychiatry and those of discourse analysis. In each case the critique is based on an incipient scandal – recidivism in psychiatry and reification in discourse analysis – which seems perpetually about to engulf those who sustain and are sustained by these discourses. After reviewing the function of these scandals as necessary for the continuation of the two discourses, the chapter then goes on to demonstrate their operation in the analysis of a particular text.

In Chapter 11, Kevin Kelly and Hilde Van Vlaenderen report on a study which originally set out to explore the relational dynamics of participation in a community health development project. The chapter explores the ways in which systematic discrepancies emerged between participants' descriptions of their own role in the project, and the descriptions of their role by others. An attempt is made to understand the discourse dynamics implied by such discrepancies in the context of community development work. In particular, notions of 'participation' and 'dialogue', which have been the primary concepts through which dialogical discursive practices in development work, are explored.

Anthony Collins and Trevor Mulder's Chapter 12 explores two crises. The first is the crisis of an individual constituted at the intersection of two discourses: fundamentalist Christianity and homosexuality. The issue here is not simply the construction of identity in discourse, but the annihilation of viable identity at the point of contradiction between discourses, and how this manifests itself as breakdown and pain. The second crisis is the issue of representation in the academy in the face of the insight that rules of discourse constitute domains of knowledge and support relations of power. In response the authors offer and experiment with ways of recovering marginalized knowledge through the transgression of discursive rules.

The final part of the book consists of two chapters. Cheryl de la Rey attended the workshop where the papers forming the basis for this book were presented. Here, in Chapter 13, she comments on the wider contexts in which the discursive turn inside (and outside) psychology functions. The cautionary note about political intention rather than technology is one that is taken up in the editorial reflections in Chapter 14. Here we draw together the methodological strands in the book, making connections with work in discourse analytic research in Europe, and marking the distinctive character of South African research.

Assembling this book has itself been an exercise in the politics and practice of discourse analysis. The research presented here is original work, in some cases the first and only forum in which the analyses have reached the public sphere. The book indicates something of the vitality and promise of discourse perspectives in informing cultural-political analyses and engagement for South African practitioners and policy-makers, as well as theorists. With the eyes of the world on South Africa marking its transition to democracy, these analyses highlight specific modes of the practice of power in language, and they will have resonances for all those in psychology and other social sciences developing forms of discourse analysis that attend to processes of culture and change.

References

Burman, E. and Parker, I. (eds) (1993) *Discourse Analytic Research: Repertoires and Readings of Texts in Action*, Routledge, London.

Foster, D. H. and Louw-Potgieter, J. (eds) (1991) *Social Psychology in South Africa*, Lexicon, Johannesburg.

Foucault, M. (1969) *The Archaeology of Knowledge,* Tavistock, London.

Foucault, M. (1975) *Discipline and Punish: The Birth of the Prison*, Allen Lane, London.

Foucault, M. (1976) *The History of Sexuality, Volume One: An Introduction*, Penguin, Harmondsworth.

Foucault, M. (1980) *Power/Knowledge: Selected Interviews and Other Writings 1972–1977*, Harvester Press, Hassocks, Sussex.

Ingleby, D. (1985) 'Professionals as socializers: the "psy-complex"', *Research in Law, Deviance and Social Control*, 7, 79–109.

Levett, A. and Kottler, A. (in press) '"She's not a feminist!" Through a lens darkly', in E. Burman (ed.) *Deconstructing Feminist Psychology*, Sage, London.

Parker, I. (1992) *Discourse Dynamics: Critical Analysis for Social and Individual Psychology*, Routledge, London.

Parker, I. (1995) 'Michel Foucault, Psychologist', *The Psychologist*, 8 (11), 214–16.

Parker, I. (ed.) (in press) *Discourse, Realism and Social Constructionism*, Sage, London.

Parker, I. and Burman, E. (1993) 'Against discursive imperialism, empiricism and constructionism: thirty-two problems with discourse analysis', in E. Burman and I. Parker (eds) *Discourse Analytic Research: Repertoires and Readings of Texts in Action*, Routledge, London.

Potter, J. and Wetherell, M. (1987) *Discourse and Social Psychology: Beyond Attitudes and Behaviour*, Sage, London.

Rose, N. (1985) *The Psychological Complex,* London, Routledge and Kegan Paul.

Wetherell, M. and Potter, J. (1992) *Mapping the Discourse of Racism: Discourse and the Legitimation of Exploitation*, Harvester Wheatsheaf, Hemel Hempstead.

PART ONE

Towards the End of Apartheid

CHAPTER 2

Discourse and racial partition in the 'New' South Africa

John A. Dixon

What was apartheid? One answer is that it was a complex system of geographic control, the remnants of which still surround us. They are visible in the contours of our cities with their buffer zones, 'natural' barriers and decentrated industrial areas. They linger in characteristic forms of spatial organization: the township, the compound, the hostel and the informal settlement. They remain part of a ceaseless discourse of territory, identity and partition. Even as its surfaces have eroded, these sediments of apartheid have endured, reaffirming the old politics of racial division. Increasingly, however, they too have become sites of ideological conflict and transformation. Space has emerged as the object of intensifying scrutiny, its management inspiring an array of political solutions, ranging from land redistribution to the formation of a neo-separatist 'Boerstaat'.

South Africa's rapidly shifting topographies frame the present discussion, which introduces two problems: (i) how do particular constructions of the landscape, and of its regulation, help to justify racial domination? (ii) what does this reveal about the relation between identity, geography, and racism? As a case study, I examine a recent dispute concerning the 'encroachment' of a black 'squatter' community into a predominantly white village near Cape Town. My analysis of this dispute isolates two discourses of partition: a liberal discourse, asserting the individual's right to an inviolable private domain, and an apartheid discourse, asserting the necessity of racial division. The differing conceptions of land rights offered by liberalism and apartheid should not, I argue, blind us to their potential ideological collusions. However distinct their visions of spatial entitlement, both discourses tend to sustain racist geographies, a process that entails, among other things, the deployment of varying constructions of 'self in space'.

My argument will incorporate discourse analysis, both as a meta-theoretical position and as a methodological practice. As a metatheory, discourse analysis posits that truth (including the truth 'discovered' by social scientists) is textually produced and delimited; that facts are not found but *made*. At first glance, the extension of this position to the analysis of space seems problematic. Concrete and visible, the topographic world appears to exist solely in a realm outside discourse, to possess an intrinsic meaning, an ontology. Its materiality rests uneasily with radical versions of constructionism. Yet if it is misguided to deny the material existence of space, it is equally misguided to deny its existence as a textual construction. After all, our understanding of the external world is determined not only by the physical landscapes we inhabit but also by the semiotic processes that render them meaningful. This metaphor of 'land-scape as text' does not, of course, imply that we live in a world composed only of symbols and signs (cf. Demeritt, 1994). Nor does it imply that the task of discourse analysis, as a methodological practice, is to distinguish where the real world ends and the symbolic begins. To the contrary, discourse analysis is a strategy of reading that seeks to dissolve language/reality dualism by showing how the 'real' objects of our understanding are constituted within texts and how, in turn, texts enable domination (Parker, 1992).

In this chapter, I will consider briefly how two texts of space, liberalism and apartheid, enable racial domination. To use Davis's (1987: 61) terms, I will consider how *physical terrain* is also ideological *location*. The location analogy aptly models the constructed and political nature of our land-scapes. Just as cinematic locations are calculated productions, so too the spaces of everyday life are manufactured and strategic. Moreover, it is often when the production approaches pure description, when its truth seems most transparent, that it is at its most elaborate and concerted. Paradoxically, *terra firma* is often simply a sign that ideology is working effectively.

Racist ideologies typically seek to naturalize racist geographies, to make racial divisions appear universal and immutable, to keep people in their 'proper places' (Jackson and Penrose, 1993; Kobayashi and Peake, 1994). In order to accomplish this, they often mobilize common-sense constructions of the link between 'race' and geography. In South Africa this process has been associated with, among other things, two interlocking narratives of African existence. According to Packard (1989a, 1989b), the entwined myths of the 'dressed native' and the 'healthy reserve' have served not only to legitimate white domination, but also to mask its contradictions (for example, to supply industry with workers on the one hand, while denying responsibility for their welfare on the other). The discourse of the dressed native has emphasized 'black' Africans' maladjustment to modern urban life, blaming this for the hardships that have accompanied white domination; correspondingly, the discourse of the healthy reserve has promoted the idea that there exists an idyllic pastoral realm to which Africans are naturally suited. Throughout the so-called segregation era, these discourses were used in virulent combination to justify the migrant labour system. During this period, the high incidence of tuberculosis amongst mine workers was attributed to their susceptibility to Western diseases and their maladjustment to urban environments. In turn, this gave white authorities licence to return workers to the more 'salubrious' atmosphere of the native reserves for periods of recuperation. Thus was the migrant's cycle of importation-deportation perpetuated. That the reserves were actually characterized by extreme poverty and desperation does not appear to have diminished the effectiveness of the ideological formation. Our purposes here require us to consider why.

Perhaps one reason is that it exploited popular images of the relation between 'race' and place. The romanticization of the African's connection to the land has long gripped the colonial imagination (see Duncan, 1993). To this day, its oppressive side diluted or forgotten, this romantic impulse persists in travelogues, postcard pictures, documentaries, even in a certain brand of progressive rhetoric that laments the destruction of old Africa and hankers for a nostalgic 'return'. The broader point is that racism is often effected through common-sense constructions of the 'race'-place nexus. This process is of course historically textured and delimited. In the eighteenth and nineteenth centuries, for example, many geographers espoused theories linking climate to morality and human development (Livingstone, 1991). They also believed that Nature (or God), having created different 'races', impelled them towards hierarchical places in the world --the rational Europeans inhabiting milder climes, the sensual Africans scattered around a torrid equator. Though supported by the science of their time, nowadays such theories appear implausible and even self-parodying; they have become unconvincing in an age less sympathetic to biological or metaphysical accounts of racial difference. Yet, notwithstanding its historical variation, spatial discourse may also fulfil some more general ideological functions. Notably, it may help to reproduce what Goldberg (1993: 48) terms the 'conceptual primitives' of racist ideology – the deeper principles of natural classification, difference and hierarchy that underpin a variety of racisms. Whether we envisage the territories of eighteenth-century geography or those of modern South Africa, we envisage a world where 'race' is inscripted in the very lie of the land, where difference appears as natural and unchanging as the physical topographies from which it issues. This racialization of space lays the foundations for racism proper. Difference frequently tips over into a hierarchy that elevates the evolution of a particular group within its particular environment. To use another South African example: the ideology of Afrikaaner nationalism locates the very origins of the *volk* – as a physically and morally superior group – in an interaction between the collective and the spatial, between the genetic stock of early Dutch settlers and the climate and terrain of Africa (see Dubow, 1992).

Geographic discourse, then, provides one medium for the reproduction of racial inequality. What is significant from a psychological viewpoint is that such discourse implicates subjectivity, for the texts of identity and the texts of space are mutually constitutive. On the one hand, specific racial identities allow us to reinvent ourselves in and across space and to invest particular places with social meaning. On the other hand, such identities are generally constituted in terms of the spatial discourses and practices that structure our everyday experience (religious, ecological, architectural, etc.). The intimate ties between identity, geography and racism have been underexplored in South Africa, even though questions of identity have featured prominently in local explanations of racial conflict (cf. Foster and Louw-Potgieter, 1991) Yet these ties are obvious to anyone who lives in this country. They are a popular conversation topic in the braai place and the shebeen alike; they are broadcast daily in the media, in parliament, in education, in the courtroom; they are intrinsic to the social categories that we use in our everyday conversation. Migrant, Boer, Sowetan, Stroller, Squatter, Bergie, Maid – each category invokes, to a greater or lesser extent, a spatialized conception of self. Each category also invokes a history of domination, none more so than that of 'squatter'.

Squatting in Hout Bay

An adequate history of 'squatting' in South Africa has not yet been written, but we can identify some key moments. Certainly, such a history might investigate the mechanisms of dispossession implemented during the segregation era and intensified during the apartheid years (cf. Christopher, 1994; Mabin, 1992). It might seek to determine the conditions under which squatting emerged as a distinguishable practice and, more pointedly, became constituted as a *racial problem*. It might explore the ramifications and mutations of these broad impulses at the level of locality (e.g. Ellis et al., 1977; Schlemmer, 1985; Horn et al., 1992). Whatever its conditions of emergence, this much is true: discussions of 'squatting' and its associated 'ills' have pervaded recent land debates in South Africa. The migration of the 'black' homeless into what were previously defined as 'white' areas has proved especially controversial. As urbanization has gathered pace, as the boundaries policed so zealously by the *ancien régime* have become more permeable, so 'squatting' on privately owned or public 'white' lands has increased.

In the Cape province, the coastal village of Hout Bay has presented a case study of this process and of the kinds of ideological conflicts it may engender. Hout Bay is located on the South West of the Cape Peninsula about 20 kilometres from Cape Town. Although most of the town was designated a 'white' area (under the now defunct Group Areas Act), it has historically accommodated a sizeable 'black' population, who have supplied labour to the local fishing industry and agriculture. During the 1970s, the first scattered groups of 'homeless' people emerged in Hout Bay – victims of both national politics and local circumstances (see Gawith and Sowman, 1992; Green, 1991). Between 1989 and 1990 these groups were joined by a further 800 or so 'squatters', whose presence drew protest from some white residents of Hout Bay. At first the newcomers inhabited beach-front land known locally as Princess Bush; however, in 1991 the Nationalist government moved Hout Bay's various 'homeless' communities to a single location on a hillside above the village. Situated between three affluent 'white' estates, the new settlement was extremely controversial and multi-plied anti-squatter arguments.

The content of these arguments was wide-ranging, covering the negative impact of squatting on tourism, the likelihood of increased crime in Hout Bay, the lack of sanitation at the hillside settlement, the capriciousness of government policy, and the damage to local ecology (cf. Dixon et al., 1994). One common line of dissent highlighted the violation of residents' rights as property owners. The Hout Bay Property Rights Association, an anti-squatter league formed in 1990, embraced this view as its *raison d'être*:

> This association: Views squatting as the illegal appropriation of private property and an infringement of the rights of property owners, recognizes that the Hout Bay squatters may be poor and homeless, possessing few resources to ensure a decent family life, but cannot permit squatting to become the norm for redressing inequalities (*Sentinel News*, July 1990).

The dispute over land rights in Hout Bay surfaced across several institu-tional contexts (for example parliament, the courtroom, town planners' meetings) and took various discursive forms (e.g., radio interviews, legal manuscripts, newspaper reports). The analysis below draws examples from a set of seventy-one protest letters that were submitted to local newspapers (*Argus*, *Cape Times*, *Sentinel News*) between 1989 and 1993. In examining these letters, I want to show how discourse about 'rights' may come to warrant racist geographies. My focus is thus limited to individuals' written constructions of spatial relations as filtered through a particular verbal genre. A more enterprising analysis might also try to establish how such constructions are entwined with concrete spatial practices (e.g. individuals' routine movements) and embodied in material forms (e.g. private property; the location and organization of informal settlement).

Whose rights?

Like any argument about rights, arguments about the right to space encompass three kinds of propositions concerning: (i) the *Subject of Rights* (who is entitled?); (ii) the *Substance of Rights* (to what are they entitled?); and (iii) the *Basis of Rights* (on what grounds are they entitled?). We can think of this threefold structure as setting the conditions of intelligibility for any rights claim. In order to be meaningful or sustainable, such claims must reiterate that structure, even if this occurs only implicitly or indirectly. It makes no sense, for instance, to speak of a right without a subject; there has to be *somebody* or *something* to which entitlement attaches. Nor is it meaningful to speak of a right without a substance; there has to be *something* to which we are entitled, some content to the right. Finally, it is unintelligible to speak of a right without a basis; there has to be some *reason* for entitlement, however obscure, ridiculous or self-evident. The threefold structure, then, is part of the grammar of the concept of rights. I have found it useful not to determine the veracity of a particular model of rights, but to use it as an analytic lever – a mechanism for exposing the contradictions of rights-based arguments, including arguments about space.

Extract 1

HOUT BAY RESIDENTS DESERVE FAIRER DEAL FROM THE GOVERNMENT

Mr Pieter Oberholzer's reply, on behalf of the Department of Welfare, Housing and Works, to the Riverside Terrace Home Owners Association's request for the government to erect a 2 m wall between their properties and the recently established squatter camp in Hout Bay was that the minister 'was trying to help within the rules regarding the spending of taxpayers' money' and that 'we can't give the residents too much hope, but we are looking at the problem from every possible angle'. The government reportedly donated R5m towards the acquisition of a permanent settlement for the squatters (whose numbers rose from a few hundred to well over two thousand during the second half of 1990) and duly identified and acquired the land on which they are now settled. The government's unilateral decision to accommodate these squatters on prime land, situated between two upmarket residential estates is sufficiently insensible. To compound this disaster by suggesting that the required wall would impede the progress of 'good neighbourly relations' is ludicrous. The majority of property owners in Hout Bay have worked hard to acquire their properties and posses-sions. The influx of thousands of indigent persons last year resulted in great hardships to residents and businesses. We have suffered continual break-ins to homes and cars, shop-lifting, squalor on the beach and privately owned land, a massive drop off in tourism and, on many occasions, threats and abuse. Many property owners have in recent months been obliged to outlay huge sums of money to secure their properties and their rights. … It is the nature of men to live among their ilk and thus residential patterns develop accordingly. Despite the fact that many of our long-established residents in the harbor area are suffering great hardship as a result of the waning fishing industry, the govern-ment saw fit to permit the influx of thousands of indigent newcomers who have little or no prospect of employment. Those of us who have toiled to maintain a certain standard of living are entitled to the protection of our property. It was the government's decision to settle the squatters on their present location, and, I respectfully suggest, it is the government's responsibility to ensure that its Hout Bay taxpayers are provided with some measure of security and peace in their homes (*Cape Times*, 7 June 1991).

Look at Extract 1 through our three-way lens. That this passage foregrounds the violation of spatial rights is unquestionable. But what conception of rights is at issue? One reading might unfold as follows. The subject of rights here is the Hout Bay property owner, the individual who has 'toiled to maintain a certain standard of living' and is 'entitled to the protection of [his/her] property'. The substance of rights refers to this individual's claim to a private sphere, a moral 'space' whose concrete form is private property and whose sanctity must be defended. But if the right to a protected domain is truly at stake in Extract 1, it is a right doubly transgressed by invasive 'newcomers' and a tyrannical state. The latter is especially heinous as it directly thwarts the substance of the rights being summoned. Broadly, this favours a minimalist model of government, in which the state's role is not to prescribe its own version of 'the good' but to preserve the sanctity of the private realm wherein individuals may pursue their own, idiosyncratic, ends. How disquieting, then, that the state whose 'responsibility [it is] to ensure that its Hout Bay taxpayers are provided with some measure of security and peace in their own homes' chooses instead to enforce 'unilateral decisions'. Finally, on what basis can we say that residents' rights have been infringed? Extract 1 stresses the individual's legitimate expectation to benefit from his or her labour ('The majority of property owners have worked hard to acquire their properties and possessions'); but this, arguably, merely indexes a more complicated set of motivations whose validity appears so obvious that it scarcely needs defending. Rarely nowadays are we pressed to spell out the precise grounds for individual rights. The tacit weight of liberal ideology usually proves justification enough.

One interpretation of Extract 1, therefore, is that it offers a classic liberal account of rights, affirming the individual's entitlement to an inviolable private sphere. This account engenders an ideal for the organization of space. It hearkens toward a world of 'frictionless mobility' (cf. Blomey, 1992), populated by individuals who can move unobstructed, carving out their own personal geographies while respecting the spaces occupied by others. Clearly such an interpretation simplifies and a list of objections can be raised. Liberalism is not a singular or static ideology: it accumulates and jettisons ideas over time; it shows different shades in different contexts; it contains not one but many constructions of the right; it accommodates a variety of political positions and effects. I wish, however, to suspend such objections and let my caricature stand. Whatever its simplicities, it captures some qualities of liberal discourse as deployed in the Hout Bay letters: individualism, a separation of the private and the public, a 'negative' conception of liberty.

Liberalism is just one discourse present in Extract 1. There is another. The discourse of apartheid posits a very different conception of rights. Its subject is not the individual but the racial group; its substance does not enshrine the individual's claim to a private realm but the group's claim to an autonomous existence; its basis lies not in the sovereignty of the individual but in the sovereignty of the racial collective, which possesses an inalienable – natural and God-given – right to preserve its separateness and distinctiveness. Only the vestiges of apartheid discourse appear in Extract 1. It surfaces in the use of categorical language and in certain characteristic forms of justification ('It is the nature of men to elect to live amongst their ilk and thus residential patterns develop accordingly'). Undoubtedly, it manifests itself most clearly in the attempt to justify the erection of a boundary wall to fence off white residents from 'squatters' ('To compound this disaster by suggesting that the required wall would impede the progress of "good neighbourly relations" is ludicrous'). Nowhere in the passage is the contrast with liberalism more marked. The racial boundary is the geographic emblem of apartheid, which, in contrast to the open, atomistic spaces of liberalism, seeks to naturalize racial partition. As many South Africans know well, the boundaries of which I speak are not purely linguistic. They derive, too, from the institutional practices that violently collate and disperse people in space; that organize topography, physical and human-made, to maximize segregation (cf. Lemon, 1990). In other words, they derive from a model of government that enforces racial separateness, even against the will of protesting individuals or 'minorities'.

To sum up, in Extract 1 there are traces of two contradictory visions of spatial entitlement, two modes whereby terrain becomes ideological location. I describe them as contradictory visions because, on one level at least, they offer opposing narratives of the right. Liberalism proclaims the sanctity of the individual's private space, whereas apartheid proclaims the sanctity of racial partition. By uncovering such contradictions, we begin to challenge the truth status of this (and any) account of spatial rights. We begin to imagine space not as something that exists 'out there', containing a fixed or unitary meaning, but as the product of a disjunctive field of discursive relations. This disruptive movement is the hallmark of many different kinds of discourse analysis. As applied to Extract 1, however, it carries certain dangers. Contradiction might be misinterpreted as the tension between an essentially democratic liberal position and the undemocratic leavings of apartheid.

Such a reading is problematic. It presupposes that liberal discourse is progressive in its political effects when it is sometimes integral to racist practice. Indeed, by disavowing the category of 'race' and equating prejudice with irrationality, liberal ideology frequently creates the conditions under which institutionalized racism can flourish (cf. Henriques et al.,

1984; Billig, 1988). At the centre of its operation is a political philosophy that affirms the moral transcendence of the individual and subordinates all other forms of identity to this rational, transhistoric 'Subject' (cf. Sampson, 1993). Clarifying the role played by the liberal subject in the production of racism, Goldberg (1993) exposes the paradox at the heart of liberal individualism, namely that its insistence upon the universal sameness of human identity helps to maintain exclusions based upon racial difference. This kind of exclusive individualism permeated arguments about space in the Hout Bay letters.

Extract 2

PLEASE STOP THE INFLUX OF THESE UNEMPLOYABLE PEOPLE

I am neither a rightwing racialist, nor a Greenpeace fanatic, and I strongly believe that a roof over one's head, no matter how meagre, is a basic right of all human beings; but I strongly feel that the way in which the squatter problem in Hout Bay has been handled is little short of criminal (*Argus*, 11 October 1992).

Extract 3

WHY DON'T THE AUTHORITIES LISTEN?

Whilst it is not for me to deny anyone the right to be allocated a piece of land, albeit the most expensive in Hout Bay, it is sheer lunacy to provide such high exposure to a third world settlement (*Argus*, 23 June 1992).

Extracts 2 and 3 provide instances of disclaimed racism (i.e., racism at once effected and denied). Each employs one of the mitigating forms documented by Van Dijk (1992) among others. Yet the power of these passages derives not merely from their linguistic form, but also from the content of the ideological system they interpolate. It is the breath-taking inclusiveness of the liberal subject of rights that lends them rhetorical force. For a moment we are placed in a world where the racial cleavages are morally suspended, where the subject of entitlement is not just some but all, and where 'a roof over one's head, no matter how meagre, is a basic right of all human beings'. It is easy to forget that both letters are calling for a race-based restriction on the 'influx of these unemployable people' into Hout Bay. The common-sense appeal of these excerpts should not, therefore, be attributed simply to the writers' virtuosity, to a dexterous use of linguistic 'resources' (behind which lies a calculating subject). The conditions of plausibility are set by the deep structures of discourse.

In a similar fashion, Extracts 4 and 5 below apply an ideologically compelling vision of human freedom. Effacing its own historicity, the so-called 'negative' conception of liberty proclaims the timeless inviolability of the individual's private domain, a sacred area where external authority must not be permitted to trespass. To many of us this conception is second nature. It informs our most cherished spatial constructs such as privacy, mobility and property ownership. It inspires our most passionate convictions such as toleration and pluralism, for as Isaiah Berlin suggests, 'Every plea for civil liberties and individual rights, every protest against exploitation and humiliation, against the encroachment of public authority or the mass hypnosis of custom or organized propaganda, springs from this individualistic and much disputed conception of man [*sic*]' (1969/ 1992: 128). This conception also impels the excerpts below, which decry the intrusion of 'unwanted' squatters and a despotic state. Intriguingly, Extract 5 conceives intrusion in spatial as well as moral terms. The geographic and the political taper off into one another as the transformation from terrain to location is completed ('The squatter community in its enlarged form will now be only 140 m from our home …').

Extract 4

THEY DON'T KNOW AND THEY DON'T CARE

I think that it is about time people sitting behind desks and living kilometres from Hout Bay were put in their places. We who live in Hout Bay not only have to live with whatever happens here but, in the end, end up having to pay for whatever gets decided by those who don't know and don't care what goes on here as long as they wield their little rod of power sitting on their fat duffs like little tin gods (*Argus*, 22 September 1992).

Extract 5

LEAVE THINGS THE WAY THEY ARE IN HOUT BAY

The squatter community in its enlarged form will now be only 140m away from our home, a home that we used to enjoy before our lives and dreams were shattered by some 'official' in the Cape Provincial Administration who decided that this was the one and only place these unwanted people could go (*Cape Times*, 25 September 1992).

Extract 5 also illustrates a discursive pattern repeated throughout my corpus of letters. To use the idiom of liberalism, there is an elevation of the right (individual freedom) over the good (racial integration) regarding the writer's personal spatial entitlement, but, in a telling reversal, an elevation of the good (racial division) over the right (individual freedom) regarding squatters' entitlement. What gives this paradoxical movement coherence is the selective deployment of the liberal 'repertoire' (Wetherell and Potter, 1992). The invocation of the libertarian 'space', and its allied subjectivities, serves to vindicate anti-squatter action. I am not suggesting here that liberal discourse inevitably sustains racist practice; indeed the protection of the individual's spatial liberties may, depending on its application, prove a progressive feature of South Africa's interim constitution. But equally it is wrong to presuppose that liberal and apartheid arguments inevitably exist in relations of antagonism or contradiction. Certainly, in the Hout Bay letters *both* discourses were marshalled in opposition to the 'squatter' settlement. Moreover, the tenacious grip that liberal conceptions exercise over everyday reasoning, especially in the 'new' South Africa, suggests that they may increasingly dominate debates about 'squatting'. They seem already to be displacing the stark separatism of the past.

Discourse, 'race' and geography

Several kinds of questions arise from the brief analysis sketched above. How can we explain the strange alchemy that binds discourse, race and geography? What are the nature of its links to racial hegemony? How, if at all, can discourse analysis break down the forms of partition that regulate our existence, that divide us from one another and from ourselves? These complex questions are already central topics within disciplines as diverse as cultural geography, history, feminism, anthropology and sociology (e.g. Rogerson and Parnell, 1989; Smith, 1989; Jackson and Penrose, 1993; Kobayashi and Peake, 1994). One approach to the analysis of 'squatting` would be to trace the historical emergence of the category itself: to analyse its 'conditions of possibility', its constitution within specific institutional practices and 'regimes of truth', and, above all, its association with particular disciplinary techniques of spatial government. Michel Foucault's writings, to which I am clearly alluding here, prefigure the fertility of such an approach (e.g. Foucault, 1975).

Lacking the ambition of a full Foucauldian analysis, the present research has explored a micro-contextual dispute about land rights, concentrating on the link between constructions of space-identity and the reproduction of racism. This kind of study can be located within an emerging tradition of social psychological work (e.g. Potter and Wetherell, 1987; Wetherell and Potter, 1992; Reicher, 1986; Hopkins et al., in press). Whatever other theoretical and methodological differences they may have, its proponents share the conviction that 'race' is a fluid political construction rather than an *a priori* essence. Accordingly, they seek to document the ideological consequences of different narratives of racial identity. In a similar vein, the present chapter has demonstrated how racism may operate by mobilizing forms of selfhood that affirm geographic belonging and exclusion. Through analysis of the Hout Bay letters, I have shown how liberal individualist rhetoric may serve to entrench the *de jure* property rights of white residents and to maintain a racist insider/outsider distinction. Correspondingly, I have shown how racialized indentities (e.g. 'squatter') are often ingrained in the landscapes – at once concrete and symbolic – within which we situate ourselves and others.

This dialectic between categorization, space and racism has important consequences for the social psychology of prejudice. It opens up domains of inquiry largely ignored within orthodox treatments of the categorization-racism relationship, which generally focus on the cognitive limitations that lead to faulty generalizations about racial outgroups (cf. Oakes and Turner, 1990) or the personality dynamics that lead to cognitive rigidity and displaced hatred (e.g. Adorno et al., 1950). In particular, it encourages us to investigate *how* categories *become* 'racialized' (cf. Miles, 1993). However much they have deplored their political consequences, social psychologists have usually taken for granted the 'reality' of racial categories, a tendency that has stifled even the more theoretically sophisticated work in the field. If instead we view racial categories as narratives, then we can problematize the conditions of their genesis and transformation. Undoubtedly, some of these conditions pertain to space; that is, the 'reality' of 'race' arises, at least in part, from its embeddedness within the organization of our landscapes and within the vocabularies through which such landscapes are comprehended. In other words, as noted earlier, the construction of space may perpetuate the 'conceptual primitives' that maintain 'race' as a natural way to hierarchize the world (Goldberg, 1993). From this vantage, spatial relations do not merely form the background or, as social psychologists are apt to say, the context of racism. They are part of its definition.

Note

I wish to thank Steve Reicher, Ian Parker and Bianca Petkova for their helpful comments on an earlier draft of this chapter.

References

Adorno, T. W. , Frenkel-Breunswik, E., Levinson, D. and Sanford, R. N. (1950) *The Authoritarian Personality*, New York, Harper & Row.
Berlin, I. (1969/1992) *Four Essays on Liberty*, Oxford University Press, Oxford.
Billig, M. (1988) 'The notion of prejudice: rhetorical and ideological aspects', *Text*, 8, 91–110.
Blomey, N. K. (1992) 'The business of mobility: geography, liberalism, and the charter of rights', *Canadian Geographer*, 36, 236–53.
Christopher, A. J. (1994) *The Atlas of Apartheid*, Routledge, London.
Davis, L. J. (1987) *Resisting Novels: Ideology and Fiction*, Methuen, London.
Demeritt, D. (1994) 'The nature of metaphors in cultural geography and environmental history', *Progress in Human Geography*, 18, 163–85.
Dixon, J. A., Foster, D. H., Durrheim, K. and Wilbraham, L. (1994) 'Discourse and the politics of space in South Africa: the "squatter crisis"', *Discourse and Society*, 5, 277–96.

Duncan, J. (1993) 'Sites of representation: place, time and the discourse of the Other', in J. Duncan and D. Ley (eds), *Place/Culture/Representation*, Routledge, London.

Dubow, S. (1992) 'Afrikaaner nationalism, apartheid, and the conceptualization of race', *Journal of African History*, 33, 209–37.

Ellis, G., Hendrie, D., Kooy, A., and Maree, J. (1977) *The Squatter Problem in the Western Cape: Some Causes and Remedies*, South African Institute of Race Relations, Johannesburg.

Foster, D. H. and Louw-Potgieter, J. (eds) (1991) *Social Psychology in South Africa*, Lexicon, Johannesburg.

Foucault, M. (1975) *Discipline and Punish: The Birth of the Prison*, Allen Lane, London.

Gawith, M. and Sowman, M. (1992) 'Informal settlements in Hout Bay: a brief history and review of socio-demographic trends (1989–1991)' *Environmental Evaluation Unit Report*, University of Cape Town, Cape Town.

Goldberg, D. T. (1993) *Racist Culture*, Basil Blackwell, Oxford.

Green, C. (1991) 'The origins and development of informal settlement in the Hout Bay area, 1940–1986', unpublished honours dissertation, University of Cape Town, Cape Town.

Henriques, J., Hollway, W., Urwin, C., Venn, C. and Walkerdine, V. (1984) *Changing the Subject*, Methuen, London.

Hopkins, N., Reicher, S. and Levine, M. (in press) 'Constructing categories and social relations in racist talk', *British Journal of Social Psychology*.

Horn, A., Hattingh, P. and Vermaak, J. (1992) 'Winterveld: an urban interface settlement on the Pretoria metropolitan fringe', in D. M. Smith (ed.), *The Apartheid City and Beyond: Urbanization and Social Change in South Africa*, Routledge, London.

Jackson, P. and Penrose, J. (1993) 'Placing "race" and nation', in P. Jackson and J. Penrose (eds), *Constructions of Race, Place and Nation*, UCL Press, London.

Kobayashi, A. and Peake, L. (1994) 'Unnatural discourse: "Race", and gender in geography', *Gender, Place and Culture*, 1, 225–43.

Lemon, A. (1990) 'Imposed separation: the case of South Africa', in M. Chisholm and D. M. Smith (eds), *Shared Space, Divided Space*, Unwin Hyman, London, 194–216.

Livingstone, D. N. (1991) 'The moral discourse of climate: historical considerations on race, place and virtue', *Journal of Historical Geography*, 17, 413–34.

Mabin, A. (1992) 'Dispossession, exploitation and struggle: an historical overview of South African urbanization', in D. Smith (ed.), *The Apartheid City and Beyond: Urbanization and Social Change in South Africa*, Routledge, London.

Miles, R. (1993) *Racism after 'Race Relations'*, Routledge, London.

Oakes, P. J. and Turner, J. C. (1990) 'Is limited information processing capacity the cause of social stereotyping?', in W. Stroebe and M. Hewstone (eds), *European Review of Social Psychology*, 1, Wiley, Chichester.

Packard, R. M. (1989a) 'The "healthy reserve" and the "dressed native": discourses on black health and the language of legitimation in South Africa', *American Ethnologist*, 16, 686–703.

Packard, R. M. (1989b) *White Plague, Black Labour*, University of Natal Press, Pietermaritzburg.

Parker, I. (1992) *Discourse Dynamics: Critical Analysis for Social and Individual Psychology*, Routledge, London.

Potter, J. and Wetherell, M. (1987) *Discourse and Social Psychology: Beyond Attitudes and Behaviour,* Sage, London.

Reicher, S. (1986) 'Contact, action and racialization: some British evidence', in M. Hewstone and R. Brown (eds), *Contact and Conflict in Intergroup Encounters*, Basil Blackwell, Oxford.

Rogerson, C. M. and Parnell, S. M. (1989) 'Fostered by the laager: apartheid human geography in the 1980s', *Area*, 21, 13–26.

Sampson, E. E. (1993) *Celebrating the Other*, Harvester Wheatsheaf, Hemel Hempstead.

Schlemmer, L. (1985) 'Squatter communities: safety valves in the rural–urban nexus', in H. Giliomee and L. Schlemmer (eds), *Up Against the Fences: Poverty, Passes, and Privilege in South Africa*, St Martin's Press, New York.

Smith, S. (1989) *The Politics of 'Race' and Residence,* Polity Press, Cambridge.

Van Dijk, T. A. (1992) 'Discourse and the denial of racism', *Discourse and Society*, 3, 87–118.

Wetherell, M. and Potter, J. (1992) *Mapping the Discourse of Racism: Discourse and the Legitimation of Exploitation*, Harvester Wheatsheaf, Hemel Hempstead.

CHAPTER 3

Peace talk and violence: an analysis of the power of 'peace'

Kevin Durrheim

What is peace? It is commonly thought of as involving consensus, but in contrast, a Foucauldian analysis offers a conception of peace in terms of power and resistance, which suggests that peace is not a consensual, terminal, or universal value. This chapter aims to investigate the nature of peace from a Foucauldian perspective. The analysis focuses on the proliferation of 'peace talk' in politics and the mass media in South Africa from the time of the release of Nelson Mandela from prison in 1990 to shortly after the 1994 elections. This period of transition from the old to the new South Africa was one of the most violent in the country's history. Concurrently, the concept of peace emerged as a significant feature of political rhetoric, and was reflected at practical and institutional levels. The 'peace movement' gave birth to peace monitors, a peace accord, a peace commission with a secretariat of peace, a national peace day, and peace-keeping forces. Television commercials advertised peace while hundreds of thousands of South Africans lined the streets in peace chains, wore peace T-shirts, blue ribbons and badges denoting peace, planted peace gardens, and generally identified themselves as peace-loving citizens.

I wish to problematize the concept of peace as employed within the South African context. Overtly, peace and violence appear as an antinomic couplet. The peace movement emerges as a good force in opposition to one that is violent. Indeed, 'peace' is used in a manner to imply that violence may be quelled by magnifying the force of peace. This conception of peace is evident in Extract 1, where Nelson Mandela addresses the nation after bomb blasts in Johannesburg immediately prior to the 1994 election.

Extract 1

I want you to look to the future with hope and confidence, because the forces of peace in this country are far more powerful (.)[1] to be interrupted in their (.) work and programme and hopes by the madmen who are now behind this violence (Nelson Mandela, SABC TV1 News, 25 April 1994).

Here peace is portrayed as possessing a strange mixture of human and natural qualities. Peace is framed in the language of the natural sciences – in terms of forces, causes, and effects. Peace is a force which has power, and which can 'do something' about quelling the violence. Physical images imbibe the concepts of peace and violence with meaning – the more we increase the force of peace, the less is the threat of violence. In addition, peace is associated with human interests – work, a programme, and hopes – in opposition to the non-human interests of the 'madmen' behind the violence. Such talk sets peace up as a rational and human force in opposition to the non-rational force of violence.

This chapter aims to deconstruct the opposition between peace and violence. This will be done first by establishing linkages between power and subjectivity, and then by demonstrating how peace talk acts as a means of 'subjectification' (Foucault, 1982). By so doing, I attempt to dispel the myth that the peace movement acts purely as a form of resistance against the irrational forces of violence. By drawing on Foucault, I argue that while peace is a form of resistance against violence, violence is also a form of resistance against peace. Consequently, peace talk acts as a force both for and against violence.

This argument constitutes a particular version of the peace movement and of the relationship between peace and violence in South Africa. It has been developed through a reflexive process of living in a culture, and reading and attempting to understand various texts relating to peace and violence. The selection of text presented in this chapter was done in an intuitive and deductive manner. I do not aim to 'test' Foucauldian theory. On the contrary, Foucauldian theory acts as an interpretative framework which itself has been appropriated through the reflexive process of attempting to understand contemporary events. The texts presented here were selected specifically to exemplify Foucauldian conceptions of power.

Discourse and power

I want to argue that peace talk acts as a mode of subjugation whose effect is not purely obedience to the 'punitive mechanics' of power (Foucault, 1976). In contrast to the effects of 'juridico-discursive' power, peace talk is productive – it produces peace-loving citizens. Peace talk functions as a form of what Foucault (1982) refers to as pastoral power. This is a form of power which not only represses, but also 'qualifies' individuals for action, thereby producing subjects. Since these power relations are reflected in relations of signification, the productive aspects of discourse form the object of analysis. Discourses such as 'peace' achieve a dual function, for by qualifying and producing subjects they secure obedience, order, docility, and discipline. Finally, I propose that the present violence may contain elements which arise through resistance to the 'government of individualization' inherent in peace talk. This form of resistance is aimed not against the repressive forces of the state, but against the productive knowledges which qualify individuals for certain actions and tie them to particular identities.

Discourse analysis (Parker, 1992; Burman and Parker, 1993; Potter and Wetherell, 1987; Wetherell and Potter, 1992) is a practice that aims to unhinge and explicate ideological/power relations that are established in the manner in which 'objects' are systematically represented and subjects are 'interpellated'. These ideological relations are bound up in the invested manner in which the social and physical landscape is presented and debated. To talk about peace in terms of 'the forces' which may quell violence is to formulate peace in a manner that demands action – from peace-keeping forces as well as from citizens who dress, demonstrate, and grow gardens for peace. To contrast peace as a social category (with a programme for action and hopes for the future) with the irrational and hopeless category of madness, is to open up a space for identity.

It is with the constructive powers of language that Foucault identifies the operations of power; not the power to negate, but the power to produce – in this instance, to produce peaceful citizens who behave in peace-loving ways. Pastoral power produces individuals as subjects.

> This form of power applies itself to immediate everyday life which categorizes the individual, marks him by his own individuality, attaches him to his own identity, imposes a law of truth on him which he must recognize and which others have to recognize in him. It is a form of power which makes individuals subjects [both in the sense of] subject to someone else by control and dependence; and tied to his own identity by a conscience or self-knowledge (Foucault, 1982: 781).

In much the same way as Parker (1992) uses the term discourse, Foucault establishes a 'constraining and productive' relationship between society and the individual. This is not a dualistic relationship where society and the individual are considered as two causally related entities. On the contrary, discursive realism breaks down the opposition between the individual and society by emphasizing an intimacy between self-understanding and power (Foucault, 1976, 1982; Parker, 1989a, 1989b). Individual identity is not an individual invention, but, through the medium of language, a person becomes an individual 'subject', 'glued in place from within by the phenomenon of responsible agency (confession) and from without by the apparatus of surveillance (discipline)' (Parker, 1989b: 60).

Foucault (1982) employs the confessional as a metaphor for the dynamics of power. The individual confessor is a subject in two senses: subject to the institutionalized scrutiny of the other who hears the confession, and the subject of the confession. Power thus operates through the production and deployment of discursive categories whereby individuals must recognize themselves, and through which they must be recognized by others. In contrast to political power, which demands the sacrifice of the individual to the collective, pastoral power aims to assure individual salvation. Unlike legal power, it looks after not the whole community, but each *individual*. Most importantly, pastoral power achieves these aims through the production of truth of the individual – 'it implies a knowledge of the conscience and an ability to direct it' (Foucault, 1982: 783). This conscience and subjectivity must be made known and must be visible to others. The confessional thus acts as a site for the scrutinized production of truth and the personal recognition of truth within the individual. It is the site where the individual is simultaneously brought into being and brought to order.

The individualizing and conscientizing functioning of peace talk in South Africa is clearly evident in Extract 2. During an interview regarding her 'peace initiatives', a Sowetan schoolgirl comments on the meaning of peace and demonstrates an imperative to confess:

Extract 2

The question of peace is not a question of the church (.) the leaders (.) it is a *question of everyone* (SABC TV1, 6 on 1, 30 March 1994, emphasis added).

Like a question, peace demands a response, not only from political, community, and religious organizations, but from every*one*. The response to peace takes the form of the confessional. As in the case of this teenager, it consists of reflecting on how one's 'peace initiatives' have been derived from a transformed peaceful self. The response that is demanded is at once a moral response of personal conscience and a response which is subject to the scrutiny of others; a response through which she may recognize herself as a moral agent, and through which knowledge is generated whereby others may know how to act.

The personal importance of peace and the imperative to confess are widely appreciated. These confessional responses find a forum in the mass media – in newspaper columns such as 'the peace-maker of the week', and in television interviews. The comments of DJ Jezzy Justice, an ANC 'warrior', take a typical confessional form:

Extract 3

I'm a man of peace. I never want to touch my Kalashnikov again. I don't even want to see it. Now is the time to forget and come together, exactly as our president points out ... A couple of weeks ago I started learning Afrikaans. We can't exist without their experience. I don't hate anybody, I love them all (quoted in the *Weekly Mail and Guardian*, 3–9 June 1994: 11).

Here peace talk functions as a confession: past actions are confessed, events that transformed one are detailed, and insights and appropriate future actions are delineated. This extract provides a good example of the dual function of the confessional. First, it brings the individual into being by offering them 'salvation' in the world as a legitimate citizen. DJ begins by stating that he is a man of peace and concludes that he hates nobody, but loves all. Accordingly, he appropriates a peaceful identity and, in this manner, is made a subject of peace. Second, the confession takes place in a public forum were DJ is subject to the scrutiny and surveillance of others. It is by these means that appropriate knowledges of peace are generated and disseminated, and panoptic surveillance and order achieved. The listener also knows how to become a person of peace and assure their own individual salvation. In this instance, this would involve disarmament, developing tolerance for all, including one's enemies, and learning a new language. According to Foucault (1975, 1976, 1982), individuals are placed in power relations by the forms of self-knowledge that are produced by objectifying individuals as subjects.

Foucault proposes three 'modes of objectification' – (i) *grammaire générale*, (ii) dividing practices, and (iii) subjectification. The *grammaire générale* refers to institutionalized bodies of knowledge such as psychology, medicine and economics, which objectify the productive subject by focusing on the individual as an object of knowledge, framing her or his activity in linguistic categories. Institutionalized knowledges thus function towards control and surveillance by supplying the categories by which individuals may recognize themselves and be recognized.

The knowledges regarding peace and violence are not generated in the formalized institutions with which Foucault was concerned. While peace studies is a subdiscipline in its own right, and much discussion of peace employs the language of 'conflict resolution', it is not within such institutions that the current proliferation of peace talk is located. Rather, the language of peace is produced within less formal and newer institutions such as the peace commission and its peace monitors, which in turn, draw on the language of political and religious institutions. A second difference concerns the urgency with which these knowledges are disseminated to the public. There is an active and immediate publication of peace through the mass media.

None the less, the knowledges of 'peace' take the same form that Foucault identifies with the second mode of objectification: dividing practices. Here 'the subject is either divided inside himself [*sic*] or divided from others' (Foucault, 1982: 778). The subject is the object of discourse; either sane or mad, sick or healthy, peaceful or violent. Dividing practices are closely related to the third mode of objectification, subjectification: 'the way a human being turns himself [*sic*] into a subject' (ibid). The individual recognizes him or herself (an object in discourse) as the *subject* of discourse. Dividing practices are related to subjectification in terms of the content of the possible categories which may be appropriated as well as by 'silencing' some identities in favour of others. In terms of this discussion, subjectification refers to recognizing oneself, and acting as a peace-loving citizen.

By these three modes of objectification the human subject is placed in relations of production and signification, and is thereby also placed in power relations. These power relations are not of the juridico-discursive form, but are associated with the production of knowledges and subjectivity. The following analysis aims to examine shared languages, knowledges, and understandings of peace as a means of demonstrating the dividing practices and subjectification associated with these texts. I aim to explore, at the level of discourse, the manner in which peace talk has taken a confessional form, and places individuals in power relations. How is a knowledge of conscience established, and why do individuals find it imperative to talk and behave in peace-loving ways? By contrasting popular images of (i) peace and non-peace, and (ii) peace-loving and peace-hating individuals, I hope to demonstrate the manner in which peace talk fulfils power functions in the Foucauldian sense.

Peace and violence: 'a dramatic story'

During the latter half of 1993, new kinds of commercials were shown on South African television: commercials that advertised peace. These were new in the suddenness of their appearance and the frequency of their screening. Also, although peace is a commodity in the form of T-shirts, bumper-stickers and badges, it was essentially the abstract concept of peace rather than commercial products or services that were advertised. With the run-up to the election these advertisements gave way to others of the same genre, specifying the meaning of democracy, reconciliation, and other closely associated 'peaceful' concepts. Since these advertisements were remarkably similar in content and style, only one will constitute the focus of the analysis. This is my reading of the visual scene.

> The scene is idyllic. A deep green hillside etched against an azure sky. Amid a cacophony of innocent screams and shouts, a group of children fly a kite. To everyone's dismay, the kite becomes ensnared in the branches of a lone tree. The children then proceed to build a pyramid by standing on each others shoulders, and thus retrieve the kite. The national peace song provides a background to this 30-second advert.

There is a difficulty here in analysing visual text in a written forum. The text must be presented as an interpretation, and the following analysis thus constitutes an interpretation of this interpretation. This is complicated by the ability of the visual media to convey meaning in subtle ways through the use of 'effects'. Thus, I have included 'subjective' adjectives and adverbs in the presentation above to try to convey my understanding of this text.

As I understand and have presented this advert, it is blatantly ideological. It portrays a consensual version of South African history – a vision of 'brotherhood'. Like these children, South Africans, it implies, have always cooperated harmoniously. As the tree interrupted play, apartheid has disrupted this harmony. However, by cooperating and working together, the advert suggests that the disruptive effects of the lone nasty obstacle of apartheid may be overcome and we may return, once again, to our initial state of 'brotherhood' and harmony. This version of South African history is ideological as it offers a valorized interpretation of the past and resolution of our problems. It masks a colonial past of conflict and division, as well as suggesting that cooperation may wipe out the inequalities of apartheid. The possibility that the children would begin fighting or cutting down the tree is not entertained.

By denying history and difference, peace talk is allied to the formulation of an 'imagined community', the nation state. By the process of remembering/forgetting described by Anderson (1991), it depicts South Africanness as a 'natural' and timeless category. By essentializing the consensuality of our 'brotherhood' and humanity, South Africans are characterized as biological beings with a common history which, like a nature, extends into the horizonless past and future. These nationalistic overtones are reinforced by the background music, the national peace song:

> South Africa: we love you
> our beautiful land
> let's show the whole world
> we can make peace in our land ...

We are connected not only in 'brotherhood', but also to a tract of land that underscores the division between South Africans and 'the whole world'. Moreover, we are part not just of any nation but, ironically, of a sexless, raceless and classless society. The 'innocence' of children, and their 'unconditional acceptance' of others, are employed to depict South African society as inherently symmetrical and consensual. Achieving peace is merely achieving what we are. Being peaceful means being true to ourselves.

In this and other representations, peace is portrayed as Utopia. It is associated with reconciliation, cooperation, equality and freedom, through which, as South Africans, our collective and personal aims and desires may be harmoniously achieved. Peace is nationalism: a race-, class- and gender-free society where *we* are bound by our humanity, our collective history, and the land upon which we live. What we need to do to achieve our true South Africanness is to cooperate and reconcile our differences. These differences were brought about by the anomaly of apartheid, which has deflected us, momentarily, from our essential unity. These images are not to be found in a single television advert. Quite the opposite, they are evident in a multitude of symbols, such as 'the dove of peace', political rhetoric, and 'peace initiatives', which have become part of our day-to-day lives.

It is also clear that peace talk is a form of resistance. In contrast to the Utopian images of peace, the vision of its antithesis – violence – is one of despair. These visions are explicit. Extract 4 is drawn from the introduction to a special section to the *Argus*, a daily newspaper which published a three-part supplement entitled '*The struggle for peace*'.

Extract 4

… even as 1993 began the prospects for renewed negotiations were bleak. The country stood precariously on the edge of disaster … Violence had become pervasive as the year began, casting a forbidding shadow over all else. There was talk of a low intensity war (special section of the *Argus*, 14 February 1994: 3).

The image of non-peace is an abyss of chaos and despair. It is the forbidding shadow of disaster. These representations of non-peace draw on the ideologies of Afrikaner nationalism (cf. Foster, 1991). The image of despair and disaster is the image of 'the rest of Africa', and particularly Angola, which from 1992 to 1994 was engulfed in a bloody civil war. Thus, while the content of 'peace' has changed from one of separate development to cooperation and unity, its antithesis remains bound to the poverty and violence of postcolonial Africa. Peace talk is resistance to South Africa following the path of 'the rest of Africa'. In this context, to 'show the whole world we can make peace in our land' is to defy the whole world by rejecting the 'Third World' status associated with Africa.

The essential feature of the semantic space lying between the representations of peace and non-peace is the starkness of the contrast. There really are only two choices: peace and Utopia, or violence and despair. Individuals must 'choose' where to locate themselves. Both the constraining and productive effects of discourse are evident in this 'choice'. It is the duty of the individual to exercise 'responsible agency' by defining him or herself as either for or against peace. Accordingly, the individual may be qualified as a peaceful and legitimate citizen. Yet, because of the stark gradient of meaning between the representations of peace and non-peace, peace talk is like a strong pressure gradient: it sweeps people towards only one pole. Peace talk makes the choice for us. In this way, peace talk opens semantic identity-space of a religious/Christian tone: who would choose evil and its attendant eternal hellfire when the goodness of heaven awaits? Peace talk has implications for individual salvation. It establishes a knowledge of conscience and an ability to direct it. Herein lies the power of 'peace'. To attain salvation individuals must recognize themselves as subjects of peace, must be divided within themselves (in the sense of incompatible peaceful and violent tendencies), and must be divided from others (the rest of Africa, violent people, etc.). Peace talk thus functions as a form of self-discipline which renders the individual docile. As I have argued, the productive power of peace talk is associated with the intensification, magnification and clarification of the opposition between representations of peace and violence.

The stark meaning gradient is manifest also in media and political representations of peace-loving and peace-hating individuals. Reflecting Nelson Mandela's distinction between the rational forces of peace and the madmen of violence (see Extract 1), F. W. de Klerk in Extract 5 explains who is behind the violence.

Extract 5

There is a new dimension to the violence in the sense that gangs or small groups of individuals, whom I prefer to call terrorists, are organizing themselves to kill people, who are innocent bystanders, at random (quoted in the *Argus*, 19 August 1990: 17).

It is immediately apparent that the category 'terrorists' is contrasted with 'innocent bystanders' to reinforce the negative moral status of the madmen of violence. However, the construction of the category 'terrorists' is complex. On the one hand, their acts are portrayed as the random and unorganized activity of gangs and small groups of individuals. In this sense, their actions take the irrational form of madness. In direct contrast, they are said to be organizing themselves. 'Terrorism' in South Africa has always been organized; specifically, to overthrow the apartheid regime. Here the word terrorist is invoked to signify a political opponent as well as to discredit their activity as irrational, and thereby silence them. While terrorists were considered forces of violence by the apartheid state, they shared with the forces of 'peace' the characteristic of organization.

'Peace' and 'violence' have had a long history as part of South African political rhetoric. Indeed, apartheid was established on the premise that separate development was the surest path away from the 'rest of Africa', and towards peace. During the age of legislative apartheid, though, bifurcated conceptions of peace and violence separated the forces of apartheid and the forces of struggle and liberation. While not articulated through advertising, 'peace' and 'violence' were clear and unambiguous categories – they were sustained by opposing political philosophies and organized through the institutions of the state and the liberation movement. It was the moves by the state and the liberation movement towards reconciliation which confused and blurred conceptions of who was struggling and whom the struggle was directed against. In contrast to the 'legitimate' and organized violence of the struggle, the forces of violence amid the reconciliation and reconstruction take on a 'new dimension' and are portrayed as acephalous 'gangs' and 'small groups of individuals' – 'balaclava gangs', the 'third force', and the 'lunatic fringe'. Since this relatively early quote of F. W. de Klerk, the forces of violence have increasingly been depicted as purposeless and unorganized. Accordingly, as reflected in Extract 1, the divide between the rational forces of peace and the irrational forces of violence has magnified.

Thus, as 'peace' has come into focus, it has slipped from view. As the category of peace is articulated and conveyed to the public through the media, so precise conceptions of who is peaceful and who is violent become more ambiguous and unclear. It becomes increasingly important to define, as unambiguously as possible, one's standing – to 'translate [a] yearning for peace into some concrete and tangible form' (special section of the *Argus*, 16 February 1994: 4).

The forces of peace are not, therefore, those of the natural sciences, where one body acts upon another. Neither are they political force in its traditional manifestation, with the police storming in to subdue the crowd. They are the forces that act upon actions by objectifying individuals, dividing them within themselves and from others, and whereby individuals turn themselves into the docile and disciplined subject of peace. The power of peace is a process of self-definition and self-discipline, held in place by panoptic surveillance via peace demonstrations, peace initiatives, peace clothing, etc.

Peace is violence

While the argument thus far has suggested that the power of peace lies in its productive and constraining effects, it has agreed with the commonly accepted notion that peace functions as resistance to violence. However, Foucault's theory of power informs our understanding of resistance by suggesting that violence also functions as resistance to peace. Consequently, peace, rather than being a force that merely acts to quell violence, also underpins violence, and thereby undermines itself.

According to Foucault (1982) freedom is an essential condition for the exercise of power, since pastoral power is based on the individual's ability to define themself as a subject. The conditions that allow the individual to 'choose' to be a person of peace imply that it is possible to choose the opposite. Given that freedom is essential to power, 'every power relationship implies, at least *in potentia*, a strategy of struggle' (1982: 794). For, 'at the very heart of the power relationship, and constantly provoking it, are the recalcitrance of the will and the intransigence of freedom' (ibid.: 790). Thus, where there are operations of power, there is resistance.

In addition to the structural principle that identifies resistance as essential to the operations of power, Foucauldian conceptions of power also inform our understanding of the 'object' of resistance. By rejecting the notion that power is possessed by individuals or institutions, we cannot view resistance as directed against the masters of power, the 'chief enemy'. Rather, Foucault argues that resistance is directed against 'the effects of power which are linked with knowledge, competence, and qualification: struggles against the privileges of knowledge' (ibid.: 781).

These two features of resistance suggest that the proliferation of violence in the country is related to the proliferation of peace. To the degree that the gradient of meaning between peace (Utopia) and violence (despair) magnifies, and 'peace' becomes hegemonic, resistance to 'peace' intensifies. This resistance is directed not against the state as such, but against the 'competent' and 'privileged' definitions of 'peace' and 'peace-loving' sanctioned by political and religious institutions. This form of resistance to 'peace' is captured in Extract 6, where 'Colonel' Leon van der Merwe, leader of the Afrikaner Resistance Movement, exercises his freedom to reject the symbols of peace.

Extract 6

White doves will not bring peace. If I'm hungry I will eat a white dove (quoted in the special section of the *Argus*, 16 February 1994: 5).

The 'colonel' shows disdain for a hallowed symbol of peace. The resistance that is evident here is directed not against the state (or even the new South Africa), but against the operations of power which suggest that to attain salvation, the individual must define him or herself as a subject of 'peace'. The 'colonel' rejects the definition of peace to which he must subject himself.

In a certain sense, the Utopia–despair conceptions of peace and violence are consensual. They appeal to the 'universal audience' (Perelman and Olbrechts-Tyteca, 1969). In Extract 6, for example, the 'colonel' rejects not peace itself, but the symbols of peace (the dove of reconciliation and salvation) and its consequences (hunger). Resistance is directed against forms of identity and forms of state associated with peace, but not against the general and vague ideal of peace as Utopia. Everyone agrees that Utopia is preferable to poverty, violence and despair. However, as soon as the details (such as political policy) of what constitutes the state of peace arise, conflict and disagreement proliferate. For example, towards the end of 1993 there was a heated political debate concerning the nature of the constitution. The political Right were in favour of breaking the country into a confederation of states, while the Centre and Left were in favour of a unitary South Africa. Both groups supported their preferences by drawing on the general and vague notion of peace. On the one hand, peace was argued to be derived from a confederation of states, while on the other, it was associated with a unitary state. In this way, the consensual vision of peace as Utopia becomes attached to particular visions of the state.

Perhaps it is true that 'peace' has always been associated with opposing conceptions of the state. However, as I have argued above, understandings of peace have changed. In particular, there has been an intensification of the opposition between peace and violence, between Utopia and despair. Consequently, it is with reference to the highly charged meaning gradient that the citizens understand and interpret political events. For some, a confederation means despair, while for others it is a unitary state that is associated with the negation of peace. Under these circumstances, violence proliferates as groups struggle against the despair associated with the fruition of opposing political ideals, and political and material struggles become superimposed on the individual's struggle against the government of individuation.

In contrast to the widespread belief that peace is a 'good' force that opposes violence, I have argued that, in South Africa, peace and violence have had a far more intimate relationship. The forces of peace are not coherent; they are not rational forces which function merely to quell violence. On the contrary, while peace talk has power to gather the citizens into 'the fold' in a peaceful manner, it also functions as a force of violence. Peace talk undermines itself in two related ways. Firstly, it establishes space for identity which may be rejected. Secondly, it is attached to particular conceptions of state which are repudiated by certain groups. With the magnification of the power of peace reflected in the intensification of the opposition between peace and violence, both forms of resistance have intensified. Thus, as 'peace' became more and more imminent with the coming of the elections, the irrational 'new dimension' of violence proliferated.

It appears as though the relationship between peace, power and violence is not straightforward. Power and violence are not simple opposites. Rather, power relationships function in multifaceted and contradictory ways, invoking both obedience and resistance: in this instance, to ensure peace, but also to sustain violence.

Notes

This chapter benefited greatly from discussion with Lindy Wilbraham.

1. In this notation (.) indicates a pause in speech.

References

Anderson, B. (1991) *Imagined Communities* (rev. edn), Verso, London.

Argus, 19 August 1990.

Argus, 14 February 1994.

Argus, 16 February 1994.

Burman, E. and Parker, I. (eds) (1993) *Discourse Analytic Research: Repertoires and Readings of Texts in Action*, Routledge, London.

Foucault, M. (1975) *Discipline and Punish: The Birth of the Prison*, Allen Lane, London.

Foucault, M. (1976) *The History of Sexuality, Volume 1: An Introduction*, Penguin, Harmondsworth.

Foucault, M. (1982) 'The subject and power', *Critical Inquiry*, 8: 777–95.

Foster, D. (1991) 'Social influence I: ideology', in D. Foster and J. Louw-Potgieter (eds), *Social Psychology in South Africa*, Lexicon, Johannesburg.

Parker, I. (1989a) *The Crisis in Modern Social Psychology, and How to End It*, Routledge, London.

Parker, I. (1989b) 'Discourse and power', in J. Shotter and K. J. Gergen (eds), *Texts of Identity*, Sage, London.

Parker, I. (1992) *Discourse Dynamics: Critical Analysis for Social and Individual Psychology*, Routledge, London.

Perelman, C. and Olbrechts-Tyteca, L. (1969) *The New Rhetoric: A Treatise on Argumentation* (trans. J. Wilkinson and P. Weaver), University of Notre Dame Press, Notre Dame, ID.

Potter, J. and Wetherell, M. (1987) *Discourse and Social Psychology: Beyond Attitudes and Behaviour*, Sage, London.

SABC TV1, 'News', 25 April 1994.

SABC TV1, '6 on 1', 30 March 1994.

Weekly Mail and Guardian, 3–9 June 1994.

Wetherell, M. and Potter, J. (1992) *Mapping the Language of Racism: Discourse and the Legitimation of Exploitation*, Harvester Wheatsheaf, Hemel Hempstead.

CHAPTER 4

Shifting sands and shifting selves: affirmations and betrayals in the process of institutional transformation

Amanda Kottler and Carol Long

In South Africa, where institutionalized oppression has been the order of the day, the question of how change is institutionalized is crucial. This chapter focuses on an attempt to deal with racial harassment at the University of Cape Town (UCT), a historically 'white' university with a long-standing liberal tradition.

In December 1992 the vice-chancellor nominated one black and one white staff member to co-convene a 'Racial Harassment Panel' (RHP). A first meeting to create this panel was held in May 1993, but the RHP did not materialize. Although the nominees had widely advertised the meeting, those present felt that key constituencies and interest groups had been overlooked or had elected not to be present. UCT's existing racial harassment policy was also considered a problematic starting point because of its focus on instances of individual racism and its apparent disinterest in 'the fundamental issue of institutional racism' (forum participant – FP). In the following months an elected steering committee, instructed to 'start again', held discussions with a wide range of UCT's organizations. This led to the idea of a forum involving all interested members of UCT, to discuss racial harassment more generally but also explicitly institutional racism before implementing any form of policy change. The forum was held in September 1993, and a decision was made to hold a workshop to define racism, racial discrimination and racial harassment and to decide practically on an appropriate policy for UCT.

The following definition arose from this workshop, held in November 1993:

> Racism: involves the irrational belief in the existence of different groups of people and the superiority of certain groups over others, or a system of beliefs and set of practices that disadvantage certain groups of people at the expense of others.

Fascinated by how a group of eighty differently gendered, aged, structurally and socially positioned people had managed to produce this remarkably sanitized definition, Kottler asked delegates at the first South African Discourse Analysis Working Conference (DAWC), held in January 1994, to discuss the definition in small groups. In this chapter we explore the process of constructing the definition and then what we loosely call its deconstruction. Our aim is to show how this kind of analysis can highlight the way text can betray the institutional group processes that gave rise to it in the first place.

Methodological process

The proceedings of the forum, the workshop and the DAWC were video- and/or audio-taped and transcribed for analysis. We use post-structuralist theories of the mutually constructing interface between institutions and subjectivity (e.g., Foucault, 1975; Rose, 1989a; Giddens, 1991) to show how the institution's organization, language and structure, i.e. its text (see Parker, 1992) influence the way the subject in turn reconstitutes its text. Clearly, it is difficult to speak outside the powerful text of the institution, but not because institutions will not tolerate disobedience or because their power is punitive. This is to oversimplify and mislead. For this reason Foucault (1975: 194) warns against describing:

> the effects of power in negative terms: it 'excludes', it 'represses', it 'censors' … In fact, power produces; it produces reality … domains of objects and rituals of truth. The individual and the knowledge that may be gained of him belong to this production.

Thus the sanitized definition was not simply constructed through 'exclusion', 'repression', 'censorship', etc., on the part of UCT's power holders. Rather, subjectivities, persuasively entangled with the institution's text, render the institution's power constitutive. In this way, within the gaze of the institution, the definition (filled with contradictions) was constructed.

Constructing the definition: framing the process The phrase 'frame of reference' was used frequently in the forum discussion. As a metaphor, 'framing' is a useful way of looking at how the process of constructing the definition was shaped and helps us to see that this happened within a specific frame, that of an academic institution. The idea of a frame allows us to examine what 'types of self' (Parker, 1992: 8) stepped into the borders of the discourses we examine and what types were excluded. It also provides 'ways of perceiving and articulating relationships' (Parker, 1992: 9) and the shifting of selves in and out of view within what at first appears to be one discourse (of transformation). In this way it is evident that the definition addresses the reader and the racist, but, by exclusion, a number of important issues remain silent. We address these issues throughout this chapter.

Affirmations: framing the space   Clearly participants at the forum and the workshop, including UCT's power holders, were all invested in facilitating the transformation of UCT's policy on racial harassment. But, introducing some sense of tension, a participant said that it is necessary to: 'have enough clout to persuade the powers that be to take the recommendations or … demands with the seriousness that it deserves' (FP).

The forum was 'perhaps the most inclusive gathering of individuals and organizations that had met in the recent history at UCT' and 'the most representative group of members of the UCT community since this process started' (a nominee). It was constructed as an open, resistant space to oppose the idea of forming an RHP. That the idea was seen as having been initiated by the Other (the vice-chancellor or 'admin') clearly framed how it was considered generally unrepresentative and how many participants felt excluded. The idea was seen as 'admin's attempt to create a "token structure" which would not counter racism. It might 'keep the sponsors happy or look good on the institution's CV' (FP) but the policy failed to make a 'bigger attack on systematic and institutional racism' (FP).

The forum space was repeatedly contrasted to the institutional space where the original policy on racism was constructed. It was therefore seen as a legitimate space from which to 'frame an alternative policy on race and racism at UCT'. It could 'tackle this thing on a more inclusive and better basis', even if it rejected the idea of an RHP and formulated 'something that is fundamentally different from the policy as conceived of by the institution' (FP).

The affirmation of this resistant space, in opposition to the institutionalized frame, allowed participants to step safely into what we shall call a discourse of resistance. However, what this actually meant was not at all clear:

> Are we a pressure group? Or are we just going to present these problems to the [institution] as a point of information? (FP).

> I think that we need to start making a something, I'm not sure whether we are a lobby or an alliance or what we are (FP).

Given what has happened at UCT since this process, which we outline on pp. 59–60 these concerns are noteworthy, particularly given that there was a fear that the forum would end up 'degenerating into some sort of legitimization of structures of power in the [institution]'. This comment clearly affirmed the existence of the discourse of resistance and the need to preserve it, but recognizing its complicated relationship with the institutional discourse gave rise to uncertainty about whether the forum could make decisions binding to UCT:

> Is [the forum] just a talking shop? ... [will] a memorandum be ... sent to the powers at administration and they will tick it or cross it and that's that? ... institutionally what kind of teeth does this body have, or can we give it? (FP).

Discussion suggested that changes coming from the forum would have to be legitimized within the institutional discourse. What was articulated within the discourse of resistance would therefore have to be transformed. Inevitably, because of the relationship between the two discourses, this did happen. A desire to 'engage the discourse that would really form part of [an institution] ... really taking change seriously' describes how the institutional discourse was infused with something of the discourse of resistance. But the need for 'enough clout to persuade the powers-that-be to take the recommendations or suggestions or demands with the serious-ness that it deserves' describes the discourse of resistance tempered for legitimacy within the institutional discourse -- transformed to 'gain clout'.

The word legitimacy is frequently used to refer to the forum's authority because it is deemed representative and because of the participative and, hence, democratic approach employed. Whether this was sufficient was never addressed. Instead, growing teeth was seen as a way of empowering the group to speak in a different voice: 'the only teeth that we will have is the teeth that we will grow for ourselves' to give '[the forum] some kind of legitimacy'. Of course, the need for teeth (to gain the clout needed for legitimacy within the institutional discourse) was, by implication, linked to the betrayal that occured.

The constant contrast between the discourse of resistance and the institutional discourse (problematically constructed in conversation as unitary and separate) reinforced the framing of the forum as a resistant space. However, frequent reference to its legitimacy led to a further problematic prerogative: that the members of this forum were united in a common goal – that there was a clearly defined harmonious and non-contradictory 'we':

> we can only have teeth if we have 32 teeth in our mouths, in other words if we have unity amongst this group, then we can be strong and have teeth (FP).

Unity is seen as strength. Coherent text – talking in the same language, holding the same goals – became an important value for action framed within the discourse of resistance. 'Talking in one voice' was to take on the apparently coherent text of the institution which provided a space to be heard. But, this limited the range of voices available and, as discussed below, its practical usefulness.

Framing racism   Forum attempts to define racism confirmed the impossibility of talking in one voice. Racism was about 'human rights',
'multicultural issues', 'alienation', 'misrepresentation'. Bringing into view
the institutional discourse, it was described as a 'social construction' and
'a perception'. These ideas were challenged by a (black) member of
AZASCO (a student liberation group), clearly positioned at that moment
in the discourse of resistance:

> I don't believe that a precondition for this meeting to go on is for us to get a
> common conception of racism. And I'm very concerned about the kind of
> language that is being used here. There is talk about 'perception' and ... about
> racism as a social construction. I know it in practical terms. I don't understand
> racism as a social construction, or as a perception, because when you talk about
> perception you are talking about something that happens inside the mind, in
> the brain. It's not there. It's here [points to skin].

Unaware of the contradictions being articulated, people's understandings
of racism were seen to be at 'different levels'. This gave rise to an idea
of a workshop to 'move forward together as much as this is possible'. To
accommodate this assumption that *everyone* wished to move forward
together and that this could be achieved only if racism is understood
uniformly we were forced to open up the frame again, to bring into view
the broader discourse of transformation.

The AZASCO participant, apparently resistant to being framed within
the discourse of transformation, and seemingly invested in what elsewhere
Kottler (1990, 1996) has called the 'differences' discourse, repeated that
people from the different constituencies represented at the forum:

> have different or conflicting perceptions or knowledge of what racism is ... for
> instance we in AZASCO have a different perception of what racism is to that
> of other people, say for instance in Congress [the vice-chancellor] or adminis-
> tration, or yourself, Comrade chairperson.

Coherence and unity were thus being presented as fictional – members of
the forum, he claimed, can have 'totally different' understandings of racism.
His inclusion of the chair, a senior black academic seemingly framed until
then within the discourse of resistance, illustrates two important aspects
of subjectivity. First, it shows that the same individual can be framed at
different times, depending on the role they are taking at that particular
moment, in multiple and contradictory discourses. Second, it shows that
it is not impossible for individuals apparently positioned in the same
discourse (for example, AZASCO members and black senior academics in
the discourse of resistance) to define racism differently. Thus what look
like coherent discourses can at different times hail or frame individuals
differently. In part, this depends on whether at that moment they are
positioned as 'subject' (acting on) or 'object' (acted upon) in that discourse.

The following exchange ensued:

Chair: What is my understanding of [racism]?
Participant: I am saying that our understanding is totally different.
Chair: No, no, what is my understanding of racism?
Participant: I said *perhaps* yours is [recording unclear] [laughter] So I remove
    you from that premise.
Chair: I am surprised how you read my mind.

Something had touched the chair; he was cross. This might have been because it had been implied that his views might be better accommodated in the institutional discourse, together with 'Congress, the VC or admin', than in the discourse of resistance where AZASCO sees itself positioned. His response did not, however, address this. Instead, he issued his own challenge and the participant – perhaps because he did not really *know* what the chair's understanding of racism was – backed down, changing his assertion into a suggestion ('perhaps'). What was equally possible, though, was a fear of authority and the chair's position, as a subject, in the institutional discourse, with the power to act on the participant as an object in that discourse. There is another possible explanation. Foucault (in Parker, 1992: 8) describes discourses as 'practices that systematically form the objects of which they speak'. Perhaps, as the institutional discourse might make the space for the 'authoritative' chair to step in, so might the discourse of transformation offer the AZASCO participant a 'conciliatory' type of self able to achieve the apparently common goal of institutionalized change.

Reframing the frame   At the end of the forum a comment that 'there is one understanding of racism that the [institution] utilizes, which may not be quite what people experience on the ground' led to the decision to hold a workshop to enable 'people on the ground' to find a definition acceptable to them. The text of the discourse of transformation remained, encapsulating the idea that until everyone spoke in the same voice (and understood racism in the same way), nothing could be done about strategies to combat racism. A workshop would enable people to 'understand one another' and 'tackle concrete issues' – to create a definition *not* to formalize or 'intellectualize' but to legitimate experiences of racism. The motivation clearly came from people whose views were also easily framed in the discourse of resistance, still apparently in opposition to the institutional discourse. However, it is noteworthy that while the space at the beginning of the forum was clearly framed within the discourse of resistance, in that it was defined as open and malleable, it had been reframed by the end. It became constricted through the introduction of institutional rules used to get the proposal for a workshop through. With the introduction of this institutional text, the reframing was facilitated. It is here that the betrayal of the discourse of resistance was first evident. A closer exploration illustrates this. A proposal for a workshop was made. Some participants were, however, uncomfortable with a possible link between this proposed workshop and another transformation conference being organized by staff and progressive student activists at UCT. Trying to deal with this (after all, this was an open space), an AZASCO participant asked if he could 'modify the proposal'. The chair, clearly positioned as a subject in the institutional discourse at this moment, said:

> No you can't, because it has been seconded ... There is a proposal before us and I think we should stick to that. It has been seconded ... it's now under discussion, and in a moment I'm going to ask, if necessary, for a vote.

Voila! The forum space is transformed from an open space for discussion to one framed by the text of a formal 'meeting', where something seconded becomes the authority. Those who were positioned as acting subjects within the discourse of resistance became positioned as objects, acted upon within the institutional discourse. The workshop, aided by the authority of the institutional discourse, continued.

Betrayals: framing the space   In stark contrast to what happened at the forum, workshop participants were never in a position to influence the process which, from the outset, was structured and task-orientated. We will now discuss the listening committee and agenda to show how these 'structures' (or text), as objects, are discourses in themselves and can and do inform the text with which we speak.

The listening committee   The workshop structure provided space for a listening committee (LC): three people who were expected to listen to the proceedings and to summarize the day's conclusions. While this might not have been the organizing group's intention, in practice it appeared on the day as if the LC was able to produce an objective rendition of the proceedings, perpetuating the belief that the different workshop voices could be collated into one coherent, non-contradictory and unitary statement. Closer examination of the LC's definition of racism, supposedly an objective, 'simple' summary of seven sub-group definitions, shows the impossibility of this task. An LC member confirmed this when he said 'some of the definitions are not reconcilable'.

We will take up one aspect of the definition: the construction of racism as an 'irrational belief', which became a focus in the deconstruction process below. In the seven definitions that emerged, racism was labeled as a 'belief', an 'attitude', a 'perception' and an 'illegitimate classification', but none suggested 'irrationality'. Only once was the idea of 'irrationality' mentioned (in discussion and controversially). The inclusion therefore came from the LC, not from the participants, highlighting how this structural aspect of the workshop and the use of the academic text of the institutional discourse produced the LC's definition. The definition's vagueness may also have had structural imperatives: if the job of the LC was objective collation, a degree of vagueness would counteract any contradictions, accusations or opposing ideas. Thus this definition had grown 'teeth' from the way in which it had successfully been contrived to speak in one voice – that voice using the institutional text because of the requirements of the situation. The LC, briefed merely to reflect back to the workshop what they were hearing and therefore meant to affirm the voice of the discourse of resistance, betrayed it because the text that set it up in the first place required it to be objective, coherent, certain – it had been sanitized in order to gain legitimacy within the institutional discourse.

The agenda The job of those present at the workshop was also framed by the predetermined agenda. This in itself imposed a very different frame on the gathering from that of the forum which was framed as an open and resistant space devoid of any agenda. In contrast, the workshop employed a task-driven approach drawing increasingly on institutional text.

The structure of the agenda helps to explain how the personal, subjective definitions offered at the forum became the sanitized one derived at the workshop. It took the following form:

— Participants discussed their experiences of racism in small groups and then fed these back to the plenary.
— Small groups defined racism, racial harassment and racial discrimination and fed these back to the plenary.
— The LC constructed their 'summary' definition – for discussion by the plenary. (Feedback occurred at the end of the actual meeting when most people had left, so discussion did not occur.)
— Participants were to decide on a practical way forward. (At the meeting, because of time constraints, another steering committee – ISCOR – was elected to do this.)

Our comment on this agenda and the actual process of the workshop involves the ordering of discussion. First, people's subjective experiences of racism were discussed. Then definitions were constructed. This might have worked, and was clearly intended, to affirm people's experiences. However, closer analysis questions this. The order suggests that after dealing with the personal 'stuff' the 'real' job at hand can happen. Astonishingly, but perhaps not surprisingly given our argument, participants' definitions began to exclude the lived and painful experiences evident earlier; participants easily shifted from using the language of experience (non-task-driven but acknowledged in the discourse of resistance) to the language of formal 'legitimate' definitions (task-driven, using the text of the institutional discourse).

Thus, there was no conspiracy and no sole author (Parker, 1992). The LC and the participants seemed to slip easily into an already available discourse of academia – the text of institutional discourse. This included those who had previously been positioned in the discourse of resistance. Some of them had, after all, as elected members of the organizing committee, been party to the construction of the agenda before the workshop. Given this, we believe that nothing would have changed had there been time to discuss the final definitions at the plenary, as planned. But the framing of discussion as 'superfluous' helped to marginalize the discourse of resistance – the open space.

Our notion is supported by the following exchange. Earlier in the workshop, a participant's suggestion of discussing the definitions 'just to get a closure' was vetoed as 'unfinished business' that an elected committee could look into at a later stage. So the definitions already 'existed', even before they were finished, as objective and unproblematic and 'existing'. This is because the LC was set up (by *all* those who constructed the agenda and who took part in the process at the workshop) to summarize the statements 'objectively'. The fact that they were able to do this was seen as legitimate enough not to warrant further discussion at the workshop.

The LC became an objective voice of authority, offering coherence and closure. This was presented as unquestionable. Its report back was constructed as a cursory formality – not a point of discussion. Here the implications of a written, subjectless definition became apparent. A member of the LC, assuming the agent of the definition to be insignificant now that the definition was on paper, commented: 'I don't know if I need to be here because we've written it out.'

Rose (1988, 1989a) argues that modern institutions govern subjectivity by inscription which makes people visible and, in this case, diagnosable. The act of 'writing out' the definition at the workshop formalized the description of what racism is, allowing no space for disagreement or debate. The definition was framed outside the discourse of resistance and inside the institutional discourse precisely because it had become objective and unitary and it was now meant to be used to describe and categorize people. Notions of 'irrationality', drawn from a (pseudo-)scientific discourse of psychology added legitimacy, and while the definition was vague because of the relationship between writing and power it was assumed that the user of the definition has the power to know – because s/he has the power to use. The turning of lived experience into writing, and of resistance into writing, has functioned 'as a procedure of objectification and subjectification' (Foucault, quoted in Rose, 1989b: 123)

The process thus far has shown how individuals have slipped out of the frame of the discourse of resistance – a discourse clearly framed in opposition to the institutional discourse – into the broader collaborative frame of the discourse of transformation. The act of defining has placed the subject under surveillance – it has offered a frame for seeing and an authoritative voice for telling. Surveillance is not part of the discourse of resistance, which opposes the power of the institution. But neither is it part of the institutional discourse. While the institutional discourse can use the definition to speak, it did not author the definition. The definition was constructed within the broader discourse of transformation which, because of its ability to 'hail' both the types of selves (i.e., that framed within the institutional discourse and that of the discourse of resistance), can make them listen as a certain type of person (Parker, 1992) – a person who wants institutional change, and to whom academic text is available, and for whom there is a pay-off (in Hollway's, 1984, terms). Being positioned within the broader discourse of transformation, using its institutional text (its language, its structures, etc.), achieved the kind of 'clout' needed to persuade 'admin' to institutionalize acceptable policies for dealing with racism at UCT.

Having looked at the way in which the definition was constructed at the workshop, we now explore the process of deconstruction by a group of psychologists at the DAWC.

Deconstructing the definition: constructing the subject

Definitions construct various subjects, the most obvious of which here is the racist subject. As indicated, although the use of the word 'irrational' in such a definition is not at all unexpected given that 'racism is most generally defined as the irrational (or prejudicial) belief in or practice of differentiating population groups' (Goldberg, 1993: 93), its inclusion became a focal point in discussion at the DAWC. In a manner reminiscent of Billig et al.'s (1988) theory of 'rhetorical constructions', in which a key term in a discourse is always constructed in an argumentative way, participants criticized both the use of the word 'irrational' and the power relations in which this term participates:

> if you set up the notion that there is a belief that's irrational and this is what racism is, it … suggest[s] that there's another belief that's rational that you can subscribe to, and what political meaning does that carry? (conference participant – CP)

With some effort, seemingly fearful that his contribution would be silenced, a black DAWC participant illustrated how this can be politically and emotionally debilitating:

> I didn't quite fully explain the political connotation because you see what happens to me as a black person, then, if I am told that racism is an irrational belief, how do I then fight it? … what does that mean for the ways in which I can take it up and challenge it? Because I'm told it's irrational [agreement].

This point, and the power of inscription mentioned above, were picked up by another participant:

> what we emphasized most strongly would be the way in which the position of the irrational gave the authority to the writer to know what racism is, and therefore to convey this to the reader – presumably both of them in a rational discourse and which effectively excluded either the writer or reader from participation in it.

Another statement 'we wondered who would decide what is irrational and what is rational' (CP), illustrated that in saying something about how the definition of irrational people is directed at rational selves who know and can define irrationality, inviting an increasingly problematic absolution:

> [The definition] doesn't [result] in 'you have to examine things', so if you're dealing with ... an instance or practice of racism, it would be quite easy to distance yourself and that invites distancing between the phenomenon and the person interacting with that phenomenon (CP).

In failing to name the reader or writer both are excluded from participation and exempted from self-examination. This is a theme throughout the DAWC achieved in different ways:

> racism involves the *irrational belief* in the existence of different groups. Well, believing in the existence of different groups is not necessarily irrational (CP).

Drawing attention to the use of a (pseudo-)scientific discourse, particularly available to the DAWC participants, the use of the idea of 'irrational' was criticized also for its negative psychological connotations: insanity, primitiveness, and the pathologizing text used 'to talk about what's going on, and that seems to suggest we are outside of that. And we fail to then look at our own racism' (CP). In this way, again the (psychologized) text exonerates the reader of the definition from racism. The use of the term 'irrational belief' returns the focus of the definition to the individual in which pathology is located, i.e., within the *racist* Other. This cleverly obscures subjectivity and agency so that racism becomes vague and empty of meaning. The definition is aimed at individuality but 'individuality' has become devoid of feeling:

> we felt [the definition] excluded feelings ... or only recognized experience in very muted ways. Um, *irrational* beliefs – that's very sanitized for talking about racism.

This vagueness became more apparent in examining how the object of racism is constructed. A participant commented: 'an irrational belief is ... a classic individualistic notion within psychology whereby only individuals exist. Groups are fallacies.' The definition also obscures reference to 'certain groups', contradictorily constructed as both fictive and real:

it looks as though there's an internal contradiction in the definition ... in the first definition based on prejudice, you've got the 'irrational belief in the existence of certain groups'. The second part ... actually deals with a 'set of practices that disadvantage certain groups'. So ... you disadvantage certain groups – there are these things called groups – and in the first part you're saying ... the belief in them is actually irrational.

Since one of the workshop aims was to find a practical way forward, a paradox emerged. If the idea of a group is irrational, then how can a group have the power to resist?

Another of the aims of the workshop was to find a way to change UCT's policy from one which disregards 'the fundamental issue of institutional racism' (FP). This was not achieved; the definition failed to identify or name the object/s of racism – a powerful example of how the text betrayed the institutional group processes that gave rise to it in the first place. This begged the question: what are the effects of the failure to name and the consequent silence?

Naming and silence   In noting that 'the state isn't mentioned which has rationalized that irrational belief system' a participant commented that the state had been excluded from its very real participation in racist ideology. Racist *practices* were constructed as devoid of political motivation. Further, describing racism as irrational makes the idea of race:

> a fiction ... it's a construction ... but it's clearly not. Its effects are not fictional in any sense and that also prompted us to talk about the rationality of racism ... the way in which it is in fact a logical system with a motivation, with interests and not to talk about that is to make it irrelevant (CP).

This participant feels and knows race subjectively, as did the AZASCO forum participant when he said he did not understand:

> racism as a social construction, or as a perception, because when you talk about perception you are talking about something that happens inside the mind, in the brain. It's not there. It's here [points to skin].

For these two participants, race identity was of central importance. Positioned squarely within the frame of the discourse of resistance, neither were invested at this moment in a notion that 'we are all the same under our skin' (Gevisser, 1995/6: 9). This idea resonates with the text of an historically important anti-apartheid similarities discourse, taken up by progressive social scientists in apartheid South Africa in the late 1980s and early 1990s described by Kottler (1996).

The DAWC conference discussion yielded a number of other concerns about the failure to name, and the always-already meaning of its silent opposite:

> We also talked ... about the all too obvious attempt ... to avoid the language provided by apartheid for a description of bodies and we talked about the quagmire that avoidance leads to ... to this kind of complete ambiguity.

Obviously the silence and absence of naming the group/s involved reflected the powerful association between the act of naming and apartheid ideology. There were more examples of how the resistance to naming denies individuals much of what is subjectively and politically important to them. For example, another participant noted that:

> while there is a valid move away from Indian, Coloured, Black, White in South Africa, leaving those things out actually takes all the usefulness ... in an important way out of that definition.

What this illustrates is how the text of the *similarities discourse* (Kottler, 1996) still clearly had an ability to continue to hail participants and prompt them to act as a certain type of self. However, some participants alluded to the problems of this discourse, now being described as the 'universalism rooted in both the dogma of hard lefties and the sentimentality of soft liberals' (Gevisser, 1995/6: 9). Failure to name 'actually perpetuates racism at some level' (CP). It excludes the practical and very real subjective experiences of racism which are 'connected to the naming of bodies and which makes the same thing said by people in different social positions mean very different things' (FP), discussed above.

A (black) participant illustrated something of this:

> in a demonstration in the face of the South African police ... you [can go to] police officers in terms of individuality, you'll soon be lying bleeding on the floor ... it's not irrational at times to perceive people as groups, nor of the existence of those groups even if the reification of those groups ... is problematic.

The silence and the evasive language in the definition was understood in terms of the South African context and a reticence to rehearse the racism of the past. But attention was also drawn to the problematic political effect of silencing, discounting (and dismissing) the history of racism in South Africa:

> It doesn't appear ... as [if] there's been a history of racism and apartheid and oppression of black people in South Africa. That's all in the past, but what we've got there is something that ... pretends that it no longer exists, or we no longer need to speak of it.

Sanitized definition Goldberg (1993: 97) argues that 'any reasonable definition of racism must in principle be able to distinguish between racialized expressions that are more or less benign'. They cannot therefore be exhaustive and often use abstract, general language for reasons as illustrated by the following statement:

> Something about these kinds of policy statements suggest we have to try and capture everything within one succinct little statement that … has all the bits logically related to each other. There's a lot that those kind of statements necessarily leave out.

The question that arises from this is what *is* the 'something' about these kinds of policy statements which requires a particular genre, and what is its effect?

In asking 'what is it about the situation [at UCT] which leads people to think that they must construct a definition?' one participant suggested that in the act of doing there was an important socio-historical naming and therefore validation of 'the existence of apartheid and the existence of racism'. He reflected that 'admin' might have said 'well, given the history of apartheid in South Africa, we need to make certain types of political statements or political proposals'.

Agency is recognized; a definition is not merely a description, and constructing one is not a passive act, but an act of reconstruction. Participants consistently used the metaphor of sanitization to describe the definition. The construction of a 'succinct little statement' meant that the debate and the concern about practical experience expressed in the work-shop had been 'washed clean'; the final definition 'speaks' in the text of the broader discourse of transformation. In this way, the definition gained legitimacy – teeth were 'grown'; it was constructed in a way congruent with institutional language, values and formalities. All of this powerfully exemplifies practices systematically forming the objects of which they speak (Parker, 1992).

The definition's practical function was, however, clearly undermined by the sanitized language used. UCT's definition was compared to another arising in a different context:

> about genre and about the ways in which this definition is formulated … I was thinking of the … striking difference between this quite extended definition … it's quite a waffly, vague and … sanitized definition … the definition used in [name of council] a few years ago … was quite pithy … racism is … *prejudice plus power*. Whether that's right or not … whether that's a better definition or not is beside the point. What's interesting is about the different context, in-stitutional contexts within which those definitions have developed … prejudice plus power is a political slogan … it's something that can be brought out at critical moments and used as part of the process of persuasion to mobilize people, whereas this is developed in an … institutional context and in a way it reflects all the sort of vagaries of [institutional] discussion's [laughter] avoidance of politics. So this is not … so much abstracted, it's not so much a general statement but it's very much located in a particular context. And then we were wondering, well what will it be used for? Is it something that people are going

to be able to appeal to ... [will it] function as some sort of legal framework? But the very way in which it's constructed opens all the options for interpretation and debate and disagreement that the different definitions offer. We wondered how it will be useful ...

The comment shows how the use of institutional text for legitimacy has paradoxically opened up spaces for silences and vagueness about whom the definition refers to, who will use it and for what purpose/s. This is in stark contrast to the stated aims of participants at the forum and the workshop. There, talk focused on combating structural racism and white male supremacy – combating the racism of groups. But the definition's political and practical usefulness is appropriately questioned. A participant pointed out this difficulty:

How do we apply this usefully to a particular situation ... where it's politically motivated around instances where one person is injured by another person? How do you take the detail of that situation and match it against such a broad definition full of its own contradictions?

Referring again to the influence of the context (a historically white, often considered elitist, institution) a participant reflected:

If you tried to contextualize this definition – it ... does not come from people who have suffered oppression. That is what I would say very clearly. That for any campus to come out with a definition, that campus is a campus that has black people who are the victim of oppression which has never been followed up, it's the follow-up of the people who were actually skirting the issues and [are] now taking part in that guilt.

It is interesting that the forum and workshop – whence came the definition – were deliberately constructed in a representative and consultative way within the discourse of resistance: they hoped to overcome UCT's historical lack of representation. The definition, washed clean as it was, gives no indication of this process and, as we have seen, shifts into the language of academia – the language of knowledge – for its legitimacy. But in also using other UCT languages – of guilt, of silence, of abstraction – it incorporates text that not only obscures the racial Object from scrutiny but also obscures the racist Object from scrutiny. Once the definition has been set down on paper, it becomes removed from the agents who put it together (doubly so since these agents silenced any agency – any subject – in the definition). It becomes open to exactly the kind of criticism it was seeking to overcome.

Implications for institutional change

The above analysis suggests that resistance that prompts institutional change is difficult because of the persuasiveness of institutional discourse and the need to gain legitimacy (or at least acceptance) from the institution. If an alternative policy is to be used by the institution, how can a discourse of resistance be maintained? It was the interface between the participants (members of the institution) and the institution (the structure which produced the definition) that allowed participants to slip into the discourse of transformation. The tension between construction and action is therefore another interface where the institution's text comes into play.

We have drawn attention to a range of political and practical problems yielded by this process. Given what has happened since 1994, we might be tempted to be nihilistic and deterministic in concluding that institutional discourse will inevitably affect institutional change. But is this position not only unacceptable because it is politically paralysing; it would also not seem to reflect some of what has actually happened at UCT. We shall briefly mention some of these changes, although neither author has recorded or followed closely any processes since mid-1994. Kottler has, however, retained an interest in these. An RHP has not materialized; ISCOR specifically decided against this idea, in order to maintain credibility. A number of working groups and forums have formed with the explicit idea of encouraging negotiation and broader participation and co-opting 'new minds and ideas' (notes on an ISCOR meeting). Discussions about racism with post-graduate students and colleagues at UCT clearly indicate that the text of 'liberal' similarities discourse makes it hard to talk meaningfully about issues of racism.

Drawing a parallel with the difficulty of talking about issues of gender at UCT, we can easily identify with this, for the same reasons. On a more positive note, press coverage in some of the local newspapers has revealed the existence of a number of apparently useful working groups at UCT. These have continued to negotiate broader participation in decision-making around issues of transformation and racism at UCT. Out of these have come booklets and mission statements and high-ranking staff appointments, which the media describe as examples of success. Thus, whilst institutional discourse did seem to influence the construction of a sanitized, abstract and certain definition of racism and could be seen to involve a process of institutional surveillance, it was clearly not a one-way process. The definition was constructed by the types of selves who at the forum were clearly framed within the discourse of resistance, but who could be, and were, hailed by the broader discourse of transformation. Whilst the definition could be used by the institution for surveillance, the text of the discourse of resistance has not been destroyed, nor have the selves who are framed at particular moments within this: the forum itself became an instrument of surveillance of the institution. Thus the power to watch is no longer one-way. Institutions are not impermeable bounded objects; they do not have exclusive and all-pervasive power. Giddens (1991) argues that modern institutions are reflexive in nature: as its 'subjects' are brought into its alignment, the institution reflexively incorporates its knowledge of them into its own frame. The institution reconstitutes its subjects as they reconstitute the institution. This is evident in how UCT has transformed itself since the workshop was held.

Conclusion

This chapter has drawn on the text of two interwoven institutions in discussing the definition of racism: the bureaucratic institution of UCT (in this case the institution of control – controlling racism) and the expert institution of psychology. The former provides the formula for a definition – a way in which the chaos can be ordered. The psychological institution has neatly ordered the chaos – those messy issues within the bureaucratic definition. Its voice is powered by knowledge (another neat device for imparting order). It is able to say something like 'this chaos can be authoritatively explained by social psychological theories of irrationality. We understand.' But discourse analysis has allowed us to understand much more. We have seen how text can betray the institutional group processes that gave rise to it in the first place and how powerful silences are in all of this. But we have also seen clearly how discourses are not static, how the language and structures exemplified in the discourses identified in this chapter have been transformed, and how the shifting sands and selves have helped to transform the insitution and the selves which occupy it.

This analysis has again brought into focus the power of the 'similarities' discourse and its continued silencing of notions of difference. We argue that apartheid may have been dismantled but racism will not go away regardless of how many policies are in place. In the context in which we have lived, we have never been 'all the same under our skin' (Gevisser, 1995/6: 9) and, while South Africa might be described as the Rainbow Nation, it is still 'black and white': race remains a core issue in all of our subjective experiences and national identities. The silence that surrounds this issue has been shouting at us for at least a decade. We must continue to question our assumptions and find ways to talk about difference without reinvoking the racializing discourse we all fear so much.

References

Billig, M., Condor, S., Edwards, D., Gane, M., Middleton, D. and Radley, A. (eds) (1988) *Ideological Dilemmas: A Social Psychology of Everyday Thinking*, Sage, London.
Foucault, M. (1975) *Discipline and Punish: The Birth of the Prison*, Allen Lane, London.
Gevisser, M. (1995/6) 'Rainbow nation is still black and white', in *Mail & Guardian*, 22 December 1995 to 4 January 1996.
Giddens, A. (1991) *Modernity and Self-identity: Self and Society in the Late Modern Age*, Polity Press, Cambridge.

Goldberg, D. T. (1993) *Racist Culture: Philosophy and the Politics of Meaning*, Blackwell, Oxford.

Hollway, W. (1984) 'Gender difference and the production of subjectivity', in J. Henriques, W. Hollway, C. Urwin, C. Venn and V. Walkerdine, *Changing the Subject: Psychology, Social Regulation and Subjectivity*, Methuen, London, 227–63.

Kottler, A. (1990) 'South Africa: psychology's dilemma of multiple discourses', *Psychology in Society*, 13, 27–36.

Kottler, A. (1996) 'Voices in the winds of change', *Feminism & Psychology*, 6 (1), 61–8.

Parker, I. (1992) *Discourse Dynamics: Critical Analysis for Social and Individual Psychology*, Routledge, London.

Rose, N. (1988) 'Calculable minds and manageable individuals', *History of the Human Sciences*, 1 (2), 179–200.

Rose, N. (1989a) *Governing the Soul: The Shaping of the Private Self*, Routledge, London and New York.

Rose, N. (1989b) 'Individualizing psychology', in J. Shotter and K. Gergen (eds), *Texts of Identity*, Sage, London, Newbury Park and New Delhi.

PART TWO

Gender, Power and Sexuality

CHAPTER 5

The psychologization of monogamy in advice columns: surveillance, subjectivity and resistance

Lindy Wilbraham

This chapter uses a Foucauldian discourse analytic approach to amplify, through exploration of structuring effects of discourse, the relationship between institutionalized knowledges, discursive practices and gendered subjectivities. Using a letter and reply from an advice column in a South African magazine as a text, the ways in which women are impelled to work in psychologized ways to effect normalization in the crisis of a male partner's sexual infidelity are examined. Psychologized technologies and practices produce rewards of power for subjection, and these powers are critically discussed in terms of an injunction towards women's ongoing vigilance in/over relationships, various strategies of empowerment available to women, and an evaluation of a Foucauldian notion of resistance.

Advice columns, knowledge and power

As a middle-class, white, feminist academic, my interest in advice columns in South African women's magazines was prompted by my own ambivalence about their operations and effects. On the one hand, I recognize the potential of advice columns to empower the individual women who read them – for example, encouraging these women to take responsibility for their own well-being, to stand firm against exploitation and abuse, and to seek support within existing institutionalized resources. However, on the other hand, I was suspicious of, and resistant towards, the ideological functions of regulation they might achieve, such as framing and resolving problems in particular ways, and the effects of exclusion that they may reproduce, such as excising reference to South Africa's legacy of unequal access to institutional knowledges and technologies, and power, on the basis of gender, race or class.

The contextualization of my ambivalence within a developing body of diverse academic and popular writings about advice columns was assisted by McRobbie's (1991) classification of three approaches to advice columns

– realist, feminist and Foucauldian – which identify underlying assumptions about knowledge and power (1991: 161–5). Although these distinctions are fairly simplistic, fetishizing differences between positions and obscuring contradictions within positions and multi-positional stances, they are used here to introduce tensions between different conceptualizations of power.

McRobbie's *realist* position assumes the transparency of discourse in the production of meaning and knowledge. Thus, 'questions' express authentic problems, and 'answers' provide information, support and/or practical coping strategies (cf. a humanist position). The dearth of South African research on advice columns is noted, but this realist view of empowerment is commonly upheld in the writings of European and American magazine editors and advice columnists (e.g. Kurtz, 1990), and in content analytic studies which have attempted to illustrate historical shifts or current trends in types of problems presented (e.g. Ratcliff, 1969), or in forms of advice offered (e.g. Brinkgreve and Korzec, 1979).

Feminist and Foucauldian positions challenge the ontological status accorded to problems and the effects of advice columns within realist assumptions. They both adopt a productive view of discourse, and add a moral-political slant to the relationships between discourse, knowledge and power. However, while Foucauldian approaches conceive of power as an individualizing tendency concerned with the physical organization of bodies ('disciplinary power'), and resistance at micro-levels (see Foucault, 1976, 1982), feminists highlight structural oppression of women ('sovereign power'), and an agenda of social transformation at a macro-level.

A (radical) *feminist* position is thus concerned with the politicization of the 'personal problems' encountered in advice columns. The exposure of hidden editing practices might reveal, for example, the framing of particular experiences as problematic for women (for example, concern with physical appearance or relationships), and valorization of resolutions which redirect women into conventionalizing feminine roles and pursuits (such as therapeutic work on the body or relationship). By this account, editors/ publishers collude with patriarchal and capitalist ideologies to dupe women into disempowerment. The formal structure of advice columns – based on individualism, privacy and intimacy – disallows critical discussion and/ or collective protest by women about gender, race or class oppression (Winship, 1987).

However, Foucault's (1975) exposition of the technology and effects of confession and the panopticon as a metaphor for self-regulation and subjection are particularly relevant to a *Foucauldian* analysis of advice columns. Here, the advice column genre's focus on sharing personal problems only feigns privacy and intimacy, for confession happens within a public media forum. The injunction to confess labours as a technology of power to establish a 'regime of visibility' in which increasing aspects of our lives become examinable, interpretable and reformable through the normalizing scrutiny of experts and the pervasive knowledges of experts (Rose, 1990: 7). This is linked within advice columns to recent trends towards information-based or service-based advice (Brinkgreve and Korzec, 1979), and the replacement of the 'agony aunty' with professional advice-givers and/or experts (Mininni, 1991).

Thus, professional procedures of motivation and mechanisms of reformation are touted, reproducing particular positions and corrective practices as agentic work towards 'optimizing experience and functioning', and thereby effecting subjectivity and normalization (Rose, 1990). Furthermore, public confession addresses a wider audience than the lonely, lovelorn, individual advice-seeker and draws in the operations of testimony and witness, whereby all readers are subjected to self-surveillance by grids of institutionalized knowledges, meanings and moralities, whether they write in to advice columns themselves or confess, monitor and labour within the safety of their homes.

Psychologization refers, in a critical way, to the processes of rendering the body, the psyche/self or the relationship visible to the normalizing discursive practices of the institution of psychology (Rose, 1990). This involves the work of reducing ideological notions of social arrangements to individual activities and proclivities.

Wholesale rejection of these norms is difficult, for the dynamic and elaborate operations of disciplinary power in normalizing discourses achieve contradictory effects (Young, 1987), viz. (a) constraining what may be known and acted upon, and regulating appropriate action or resistance; and (b) producing the rights, strategies and resources that facilitate action and 'care of the self' (Foucault, 1986: 43). Thus we depend on expert techniques for enhancing our capacities as individuals; we choose strategies and act on promises of health, well-being, fulfilment, tranquility or autonomy in order to care for and 'actualize' ourselves. This 'entrepreneurial self', through bolstering dominant forms of subjectivity, produces a sense of control and directedness in individual lives, e.g. choice, agency, desire, responsibility, morality and self-discipline (Rose, 1990).

In this chapter, I explore a construction of infidelity within psychological discourses, and the positioning of women as emotional workers and enforcers of monogamy-rules in the practice of heterosexual relationships. I sustain a critical focus on issues of power – attempting to produce, for example, a reading of an advice column extract that is disruptive of taken-for-granted assumptions – and conclude with an evaluation of a Foucauldian notion of resistance.

Reading a South African advice text

The text selected for analysis in this chapter is from the 'Janet Harding's Lifeline' advice column in *You* magazine (*You*, 1991). The chapter is a fragment of a larger study, which compared the operations and effects of eight different sites of advice in three South African magazines: *You* and two 'white women's magazines', *Fair Lady* and *Femina*. Aspects relating to the comparison of these sites of advice have been published elsewhere (e.g. Wilbraham, 1996a and 1996b). *You* magazine is a so-called family magazine, which is targeted at an English-speaking, general interest population. Female readership of *You* is estimated at 65 per cent, but readership statistics indicate that it reaches a broader spectrum of South African readers in terms of gender, race or class (e.g. 57 per cent white; 43 per cent black) than either *Fair Lady* or *Femina* (All Media Products Survey, 1992). I return to anomalous issues relating to the readership of *You* magazine at various moments during this chapter.

The advice text analysed here was selected as it was explicitly concerned with the operation of technologies of normalization in an instance of infidelity, and contradictory issues of dis/empowerment for women. The heterosexist positioning of women (as suffering wives) and men (as compulsive adulterers) might be interpreted as a pre-selection bias in gendered representations within advice columns. However, I should make clear that I make no claims to generality of practices of infidelity beyond this text, and acknowledge that other readers and/or texts might produce varying discursive foci.

Thus this advice text is used as a 'surface of emergence' for the psychologized, discursive construction of monogamy. The hidden editing operations of an intertextual chain – for example, from original to published version – highlight Barthes' (1977) notion of the 'death of the author'. The text is, thus, severed from authentic authorship by any particular individual (advice-seeker or advice-giver), and original aims and intentions are deconstructed in my interpretation. Question and answer sections are marked Q and A, not to differentiate authorship, but as part of an interpretation of a formal, rhetorical technique used in advice columns to set up institutionalized resolutions as unassailable truth.

Analysis of the psychologization at work in this text proceeds through intuitive exploration of the connotations invoked. For example, examination of how monogamy is constructed as an object within psychological discourses focuses on the particular dialogue, statements and metaphors that are set up in this advice text. The analytical strategy here is to approach the text as an 'addressor', i.e., how it addresses and produces an audience. Parker (1992) has suggested the following questions as germane to a focus on subjectification: who is being addressed by this text?; what are they expected to *do* when addressed? (e.g. adopt particular perceptions and positions, and perform appropriate, reformative work); and what rights/ powers does this discourse bestow on these subjects to speak (1992: 10).

A goal of such an analytic procedure is to explore the reproduction of power relations and ideological effects achieved through deployment of institutionalized discourses. Within advice texts – where rigorous editing guarantees the production of unidimensional, seamless meanings – Derridean deconstructionist techniques are invaluable for their focus on power issues. Through identification of oppositional terms, deconstruction provides a way to bring absent or implicit terms into visibility, and to show how institutionalized knowledges (e.g. psychological discourses) maintain dominance through the silencing and/or marginalization of these oppositions (e.g. Parker, 1988).

Having outlined a methodological orientation, I will now illustrate how this informed my reading of a particular text.

Monogamy rules: will I ever get over his affair?

'Will I ever get over his affair?' is the title of the advice text reproduced below. Titles are editorially inserted in most South African advice columns. Mininni (1991) has interpreted this as a formal device to assure anonymity. I emphasize the link between documented shifts towards information-based advice issued by experts, and anonymity operating through 'death of the author' strategies in advice texts.

Q I have been happily married for 30 years, having got married at 17. We've had the usual ups and downs, but basically our marriage has been good and my husband and I were considered an ideal couple. However, about four months ago, I discovered he was having an affair with a girl of 20 he met at the office. He has begged me not to leave him and says he loves me more than ever, but I feel betrayed and bitter and my self-confidence is shattered. It is difficult to sleep with him knowing he has slept with her. I feel separated from him and so furious with her and feel the magic has gone out of our marriage. We don't want to go to a marriage counsellor, but I feel the need for outside help. Does the pain ever get better? Can I ever trust him again? And will our marriage ever be the same again?

A The crucial issue is how much you both want your marriage to work, and a lot now depends on how you handle it. Recognise that along with your marriage facing a crisis, each of you is experiencing your own personal crisis. You probably feel so hurt, shocked and generally unnerved that it's impossible for you to consider forgiving him, letting the affair go and rebuilding a relationship. You're probably also too uncertain to make a reinvestment of trust. No doubt you're very angry, which will further block any positive feelings within your marriage. But try to gain perspective – regard this as a crisis in your marriage rather than an event that is bringing the relationship to an end. Understanding that may give you more equilibrium with which to confront the crisis. Remember that both you and your husband want your marriage to work – and remember too that a crisis can be used as an opportunity to test the commitment and make it work. It *is* possible with love and determination and as there are people out there who can help you both, why not use them? Talk to your husband about outside guidance – your marriage is worth it. Contact a counsellor at the Family

Life Centre on (011) 833-2051 in order to work through your feelings – not to negate them, but to allow other, more constructive feelings and thoughts through as well.

Foucault (1986) introduces his discussion of power relations in monogamy by referring to it as 'the monopoly on sexual pleasure' (1986: 165), with monopoly connoting sole privilege, exclusive control or possession. Foucault's detailed historical analysis traces the development of Christian censure of non-procreative sexuality into the 'conjugalization of sexual relations' (ibid.), i.e. where the state of marriage coincides with and contains sexual activity, precluding the pursuit of carnal experience else-where. Thus, when the incipient requirement of symmetrical fidelity breaks down – as in the husband's adultery in the above text – a 'crisis' ensues (e.g. socio-moral outrage as conventionalized relationship rules are flouted, betrayal of trust, etc.), requiring a renegotiation of sexual monopoly, and power, in the marriage or relationship.

The florid details of this particular adulterous affair – who did what to whom, when, how often, and why – are not of concern to this analysis. My reading focuses on what psychologization (in A above) does to this compelling narrativization, and some of the effects which are thereby reproduced for women-readers. I will argue that these dis/empowering effects serve to structure (a) such an event as 'a crisis', (b) a will to therapy, and (c) an imperative for ongoing relationship-work and vigilance. It is noted as a reflective comment on the analytic process that the production of these effects into a linear narrative is fraught with points of overlap and rupture, intertextual reference and refraction through my own subjective positionings.

'Crisis' The advice text presents a woman's account of the effects that the discovery of her partner's infidelity have wrought on their marriage, viz. a cataclasmic shift from 'the usual ups and downs', to a state where 'the magic has gone out of [the] marriage'. The disruption of 'the usual' and the loss of magic – to which I return below – is specified to be associated with 'shattered' self-confidence, betrayal, bitterness, pain, mis-trust, anger (with 'the other woman'), and sexual/intimacy derailments (e.g. 'it is difficult to sleep with him', and feeling 'separated from him'). The advice columnist, almost parodying humanistic therapeutic techniques to convey acceptance, understanding and non-judgement (e.g., Rogers, 1961), faithfully reflects back the laundry list of symptoms ('You probably feel so ... hurt, shocked, unnerved, uncertain, angry'), thereby normalizing these emotional responses. However, a notion of 'crisis' is introduced which has to be normalized via psychotherapeutic technologies.

Thus the emblematic repetition of 'crisis' – repeated five times in A – achieves at least three effects. First, it reproduces this event, and the emotional experience thereof, as a crisis: a catastrophe, a disaster, with dire and destructive intra-subjective (i.e. emotional or psychic) and inter-subjective (i.e. relational) consequences. A similar argument has been put forward with respect to talk about jealousy in heterosexual relationship practice (Stenner, 1993). In this advice text, the wife's account gains definition through being slotted into a body of institutionalized knowledges and professional experiences of the effects of adulterous affairs on marriages (i.e. similar 'cases'), via the advice-giver's accredited professional status within a crisis-counselling psychological organization, Lifeline. This operates to forge a perceptual grid whereby women/readers are enabled normatively to recognize and expect the discovery of asymmetrical fidelity as a crisis.

Second, the advice columnist achieves a psychologized reformulation of crisis: from dangerous node, destructive disaster or condition of uncertainty, to positive/constructive turning-point or decisive moment (cf. Parker, 1989). Thus the crisis is rearticulated in terms of its 'therapeutic opportunities' (Rose, 1990: 245), viz. 'an opportunity to test commitment and make [the relationship] work', to 'work through feelings' and 'to allow more constructive feelings and thoughts through'. Rhetorically, this shift in perspective is achieved by first establishing normalizing agreement, acceptance and common ground through the technique of reflecting back, and then by introducing the contradictory reformatory imperative signified by the adversative conjunction, 'but': '*But* try to gain perspective – regard this as a crisis in your marriage rather than an event that is bringing your relationship to an end.' The initial state of reinforcement and acceptance labours to mask the ideological effects of the psychotherapeutic normalization (Mininni, 1991).

Third, three distinct crises are identified by the advice columnist: the wife's personal crisis, i.e. emotional devastation; the husband's personal crisis, which is unelaborated (a moment of weakness? a middle-age crisis? sexual frustration?); and the marriage's or relationship's crisis, i.e. a commitment test. Psychologization permits anthropomorphic attribution of life to the relationship (cf. a third 'body' in a union between individuals: Coward, 1984), and structures an injunction to introspective reflexivity, and talk, about the relationship's nature, health and crisis. That the husband's personal crisis is not permitted to emerge in the above advice text sets up the symbiotic duet between the crises of the wife and the relationship, and lays a discursive foundation for the positioning of women as willing and malleable subjects of psychotherapeutic techniques for the self and the relationship.

The will to therapy It is the wife – and the female reader addressed by this advice text – who is positioned as responsible for the normalizing 'emotional housework' of heterosexual relationship practice (cf. Wolf, 1990). She discovers the affair, she recognizes relationship trouble, she confronts and articulates the crisis, she seeks assistance from experts, she confesses her inability to keep her partner sexually faithful (via writing into an advice column). Furthermore, she must now work through her own feelings to 'allow more constructive feelings through', to forgive her partner, to rebuild the relationship, and to persuade him to enter marriage guidance counselling.

The will to therapy pivots on and is structured by the rearticulation of crisis. Tension is set up between negative-destructive and positive-constructive poles, and it is revealed to the wife/women readers that particular emotions and thoughts (bitterness, betrayal, anger, etc.), however 'normal', will block therapeutic resolution of the crisis. The advice columnist's institutionalized expertise enables profferment of reliable information on the wife's emotional state ('*You probably feel* [so hurt, shocked, etc.]' and '*No doubt you're* [very angry]') to establish logical, conscious sequences of cause and effect. Resolution and reformative work are set up in similarly informed completions and narrativizations: 'It *is* possible [to make the relationship work]', *provided* particular perspectives, positions and practices are adopted.

'Making it work', then, is associated with several normalizing prescriptions that reproduce psychotherapeutic technologies as extremely difficult for women to resist. First is the invocation of 'love and determination' in the negotiation of this relationship crisis. The wife's account avoids explicit mention of love, establishing instead, via her emotional devastation, a sense of power over her partner who has 'begged [her] not to leave' and 'loves [her] more than ever'. However, her emotional devastation and her desire to 'save' her marriage is read as proof of her love. This reproduces women as inherently possessing the requisite love and determination to work at saving or maintaining relationships, and structures a will to therapy to prop up, or reveal to women, these normalizing injunctions of feminine subjectivity.

The work of this psychotherapeutics, via the invocation of 'love and determination', reproduces a belief that women are empowered through the successful psychologization of the interiority of their selves and relationships. Through acceptance, forgiveness and articulation of clearer emotional needs ('talking about it'), a greater sense of control in/over the relationship may be negotiated. This coercive institutionalized interpretation silences other possibilities for the empowerment of women in the advice text. For example, feminist psychotherapies may challenge the spiralling emotional exposure and inwardly looking vulnerability for women in these practices (e.g. Hare-Mustin and Marecek, 1986; Burman, 1992). Hence this situation may alternatively be seen to present possibilities for the development of wives'/women's autonomy – to exit from a relationship, to pursue extra-relationship interests and a career, to forge emotional and financial independence – and/or as an opportunity to express anger, e.g. collective protest against the patriarchal exchange of women as objects.

Similarly, while 'normal' emotional devastation (bitterness, mistrust, anger, etc.) is referred out to an-other therapeutic space to be worked through, other emotions and options are 'abnormalized' through their absence in this forum. These allegedly inappropriate responses might offer women modes of resistance to dominant meanings of infidelity, and an individualizing sense of power. Thus, for example, the discovery of infidelity might be ignored altogether; a sexual partner may be contractually shared; there might be relief at a legitimate opportunity to dump a partner; or the exactment of various forms of revenge, such as withholding sex, having an affair yourself, divorce, exorbitant alimony, etc.

Foucault (1986) wryly notes that, in patriarchal discursive practice, a husband's adultery is perceived as a harmless indiscretion or weakness. Along similar lines, Hollway (1989) identifies several discourses that operate to construct gendered subjectivity in heterosexual practices of sexuality, viz. the *Male Sex Drive discourse*, which positions men as naturally and opportunistically seeking sexual variety (with women as their objects); and the *Have-Hold discourse*, which positions women as needing to contain sexual activity within committed, emotional bonds (with men as their objects). If a husband's indiscretion becomes publicly known, or indeed is publicly challenged by a wife, she risks losing her subjective status, i.e. as a wife or partner capable of monopolizing his sexual pleasure.

Thus Foucault (1986) concludes that a wife – and by implication, the woman-reader – is obliged to privately concede to, forgive or tolerate her husband's indiscretions because (a) it saves her social or sexual honour as a wife, and (b) it proves her continuing love and affection for him (1986: 175). Foucault's vision produces a chilling interpretation, through echoes with 'love and determination' in the above advice text, of the patriarchal underpinnings of gendered subjectivity, institutionalized psychotherapeutics and capillaries of power in heterosexual relationship practice.

The second normalizing prescription invoked in 'making [a relationship] work' is a willingness to subject oneself in, and have the relationship objectified by, a psychotherapeutic technology, purveyed by particular professionals, practitioners and/or experts: '[A]s there are people out there who can help you both, why not use them?' This rhetorical question disguises itself as a choice or option, but serves as an imperative injunction. The consequences of not following this directive are to remain in a state of uncertainty, irresolution and crisis, and to suffer ignominious interpretation of one's motives as lack-of-love for a partner, or lack-of-determination to save the relationship.

The referrals out to experts portray these experts as occupying a physical and/or therapeutic space external to the (interior of the) relationship itself and external to the advice text, e.g. 'people out there [who can help you]' and 'outside guidance'. This achieves a profession-policing function: to keep the nature of the psychotherapeutic work, done in that other space, invisible, that is expert knowledges which must be sought out and paid for. 'Work', repeated three times in A, is set up as the oppositional term for the repetitious 'crisis': crisis needs work, and work will resolve crisis. Thus this wife – and, by implication, the addressed woman-reader – is instructed to 'contact a counsellor' and to persuade her husband/partner to enter marriage guidance counselling.

Beyond the advice column genre, then, women's personal or relationship 'failings' are subjected to proliferating forms of psychologized scrutiny in the privacy of therapy rooms and/or domestic homes. This seldom achieves, outside academic debate, the political attention which could inform arguments of gendered, classist and/or racialized oppression in everyday, taken-for-granted practices (Coward,1984). In the South African context of *You* magazine's touted readership statistics, for example, referrals out might be read as producing an exclusionary effect which delimits access to psychotherapeutic empowerment for those women-readers who live within time and/or financial constraints, or resource-challenged environments (e.g. working-class or rural African women).

'Work' also stands in opposition to a construction of magic in relationships, viz. 'the magic has gone out of [the] marriage'. Magic invokes, in its disappearance, a longing for a lost sense of enchantment, romance, mystery, unpredictability and the non-rational, i.e. aided by forces of nature or the spirit-world. Psychologized knowledges, and conscious, rational, professional, scientific work, are called in to replace lost innocence about the function and dysfunction of relationships, the psyche and emotional needs. Ironically, the silence that surrounds the operations of this reformative work in this advice text produces a sense of mystery and magic about the effects it advertises.

Relationship vigilance The professional policing of the nature of psychotherapeutic work in the above advice text produces several other effects. First, the details and consequences of the crisis, as an *avoidable* disaster, are framed – e.g. through checklists of symptoms of emotional and relationship wreckage – and then reinforced through professional opinion. Although appropriate routes for reformation are laid down, these symptoms of crisis might be read as serving a pedagogic function via 'shock tactics'. On the informational agenda is a taken-for-granted monogamy rule in relationship practice, and women's subject positioning in terms of that rule, e.g. policing it, forgiving its contravention, etc. (cf. Hollway's Have-Hold discourse). The guilelessness of the 47-year-old wife in a 30-year-old marriage thus serves as a relationship-lesson for women readers. This wife had mistakenly relied on 'the usual ups and downs', and on 'relationship magic': she was not *vigilant* enough.

Vigilance is intended to connote a sense of watchful surveillance and institutionalized reflexivity over the relationship as an object. Following the Foucauldian notion of psychologization, individual emotional states related to vigilance – e.g. mistrust, anger or jealousy – are understood to be produced and structured by the normalization of monogamy rules and their contravention (see Stenner, 1993).

An invocation of relationship vigilance as women's work in the context of Foucault's comments on private agreement between spouses emphasizes the uneasy silences in advice texts around the negotiation of monogamy rules in relationship practice. Is monogamy explicitly contracted, or just expected as part of an unspoken, conventionalized, relationship deal? *Who* speaks, and *when*: after a partner's infidelity has wrought its promised damage, or before this? In anticipating sexual infidelity, how do we avoid the sting of sexist discursive assumptions or double standards (e.g. men 'cheat' more than women)?

These questions highlight several (related) approaches to women's positioning as sexual relationship vigilantes. Following popular media representations of why men have affairs, women learn to defuse the potential danger by, for example, keeping men sexually or emotionally satisfied, and being watchful for 'warning signs of [male] dissatisfaction' as evidence of relationship trouble (e.g. working long hours, drinking too much, avoidance of sex, etc.) (Livingstone, 1987). In the above advice text, male contravention of the monogamy rule offers women active reformative positioning: to discover and confront a partner's infidelity, and to seek counselling to defuse the ensuing emotional and/or power conflict between partners.

Second, however, the details of the crisis serve to highlight this as a normative or *unavoidable* event in the developmental passage of most committed relationships. Thus adultery happens even to apparently 'good marriages', in which there would be no manifest warning signs – for example, the wife in the above advice text thought her marriage was 'good', and they were 'considered [by others] to be an ideal couple'. This construction of normative male infidelity temporarily excuses the wife's lack of vigilance, and repositions her as the catalyst of reformative, post-adultery, relationship work. The wife's final question – 'Will our marriage ever be the same again?_ – muses nostalgically on the future of the relationship. Speculation on an outcome in this instance is spurious; but the positioning of women who have witnessed this wife's confession will arguably shift towards relationship vigilance.

Third, the details of this crisis, and the touted success of engagement in psychotherapeutic work, limit the options that are available to women in similar circumstances. Thus, while Rusbult (1987) mentions 'exit [from a relationship]' as a valid, and often individually empowering, strategy to counter relationship dissatisfaction, its absence in this advice text is marked.

It would appear that there is an invocation of a hierarchy of different types of extra-relationship affairs (e.g. naughty lapses, flings, secret versus discovered affairs, serious versus harmless affairs, etc.), a hierarchy of different types of relationships (e.g. good, strong, distant, abusive, etc.), and a network of normative relations and predictable psychotherapeutic outcomes between these hierarchies.

The effect of these normalizations for the wife in the advice text is that her husband's affair – although it is not stated that his affair is over – does not constitute legitimate grounds for her to exit the marriage, i.e. when 'love and determination', and psychotherapeutic work, might rescue it. Advice columnists appear to reserve the right to issue permission to exit in particular instances of extreme physical and/or emotional abuse (e.g. ritual affairs, domestic violence, etc.), presumably because such relationship breakdown is perceived to typify the failure of psychotherapeutics. Psychologization thus opens up women's motives for wanting to terminate relationships to public and private surveillance, and redirects women back into a spiral of relationship vigilance.

This is not to say that women are necessarily disempowered by these practices. Indeed, assuming a psychologized position produces rights to speak, with powerful institutional support, and to take a positive and proactive stand against a partner's infidelity.

Resistance: constraints, disruptions and objections

Is it possible within the technologies of power I have unpicked in the above advice text – the confessional examination and disciplinary surveillance of psychologized knowledges of monogamy – to conceptualize the resistance which, Foucault (1976) claims, is inscribed as 'an underside' or 'an irreducible opposite' in all power relations (1976: 96)? Rather than producing radical rupture or transformative change, however, Foucault explains that resistance, always from the 'inside of power', is individualizing: 'no single locus of great Refusal, no soul of revolt ... or pure law of the revolutionary', but shifting, spontaneous points or knots of resistance that 'inflame certain parts of the body, certain moments in life' (ibid.).

At its most optimistic, a Foucauldian reading might posit the advice column as epitomizing the operations and effects of resistance. Crises and problems are re-read as nodes of resistance – e.g. a moment of non-monogamy which disrupts an otherwise 'good' (read 'docile') relationship – within existing frameworks of institutionalized knowledges and practices. The repetitiousness of these resistances, i.e., the same problems, cyclically patterned, year in and out (e.g. Coward, 1984; McRobbie, 1991; Mininni, 1991), and the repeated marketization of technological resolutions to these problems (e.g. psychotherapeutic counselling), are read, at a globalizing level, as a sign of the ongoing recalcitrance of women's relationships with men, and as a sign of the persistent need for institutionalized reinscription.

However, while I have attempted, during this analysis, to *produce* moments of my own resistance, this Foucauldian account is in tension with feminist and other political projects. In this concluding section, I return to the schism between 'sovereign' and 'disciplinary' models of power – and to my ambivalence – to evaluate briefly the operations and effects of Foucauldian resistance within the advice column genre.

Locating instances of intentional resistance by individual advice-seekers in the advice column genre proves to be problematic. The formal structure of advice columns operates to suppress resistance in several ways. First, pre-selection bias frames experience deemed to be in need of normalization. This has less to do with the rigorous editing practices demonized by feminist critics than with the normalization of the audience produced, in the longer term, by these editing practices. Thus 'problems' are forged within an audience of regular readers, steeped in the ideological content and structure of advice columns and/or magazines. Women for whom monogamy is 'un-problematic' are invisible, having either successfully negotiated conventionalized monogamy rules in heterosexual relationship practice, or resisted them in creative ways, such as active non-participation in the advice column genre, or negotiating unconventional relationship rules.

Second, the question and answer format reinforces power-knowledge relations and professional hierarchies, for example between knowledge-seeker and knower or expert. Within a confessional space, Foucault has drawn attention to 'the authority who requires the confession, prescribes and appreciates it, and intervenes in order to judge, forgive, console, reconcile' (1976: 61). The question and answer form, like an adjacency pair in conversation analysis, permits the authoritative expert the 'last word' according to privileged access to institutionalized bodies of knowledge, to which no response (e.g. contestation, refusal, rejection, ridicule, non-compliance, etc.) is visible in published form.

Having made these points, I should make clear that such an approach moves dangerously near to claiming identification of a reality beyond discourse, i.e. individuals, or original authors, whose 'real' experience is textually distorted or obscured by the devious intentions of editors. Advice texts, as addressors, acquire and participate in *another* reality through discourse, and in addressing an audience of readers in particular ways, produce particular meanings and positions (Parker, 1992: 9–10). This is in keeping with the shift from author to text in contemporary analyses of cultural texts, and a focus on how texts are read or received by different audiences of individuals.

British Foucauldian feminists' writings on the advice genre have explored the complex ways in which women resist the prescriptive positions and practices that forge feminine subjectivity (e.g. Coward, 1984; McRobbie, 1991). Advice columns might be written and read for reasons other than the truth, such as ridicule, *schadenfreude* (pleasure in others' misfortunes), voyeurism and entertainment (cf. soap opera), and are set alongside knowledges and options received from other sources. Thus, women are not seen as ideological 'victims' of these texts.

These ideas highlight an important direction in which the analytic work in this chapter might be extended, viz. generating dialogue and discussion – among women from varieties of positionings in South Africa – around readership of advice texts. Analytic interpretation of this talk could access the variability of meanings and practices produced by advice texts, while addressing particular moments of individualizing resistance to, or cultural and/or class disruption of, dominant psychologized subjectivities.

My reading of an advice text in this chapter is intended as such a moment of ambivalence about and resistance to modern subjectivity. Following Parker (e.g. 1989, 1992), I see deconstruction/discourse analysis as an opportunity to explore ideological operations and effects of discipline and confession, and to unravel the discourses and texts that hold these technologies of power in place. My resistance is forged within a particular set of institutional positions (academic, white, middle-class, feminist, etc.), and this 'is therefore always-already incomplete' (Stenner, 1993: 130). However, reflection on my unease about the incompleteness and/or usefulness of my resistant analysis within a South African context has turned, first, towards frustrated contemplation of the apparently inescapable effects of power-knowledge and normalized feminine subjectivities; and second, towards the fairly disturbing similarity between discourses (e.g. about heterosexual relationships) encountered within South African advice columns and First World academics' analyses of European and/or American advice columns.

Both these reflections highlight, perhaps, the ambiguous positions occupied by white women in a South African context, who share with their European and American sisters – through historical processes of colonialism, globalization, institutionalization of knowledges and consumer capitalism – First World, white, middle-class, self-reflective norms and values, and a seeming smorgasbord of knowledges and life-options from which to choose. I will now address very brief comments to these and other issues related to resistance and empowerment in South Africa.

The elaborate operations of power in psychologized constructions of monogamy in psychic and relational practice have become taken-for-granted truths for women occupying particular positions in South Africa. Emotional needs for monogamy, for example, are produced and structured by these truths: caring for ourselves requires the adoption of these perspectives and practices, and contravention produces predictable psychic risks and damages. This reduces moments of resistance to alleged inappropriateness, e.g. cultural practices of polygamy, so-called open marriages, having an affair to exact revenge on a faithless partner, or multiple 'casual' sexual encounters. Furthermore, monogamy is over-determined within other institutionalized discourses which are deployed to discourage resistance to psychologized truths. For example, medicalized discourses promise HIV/AIDS, unwanted pregnancy, and sexually trans-mitted diseases as consequences of non-monogamy.

A mode of resistance available to women ensnared within the above discursive determinism is reversal/rejection of the conventionalizing sub-ject positions and practices; for instance, monogamy might be replaced by sexual permissiveness. Hollway (1989) discusses the contradictory liberatory effects for women of adopting positions of resistance to conventionalized feminine positioning in Have-Hold discourse within a *Permissive discourse.* This discourse resists notions of 'relationship' and celebrates sex as a 'natural drive' in both women and men. The dangers for women of adopting such subjective positioning involve enhancing men's patriarchal power and rights to opportunistic sex without emotional bonds, attempting to advance an argument that women's sex drives are equal to men's fictive ones, and making women feel guilty about having relationship needs (Hollway, 1989: 56).

Hollway's examples emphasize that while resistance to monogamy rules may produce individualizing moments of power, these are informed by and contained within two related social frameworks. First, discursive frame-works of incremental meanings and knowledges about subjectivity, i.e. how do we retreat from, or un-learn, psychologized knowledges about emotional needs? If it is young, white, South African women who are targeted for empowerment through advice columns, for example, is it beneficial to these women to resist psychologized knowledges? Second, socio-structural frameworks that police access to empowering institu-tionalized truths, and thus police resistance to them. In the South African advice text from *You* magazine, with its implication of a statistical spread of readers from varieties of social groups, the silence around class- or race-based access to psychologization through apartheid health care facilities is a case in point.

Many rural African or working-class women in South Africa, for ex-ample, do not have the autonomy or status to support either enforcement of monogamy rules in the practice of heterosexual relationships, or the consequences of their own individualized resistances to these psycho-logized rules. These women may face domestic violence, desertion by men, economic hardship and/or responsibility for children, etc., as a result of the assertion of their rights (Strebel, 1992).

Thus it would seem that resistance can not be seen to operate in uniform ways in an intricately stratified South African context. Also, individualized resistance to monogamy rules and/or feminine subject positions by white or black women cannot achieve effects which challenge the structural oppressions of gender, class, race or culture. There are, therefore, dangers of idealism inherent in an analysis which claims to 'expose the lies of ideology' (Parker, 1989: 66), or attends to language at the expense of macro-structural power relations 'which endure when text stops' (Parker and Burman, 1993: 158).

These comments are germane to feminist ambivalence about the operations and effects of a Foucauldian model of disciplinary power and resistance. For example, a celebration of local operations of power in specific situations or relationships removes the sting of structural oppression. Foucauldian resistance is located at an intangibly diffuse micro-level, i.e. in terms of 'swarms' or 'capillaries' of spontaneous individual resistances distributed within shifting institutionalized relations, rather than directed struggle (Burman, 1991). Thus, the all-pervasiveness of this analysis of power, which necessarily contains resistance, threatens to usher in 'an exhausted and passive fatalism and surrender of political vision' (ibid.: 331).

The difficulty of maintaining demands for politicized agency, collectivity and transformation in an approach to advice columns is precisely that, although problems, emotions and, indeed, the imperatives for women to police monogamy in relationships, may be socially, politically, institutionally or discursively produced, it does not mean that we experience these things as such. Neither does it mean we should be denied the rights, or the power, to seek individualizing relief through institutionalized reformative technologies.

However, to accept the hegemonic, globalizing, white, middle-class, feminine subjectivities that operate within the technologies of institutionalized power-knowledge in South African advice texts is to deny the position of South Africa as a (newly) African state. My response to the implied question as to 'how do we escape discourse?' (Parker, 1992: 20), lies in the analysis of discursive practices of resistance (my own and others') to the recipe of seamless truths offered in advice columns. I acknowledge that my version – as a text – is embedded in the very practices of psychologization and power it seeks to expose, but this embeddedness has, productively, facilitated a critical (albeit ambivalent) gaze. As Hollway (1989) suggests, it is awareness of contradictory empowering effects produced by particular discourses that serves as a first step towards resistance and/or discursive and social transformation. Through encouraging reflexive engagement with complex questions relating to subjectivity and power, I would hope that the advice column genre might constitute a key arena of struggle in which South African women are able to forge new sets of cultural identities.

References

All Media Products Survey (1992), Markinor, Johannesburg.

Barthes, R. (1977) *Image-Music-Text*, Fontana, London.

Brinkgreve, C. and Korzec, M. (1979) 'Feelings, behaviour and morals in the Netherlands: 1938–1978: analysis and interpretation of an advice column', *Netherlands Journal of Sociology*, 15, 123–40.

Burman, E. (1991) 'What discourse is not', *Philosophical Psychology*, 4 (3), 325–42.

Burman, E. (1992) 'Identification and power in feminist therapy: a reflexive history of a discourse analysis', *Women's Studies International Forum*, 15, 487–98.

Coward, R. (1984) *Female Desire*, Paladin Books, London.

Foucault, M. (1975) *Discipline and Punish: The Birth of the Prison*, Allen Lane, Lonodon.

Foucault, M. (1976) *The History of Sexuality, Volume 1: An Introduction*, Penguin, Harmondsworth.

Foucault, M. (1982) 'The Subject and power', *Critical Inquiry*, 8, 777–95.

Foucault, M. (1986) *The Care of the Self*, Pantheon Books, New York.

Hare-Mustin, R. T. and Marecek, J. (1986) 'Autonomy and gender: some questions for therapists', *Psychotherapy*, 23, 205–12.

Hollway, W. (1989) *Subjectivity and Method in Psychology. Gender, Meaning and Science*, Sage, London.

Kurtz, I. (1990) 'Perennial Problems', *Cosmopolitan*, December, 84–7.

Livingstone, S. M. (1987) 'The representation of personal relationships in television drama: realism, convention and morality', in R. Burnett, P. McGhee and D. Clarke (eds), *Accounting for Relationships: Explanation, Representation and Knowledge*, Methuen, London.

McRobbie, A. (1991) *Feminism and Youth Culture: from 'Jackie' to 'Just Seventeen'*, Macmillan, Houndsmills, UK.

Mininni G. (1991) 'Diatextual analysis of the advice column,' *Rassegna Italiana di Linguistica Applicata*, 23, 73–81.

Parker, I. (1988) 'Deconstructing accounts', in C. Antaki (ed.), *Analysing Everyday Explanation: a Casebook of Methods*, Sage, London.

Parker, I. (1989) *The Crisis in Modern Social Psychology, and How to End it*, Routledge, London.

Parker, I. (1992) *Discourse Dynamics: Critical Analysis for Social and Individual Psychology*, Routledge, London.

Parker, I. and Burman, E. (1993) 'Against discursive imperialism, empiricism and constructionism: thirty-two problems with discourse analysis', in E. Burman and I. Parker (eds), *Discourse Analytic Research: Repertoires and Readings of Texts in Action*, Routledge, London.

Ratcliff, R. (1969) *Dear Worried Brown Eyes*, Robert Maxwell, London.

Rogers, C. R. (1961) *On Becoming a Person: A Therapist's View of Psychotherapy*, Houghton Mifflin, Boston.

Rose, N. (1990) *Governing the Soul: The Shaping of the Private Self*, Routledge, London.

Rusbult, C. E. (1987) 'Responses to dissatisfaction in close relationships: the exit-voice-loyalty-neglect model', in D. Perlman and S. Duck (eds), *Intimate Relationships: Development, Dynamics and Deterioration*, Sage, Newbury Park.

Stenner, P. (1993) 'Discoursing jealousy,' in E. Burman and I. Parker (eds), *Discourse Analytic Research: Repertoires and Readings of Texts in Action*, Routledge, London.

Strebel, A. (1992) "'There's absolutely nothing I can do, just believe in God'":
    South African women with AIDS', *Agenda*, 12, 50–62.

Wilbraham, L. (1996a) "'Few of us are potential Miss South Africas, but ... '":
    psychological discourses about women's bodies in advice columns', *South African
    Journal of Psychology* 26, 53–65.

Wilbraham, L. (1996b) 'Avoiding the ultimate break-up after infidelity: the market-
    ization of relationship-work and counselling in a South African advice column',
    Psychology in South Africa 21, 27–48.

Winship, J. (1987) *Inside Women's Magazines*, Pandora, London.

Wolf, N. (1990) *The Beauty Myth*, Vintage, London.

You (1991) 'Janet Harding's Lifeline', *You*, 25 July, 144–5.

Young, A. (1987) 'How medicine tamed life', *Culture, Medicine and Psychiatry*, 11,
    107–21.

CHAPTER 6

Let's talk about sex: liberation and regulation in discourses of bisexuality

Jocelyn Blumberg and Judith Soal

Within the modern era issues around sexuality and sexual practice have taken hold in the social and political domains, leading to the emergence of a wide range of discourses relating to sex (Foucault, 1976; Parker, 1992). These discourses proclaim our subjection to an era of sexual repression and demand a move towards sexual freedom, in both political and personal spheres (Rubin, 1987). Talking about sexual issues has come to be considered a liberatory practice often undertaken in an attempt to resist hegemonic sexual mores. Through consciousness-raising and mutual support, people are encouraged to share personal experiences and dilemmas as a move towards personal empowerment, as well as social and political change (Hutchins and Kaahumanu, 1991).

Our interest in 'sex talk' was prompted by ambivalence around the operation of discourses of sexual liberation in our personal lives. This ambivalence could be contextualized and explored within a post-structuralist framework. Following this approach, language is seen to be organized into socially and historically constructed discourses, which constitute knowledge and confer power. It is through inciting an investment in hegemonic discourses that power/knowledge serves to construct and regulate subjectivity in the service of a particular social order (Rose, 1990).

In this light, and in sharp contrast to discourses of modern sexual repression and liberation, Foucault (1976) suggests that the politicization of sexuality is based on an inadequate conception of power/knowledge in the construction of sexual experience. While Foucault does not minimize the repressive power of institutionalized forms of sexual oppression, he argues that this power is also produced and reinforced in the micro-practices of our everyday lives. Furthermore, he suggests that the notion of sexual repression and thus sexual liberation fails to recognize the role of power/knowledge in constructing its subjects (Henriques et al., 1984).

The perception that 'sex talk' can be liberatory relies on the liberal humanist assumption that an inherent truth exists within the individual and that an examination of sexuality and a confession of long repressed sexual desires is necessary to access this truth (Foucault, 1976). Through this we are promised self-fulfilment, self-knowledge and meaning (Parker, 1989). According to Foucault (1976), confessional practices and the assumptions upon which they are predicated, while ostensibly promising liberation, ultimately constitute a subtle and complex form of regulation. Confession serves to construct 'inner desires', as well as to reproduce and normalize certain truths, generally those prescribed by the discourses dominant in the confessional forum. If, following Foucault, we assume that confession operates in the constitution of meaning, practice and understanding, then we must recognize that through the confessional act we are actively implicated in the regulation and government of self and sexual practice (Foucault, 1976; Parker, 1989).

Working from these theoretical bases, we explore the dynamics of liberation and regulation in a discussion between a group of women who identify themselves as bisexual. By forming a bisexual women's group, they explicitly created a confessional framework to discuss sexuality.

Bisexual women and discourse

The participants were members of a bisexual women's group, including one of the researchers, which had been meeting fortnightly for about eighteen months. The group was formed largely in resistance to the alienation experienced both from heterosexual discourses and from the lesbian discourses dominant in the feminist organization to which they belonged. As such, it was intended to serve a supportive as well as 'consciousness-raising' function. The group comprises three black and four white women who are predominantly university educated, and would identify themselves as feminists. There is a strong investment in progressive discourses within the group, as well as exposure to psychoanalytic discourses through therapy or through studying psychology. The women are also friends.

Guided by the methodological process documented by Hollway (1989) we felt comfortable with seven women, since 'the information derived from any participant is valid because that account is a product (albeit complex) of the social domain' (ibid.: 15). The analysis allows an understanding of the discourses available to these participants and should not be considered representative of all bisexual women. Furthermore, the accounts of participants should not be viewed as fixed and enduring or as a representation of their true selves, rather, the texts should be viewed as 'transindividual' (Parker, 1992: 7) and dynamic. We chose to collect the text through a focus group discussion, which typically facilitates open and unstructured dialogue. Since this is similar to the usual style of the group's meetings, we hoped it would constitute a relatively non-threatening environment. We also hoped that participants' accounts might be stimulated by the accounts of others, allowing us to explore the dynamics of the group, in particular the operation of 'confession'. Having gained the group's agreement to participate in the study, we tape-recorded a two-hour discussion around sexuality and intimate relationships.

The discussion was transcribed and analysed using discourse analytic methodology. Our method of analysis is largely Foucauldian and has been guided by the work of Henriques et al. (1984), Hollway (1989) and Parker (1992). The analytic process involved gaining familiarity with the data through repeated reading of the transcript. Drawing on our knowledge of the literature and our own intuition, we selected themes we felt were pertinent to an exploration of liberation and regulation in the confessional forum. In this way, salient discourses were analysed with close attention to their social and historical context and their function in relation to structures of power/knowledge. The analysis is necessarily selective. Our positioning as white, middle-class, university-educated women, with invest-ments in psychoanalytic and feminist discourses, as well as our various sexual perspectives, has necessarily shaped our analysis, which should be viewed as another text open to reinterpretation. In the interests of anonymity, pseudonyms are used. Parker's (1992) transcription conventions were utilized.

The first section of the analysis examines ways in which sexual identities are defined in and through language and discourses. We explore three subject positions within broader discourses of bisexuality taken up by participants and examine their implications for the construction of sub-jectivity, as well as the degree of power afforded by each. The second section focuses on discourses emerging in discussion of intimate relation-ships. Again the focus is on the extent to which accounts are governed by, and/or resistant to, dominant discursive injunctions, as well as on the role of the confessional forum in the construction of experience and understanding.

The construction of sexual identity

The group's focus on issues related to bisexuality necessarily encouraged discussion of sexual categorization, marginalization, and the transgression of hegemonic sexual prescriptions. In this section, we explore how political, social and moral discursive injunctions lead participants to take up multiple (and often contradictory) subject positions in order to present 'desirable' images of their sexual selves.

The normal bisexual The first subject position constructs a picture of the normal bisexual – in this forum, a woman who sleeps with, or is sexually attracted to, both men and women. This position resists assertions from both heterosexual and homosexual discourses, which suggest that bisexuality is unnatural, deviant and rooted in confusion. Bisexuals are often portrayed as 'trying to get the best of both worlds', or as choosing the position in the interests of being trendy. Even progressive discourses present bisexuality as a politically impure option (Hutchins and Kaahumanu, 1991). In this sense the legitimacy of bisexuality is undermined. With reference to these constructions, Sonia relates:

> A gay man, um introduced me to his family as: 'this is Sonia, my only white lesbian friend' and I said 'I'm not lesbian, I'm bisexual', and he said 'you must stop repressing or suppressing your own homosexuality'. /angry mutters/. And I had this kind of intellectual argument with him. And then I went home and I just cried, I was so upset, I was angry when he said this and then I actually, afterwards I realized I was really really hurt.

Sonia argues that bisexuality should be seen as a natural sexual category or orientation:

> It's not as if I chose to be also attracted to women just because I had lots of friends who did. So a lot of this stuff just has to do with desire. At some stage one chooses to live out one's desires, one also has the sort of confidence to do it.

Sonia's statements here point to a desire to normalize bisexuality, to present herself as ordinary and well-adjusted, and bisexuality as a legitimate sexual practice. The position gains credibility by constructing bisexual desire as essential or inherent, as opposed to a position mediated by the social milieu. This is reinforced by implying a process of 'working through' and resolution.

In an interchange between Sonia and Susan, the positioning of bisexuals as an oppressed, minority group is developed:

> Sonia: It's about being part of a minority really, a minority within a minority, not fitting in anywhere in particular, not fitting in with the straight world or the gay world. And not being accepted by either.
>
> Susan: And more than that being criticized (.) being ostracized by both.

This position presents bisexuals as marginalized by mainstream ideology and capitalises on the 'repressive hypothesis' (Foucault, 1976): Bisexuality is politicized and power is derived from discourses of 'minority rights'. However, in attempting to facilitate the equal participation of this minority group in the institutions of the dominant culture, it is necessary to normalize and legitimize bisexuality. This endeavour ironically results in a trivialization and depoliticization of sexual preference. Bisexuality is constructed as a third sexual category alongside hetero- and homosexuality and the focus is shifted from the need for social change to that for personal change, thus conforming to, rather than challenging dominant values.

Within this group, the normalization of bisexual practice simultaneously works to define and police that practice. The necessity to consistently position oneself within a fixed sexual category constructs the parameters of one's sexual expression. There may be the expectation that one must consistently 'perform' bisexually:

> Jackie: I was joking to Rosie earlier that if I'm going to stay a part of this group, I'm going to have to stop sleeping with so many men!

In this light, it seems that the 'normal bisexual', position may not always be a liberatory one. Through the process of confession, the group defines parameters around bisexual practice in such a way as to potentially regulate and constrain the experience of group members.

The sex-radical A second subject position emerging in accounts is that of the 'sex-radical', which celebrates and capitalizes upon transgression:

> Sonia: I think my identity, my sexual identity has developed to a point now where (.) almost bisexual has become too limiting, because it really just talks about behaviour like fucking men, fucking women, whereas I think how I feel about sexuality is much wider than that. So now I would call myself sex-radical, or queer, which also defines itself as removed from mainstream, kind of heterosexual behaviour, or even sort of homosexual behaviour that replicates heterosexuality quite closely.

And following on from Sonia's description, Jackie says:

> Ja, I mean I think for me it does encompass a lot more than just talking about who you sleep with. And also that whole thing of non-monogamy and looking at alternatives that aren't just about sleeping with men and women.

Here, bisexuality *per se* is presented as being limiting and conservative. The 'sex-radical' position encompasses more than talk about the gender of sexual partners, it constructs a particular outlook towards sexuality and intimate relationships. It rejects monogamy and encourages exploration of unconventional modes of sexual expression.

Even more than the previous position, sexual practice and sexual identity are strongly politicized and prioritized. This position is explicitly defined in opposition to the norm, as one of deviance.

> Sonia: I think what that position also would argue is that it is not as if there's just a sort of a bowl full of different positions and you can just pick any one of them, with some activities or sexual orientations there's more coercion. I mean in terms of heterosexuality and monogamy there's more coercion. Other forms of sexual expression are just much more taboo, like cross-generational sex. It's a much more difficult position to maintain. The sanctions against that are much stronger than the sanctions against bisexuality for instance (.) and I

think that there are sexual behaviours that are more transgressive than others and therefore you're more isolated when you do them.

By resisting the coercive injunctions of the hegemonic discourses of sexuality and taking up a more taboo position, one is necessarily isolated. This emphatic embracing of 'otherness' may provide a certain amount of power and sense of self through its transgressive nature within discourses in which transgression is celebrated. However, this power is also limited since deviance is on the whole socially devalued (Flax, 1990). In this sense the taking up of an explicitly deviant position serves to leave intact and to reinforce the hegemonic discourses of sexuality. Furthermore, embracing transgression and devaluing 'normal' sexual practice can be similarly coercive in that transgressiveness becomes the standard against which we are assessed.

Both the 'normal bisexual' and 'sex-radical' positions insist on the right to lay claim to particular sexual identities. They maximize sexual identity, and allow these women to carve their niche in the world, separating 'us' from 'them'. They provide power, meaning and a sense of freedom, but simultaneously disallow the taking up of other positions: when sexual identity is maximized, other aspects of self and behaviour are regulated accordingly. The problems of fixing sexual identity are taken up and illustrated with the next discursive position, which we call (ironically) the 'non-labeller'.

The non-labeller This position problematizes the system of sexual categorization and points to the ways in which one is confined by definition on the grounds of sexual orientation or practice.

> Alex: Ja, I was quite cross the other day when I was sitting talking and someone said: 'Oh but Alex's straight,' and one of my friends said: 'No she's not she's bisexual.' I was, I thought: 'Fuck you all,' I thought.
>
> Susan: That's interesting though that you that you defy description.
>
> Alex: But I was described as a bisexual by a gay woman who sleeps with men but calls herself a dyke!

In another instance, Susan says:

> Susan: I was just thinking about this whole thing of labels and that (.) probably one of the things that, as a group, is probably helluva characteristic of us individually is that we are all people who reject or who would try extremely hard not to label ourselves, and maybe saying that we are bisexual is, like Sonia said, sort of [limiting].

This position attempts to reject categorization and generalization and provides an interesting contradiction to the previous positions. However, participants remain trapped within this system of labelling or self-definition in sexual terms, since it provides the vocabulary whereby they understand and present themselves. The prioritization of sexual identity is seen as a political responsibility so as to conscientize and liberate oneself and others.

> Susan: ... using it politically, using it when people ask you because for most people, especially in South [Africa], that's radical enough, just to say that you are bisexual is such a huge bloody thing. /Mmm's of agreement/ Never mind all the kind of variations on it that Sonia's mentioned. And maybe that's necessary, that's why one would use it. Not because its like this label and this defines my sexuality. 'Cos I mean then I think it can become just as limiting as saying: 'I'm a lesbian'.

Further contradictions emerge later when one of the researchers is challenged by Sonia about her own sexual orientation. This suggests that definition by sexual orientation remains necessary:

> Sonia: So Rosie, what's your sexuality?
> Rosie: /laughter/ I was waiting for that!
> Susan: Has everybody been giving you meaningful glances every now and then?
> Sonia: There's no right or wrong answer. /laughter/

When placed in an insider–outsider position there is a reversion to definition along the lines of sexuality.

This analysis suggests that these women are attempting to accomplish contradictory objectives: first to challenge the scope of existing sexual identities, and thus necessarily constructing new categories (the 'normal bisexual', the 'sex-radical'), and second to challenge the existence of any sexual categories at all. This leads to a stalemate whereby they remain fixed within and regulated by the dominant system of sexual categorization.

Discourses of relationships

Much discussion in the group involved talk about intimate relationships, although many dilemmas raised are not peculiar to bisexual women. What is different about this group is the level of reflexivity and awareness of the role of ideology and stereotypes in shaping practice. This awareness has similarly been encountered in work around 'progressive' heterosexual relationships (e.g. Hollway, 1989).

New model relationships A permissive approach to sexual encounters has gained increasing acceptance as an alternative to discourses that uphold the sacred and serious nature of sex (Hollway, 1989). Permissive discourses assert that sex is a pleasurable and natural activity, which should be freely enjoyed between consenting partners without the need for long-term commitment or institutional sanction. Although permissiveness has been taken up in many forms, our analysis highlights a rejection of nuclear relationships in favour of what we term the 'new model relationship'.

> Sonia: But then also what does one do with culture? Because families, nuclear families are part of Western, modern Western culture but I think nuclear families fuck up children quite badly.
>
> ... monogamy is a sort of conventional. (.) I mean psychology will teach you that that's an ideal, you know a long-term intimate relationship is part of the developmental process so you can develop like a good, normal human being.

These ideas come from an intellectual rejection of the naturalness and desirability of nuclear relationships, which are seen to be unhealthy and to restrict people's individuality. There is a rejection of the coercive nature of psychological discourses that dictate truths about healthy, mature modes of sexual expression. Heterosexual relationships are seen to support patriarchy and capitalism, and homosexual relationships to replicate rather than challenge the institutionalized norm. The criticism of the nuclear prescription also comes from personal disillusionment and experiences of relationships that have not achieved an idealized nuclear harmony.

> Susan: I'm saying: monogamy's not the important thing, long-term commitment is not the important thing. What's important is now, what's important is that there is honesty and respect.

The group discusses an alternative to the nuclear relationship – a new model for relationships or sexual encounters. This attempts to address both the intellectual criticisms of nuclear relationships and personal disillusionment with relationships that can cause as much pain as they do pleasure. It tries to present a formula to avoid pain. The model suggests that we do not own our sexual partners, that we cannot expect them to give meaning to our lives or to make us complete. All we can ask for and all we must give is honesty, consistency and clarity. It assumes a rational consistent individual, and suggests that we will not (or cannot) be angry or hurt if our partners are honest and upfront from the start.

The 'new model relationship' assumes a clean discursive slate, it ignores the irrational and contradictory aspects of discursive investments. However, the 'baggage' left by more conservative discourses of relationships becomes evident in the women's talk.

Meaningful relationships Conventional approaches to sex and intimacy construct the idea of the 'meaningful relationship' – a (heterosexual) monogamous pair who have sex together and ultimately marry and have children (Hollway, 1989). When sex is added to a friendship, it is seen to take on a new significance, an elevated status, becoming infused with particular meanings and expectations. These discourses present a meaningful loving relationship as a natural desire, a sign of emotional maturity and health, as well as a means to achieve happiness and fulfilment. Investments in these discourses become clear in the following extracts:

> Alex: I'm feeling very vulnerable, wanting a relationship more than anything really.
> Jackie: What do you think that would give you though?
> Alex: Umm, I think stability.
> Pam: With men – it never lasts.
> Sonia: With me it doesn't last with women either! It just never lasts. There must be something wrong with me.

We can see that the promise of the 'meaningful relationship' is deeply embedded. There is an implication that if we are not able to realize the fruits of this promise there must be something wrong with us; we need to 'act upon ourselves' (Rose, 1990) by becoming more attractive, more loving, tolerant, expecting less, working harder and so forth, so as to be worthy of this relationship. The responsibility for this work is typically placed on women. While a feminist analysis might blame heterosexual relationships for the perpetuation of this dynamic, the discussion here suggests that this extends into relationships where both partners are women. Simply changing our practice (not being exclusively heterosexual) does not free us from the injunctions that accompany our gendered subjectivity.

Because of a rejection of traditional relationship structures, it appears that these women hope to fulfil their desires from within the 'new model relationship'. However, this model contains a similar need to act upon oneself in order to achieve success:

> Sonia: It's a fear of being rejected because for some reason, I fear rejection from lovers but not from friends. I think it has to do with expectations and investing things in another person. I wish that I could have the kind of relationship where I wouldn't have expectations or I wouldn't feel insecure or feel those things. I just have this idea that it's possible.

Here, Sonia rejects the idea that relationships can fulfil her expectations, but still can't escape or deny them. She blames herself for having such expectations and for feeling insecure. This suggests a different motivation for talking about relationships in this forum. Despite an explicit desire for such talk to be liberatory, it could be that the group provides a space to perform this 'self work' so as to be able to realise the promise of relationships.

The implications of contradictory investments in the 'new model'/ 'meaningful relationship' discourses become more evident in the following, rather lengthy discussion, which is presented here interspersed with comment.

Jackie: So what was Victor, what was your relationship with him?

Sonia: Well, that was a fling or an affair and it was a couple of weeks so …

Jackie: But it didn't come with any of those horrible things (.) insecurity (.) 'cos you weren't invested or why?

Sonia: Well, I think because there wasn't this emotional (.) I wasn't in love with him but also because there was this incredible honesty right from the start. I knew what was going on, so I knew what I could expect and what I couldn't expect. So that also made it easier not to have expectations. I also knew that I would be told if things changed, which did happen, so it wasn't as if I was all the time thinking: 'Oh this is going to end, why is it going strangely' or whatever, because I knew that the agreement would be that we would be fucking and that if he didn't want to any more or I didn't we would just tell and that's what happened and it just made things so easy.

Jackie: So the honesty was really important

Sonia: I think it's incredibly important and I can really say that although I'm sad in a way because I really enjoyed fucking him and I'm sad it had to end, but I experienced no pain. I experienced some sadness, but absolutely no pain, and that to me was amazing because I had this very nice fling with someone, and it ended, and it didn't disrupt my life.

Our positioning as researchers in feminist and psychoanalytic discourses aroused a sense of discomfort with this extract. We felt that Sonia was in a vulnerable position in relation to this man who seemed to be able to dictate the parameters of the relationship, despite her assertion that it worked for her. We wondered whether we would have felt as uncomfortable had she been describing a relationship with another woman. In this case we felt that she was rationalizing, trying to make her experience a testimony to the success of the model. It raises the important question of whether knowing that something is going to end will protect one from pain. It seems that Sonia's investment in the 'new model' serves to silence and disallow any feelings of hurt and anger.

Susan: I think Sonia's experience is ideal. I've never been able to do that, I really try. I actually think that it takes two people that have the same amount of respect and commitment to that. And it doesn't have anything to do with monogamy or the nature of the relationship, perhaps it's just a matter of honesty.

Jackie: So what's gone wrong? /laughter/

Susan: Well, I like to blame the other people. /laughter/ I like to think that I'm committed to that, but that the people that I've got involved with haven't been, and that maybe one articulates that to people at the onset, OK, and then either they're not able to be that honest or otherwise they don't believe that that's actually what you want. I've had that quite often that I'm saying monogamy's not the important thing, long-term commitment is not the important thing. What's important is now, what's important is honesty and respect, and they say ja, but they don't actually believe me. /Murmurs of agreement/. So then I've been lied to, and I've been let down in spite of having tried very hard to establish that from the beginning.

This extract expands on the qualities necessary for the success of the new model relationship. You need to be quite resolved about what you want, capable of a high degree of honesty, committed and respectful. Most importantly, partners must be as capable and committed as you are. In some ways this is a nice change from women taking the blame for failed relationships, but it also assumes a high degree of rationality and consistency in personal desires and expectations. The next speaker throws a spanner in the works:

Jackie: Well, I've maybe agreed to things that haven't been ideal because I want what's happening. So with Mark now, we're both saying OK, it's not a big relationship, it's not a big thing, I'm saying: 'No I don't want anything,' but maybe I actually do, you know. I just feel that I can't say that. It's like, it's not OK at a very early stage to say: 'Well actually I'd like more, I don't want just a casual thing, I'd actually like more.'

Pam: Because you feel you might be asking too much? You just accept what's available, rather than ask for more?

Jackie: Ja (.) it's not at all OK these days to start saying: 'I'd actually like something committed.' Whatever that means. I don't know, maybe by committed I just mean consistent? Which is what you are saying?

This extract shows that the 'new model relationship' can also be limiting and prescriptive. Since we aren't supposed to want 'too much' from our partners, what happens if we feel that we want more than a commitment to honesty? Jackie finds it necessary to pretend that she does not want any kind of serious relationship, maybe setting up the kind of pattern that causes partners to disbelieve Susan, in the previous extract. Within this forum, it seems that expressing a position that exposes the negative implications of an allegiance to the 'new model' is difficult for Jackie, because she almost immediately retracts this, and capitulates to the preferred 'line' of the group. This instance clearly highlights the way in which the confessional act can shape experience and understanding.

Sonia: Ja, I think what I basically want in any kind of fling, affair, relationship is (.) predictability. When I broke up with Neville last year that was the thing that freaked me out, I thought there was so much denial from his side. He said one thing, and did another thing, and I said to him: 'But why, just if you were honest this wouldn't have been so painful.' But maybe he was just really confused, he really didn't know, so he couldn't be honest. He couldn't say: 'This is what I want and this is what I don't want, this is what I can deal with,' because he himself didn't know.

Jackie: You mean he wasn't actually going out to hurt you. That's just the way relationships are set up, all the games?

Sonia: Ja. So unless you get involved with someone who is very secure in themselves so that they actually do know. But fuck, even if someone could just say: 'I'm confused listen, I just don't know'.

Susan: But people never admit that they are confused.

Jackie: But when I'm talking to Mark I'm not confused, you know …

Here Sonia acknowledges the irrational aspects of interpersonal relationships: that it isn't simply a matter of honesty and dishonesty. Nevertheless, her account remains infused with the values upheld in psychological discourses, which emphasize the need to 'act upon oneself' to achieve maturity, inner security and resolution. Again Jackie raises a problem, but the group don't pick up on it and she doesn't pursue the matter, possibly because she does not want to position herself as one of the dishonest, unresolved types to be avoided in relationships.

Discourse and 'liberation'

This exploration of women's talk within a confessional forum necessitates a questioning of its liberatory function. As suggested by Parker: 'A paradoxical consequence and twist to this process is that an individual seeking 'awareness' and 'liberation' risks becoming bound all the more tightly in the meshes of modern culture.' (1989: 61). The positions emerging within the group construct a lens through which participants assess themselves and others. These privileged discourses restrict the possibility for the emergence of alternative positions and are simply reinforced during group discussions. While this might be affirming at times, it also silences dissenting voices and allows little space for transformation. Furthermore, the belief that liberation can be achieved through intellectual critique and awareness effectively implies that we can escape discourse, and ignores the continued effect of hegemonic discourses on feelings and desires. When difficulties are experienced with liberating the self from 'unprogressive' desires, they are attributed to individual weakness or inadequacy, in this way reinserting us into the process of self-regulation. While we do not want to undermine the importance of this group for these women, or to disregard its role in challenging dominant sexual prescriptions, this analysis suggests that the confessional forum of the bisexual women's group may serve to construct additional self-regulating values and standards.

We have attempted to locate the participants' initiatives towards liberation within prevailing discursive frameworks, and to avoid attributing blame. However, our analysis inevitably sets up another lens through which participants are assessed, obscured through its construction as feminist research aimed towards empowerment (Burman and Parker, 1993). The assessment becomes all the more powerful because of its presentation as 'expert knowledge' and there is a danger of again regressing to the notions of definitive truth and individual culpability (Parker, 1992). The potential for discourse analytic research to be perceived as a personal criticism or attack is exacerbated by the largely inaccessible nature of post-structuralist notions such as 'death of the author' and 'multiple subjectivities'.

We recognize that our analysis constitutes an alternative (rather than final) reading of the text. As such, it comes to constitute yet another text, embedded in similarly regulatory discourses. None the less, if this is to be a useful venture, we need to avoid the trap of interpretive regress and the ensuing political immobilization (Burman and Parker, 1993). If not, we cannot engage with the very real and painful problems that we experience in this sphere of our lives. Research of this nature can be effectively utilized by highlighting the contradictory effects of discursive investments and thus reframing and juxtaposing texts so as to create space for further manoeuvre and resistance (Parker, 1992).

Note

We wish to express sincere thanks to Lindy Wilbraham for her guidance and support during this project. We would also like to thank the group of women for agreeing to participate in the study and for sharing intimate and at times painful experiences with us.

References

Burman, E. and Parker, I. (eds) (1993) *Discourse Analytic Research: Repertoires and Readings of Texts in Action*, Routledge, London.

Flax, J. (1990) *Thinking Fragments*, University of California Press, Berkeley, CA.

Foucault, M. (1976) *The History of Sexuality, Volume I: An Introduction*, Penguin, Harmondsworth.

Henriques, J., Hollway, W., Urwin, C., Venn, C. and Walkerdine, V. (1984) *Changing the Subject: Psychology, Social Regulation and Subjectivity*, Methuen, London.

Hollway, W. (1989) *Subjectivity and Method in Psychology*, Sage, London.

Hutchins, L. and Kaahumanu, L. (1991) *Bi Any Other Name: Bisexual People Speak Out*, Alyson Publications, Boston, MA.

Parker, I. (1989) 'Discourse and Power', in J. Shotter and K. Gergen (eds), *Texts of Identity*, Sage, London, 56–69.

Parker, I. (1992) *Discourse Dynamics: Critical Analysis for Social and Individual Psychology*, Routledge, London.

Rose, N. (1990) *Governing the Soul: The Shaping of the Private Self*, Routledge, London.

Rubin, G. (1987) 'Thinking sex: notes for a radical theory of the politics of sexuality', in C. Vance (ed.), *Pleasure and Danger: Explaining Female Sexuality*, Routledge, Boston, MA.

CHAPTER 7

Credibility, plausibility and autobiographical oral narrative: some suggestions from the analysis of a rape survivor's testimony

Jane Foress Bennett

The seeming antonymy of representation and silence has been my nemesis, born as I was in the later twentieth century and raised in a culture for which the term 'whited sepulchre' is generous (generous because too tidy). Promising everything from predication to god, language delivers only latticework, a collection of sticks and gaps, not even – except in the most gross of contexts – a gate through which to pray or howl. I've sometimes thought that if one wanted to discover a scholar's secret knot of a heart, what you have to do is examine what it is he, or she, 'works on'. Held up to the light, more than one academic inquiry might suggest a source of pathology, a hint of personal terror; for me, if I am asked, 'well, what are you?' (this is not always asked in an academic context) I say, 'I'm a linguist'. Which should mean that I am compelled by what can be, or is, said; it should mean that I have faith in sound as communication. But I do not, in fact, have faith in 'sound as communication' at all; pathologically, I think about language because I live – in a both personal and historical way – within and across the failures of language; if I 'am' a linguist, this is probably not rooted in any love, or trust, of speech; my claim to 'linguistic' research is probably the flummoxed rearguard action of one who has her doubts about voices and especially about ears, not least her own.

This scepticism about the practice of 'attention' lies at the heart of research I completed two years ago whose focus is on the noetics of rape in mainstream New York. The term 'noetic' is borrowed from Ong (1981), who used it to describe the way in which experience becomes represented, transformed, exchanged, and canonized within a culture. The interests of the original research lay in the shape of a complex noetic battle – the battle between representations of the experience of sexual violence and social discourses whose paradigms of 'gender,' 'sex,' 'heterosexuality' and 'law' occlude, preclude and disperse that experience. In this chapter, it is through the autobiographical oral narrative of a North American woman's experience of sexual violence that certain key questions about the representation of subjective 'truth' are explored. In the current moment of South African transition, where issues of historical abuse and culpability are at the forefront of the possibility of the construction of a new dispensation, it is crucial that the complexity of 'social memory' and 'subjective truth' be examined. (This chapter was prepared first in 1994, and then revised in late 1995 for publication. Work on the establishment of the Truth and Reconciliation Commission began in mid-1995, in South Africa.) Despite their roots in an American setting, I hope that the observations that follow may have something to offer to the South African discourse of historical abuse and current accountability, one recently institutionalized through the Truth and Reconciliation Commission, and one whose shape will have dramatic influence on the meaning of being 'new' South Africans.

Introduction to questions of language and pain

In Elaine Scarry's (1985) *The Body in Pain,* she claims that to the question, 'What is at stake in material making?' the scriptures of Judeo-Christian tradition respond, 'Everything'. In the imaginings of a creator God, the projective value of the human body becomes the integral thread of narrative; the real of flesh, fragile and often bewildered, is made into the omniscient Word as an act of substantiation. Construction, handiwork, the possibility of the artefact/the other, language itself, spring from the intimate knowledge not of the body as whole, but of the body as wounded, broken, in pain, the body un-made. In the opening moves of her philo-sophical reading of human pain for Western political epistemology (ranging from the Old Testament to Marx), she speaks of physical pain as the unrepresentable, the unseeable, the experience that ineluctably confirms the meaning of humanity for the sufferer, and – simultaneously – creates doubts about that very meaning for anyone who, from within the safety of their own skin, watches.

I was struck, on first reading Scarry, by a memory of a speech I had once heard given by Jamaica Kincaid (given at Barnard College, Columbia University, 1991). Speaking of her passion for language as intimately related to the long cruel story of the colonizations of her homeland, Jamaica, she said of English imperialism, ' It wrecked something. It wrecked everything. And it left something other than the violence I just described, or would have liked to describe. It left something, and in some of us it left language.' Later on, in the same speech, she talks of the axe-head of violence sunk into a tree split forever into two branches – knowledge of pain, and knowledge of language. Both Scarry and Kincaid understand the possibility of representation as bound into the fact of horror: physical pain, human indifference, colonialisms; both theorists work from the assumption that language is therefore, by definition, essentially incapable of the representation of the content of trauma; a symptom of its form, language can represent pain only in its failure to *be* language, its willingness to forgo sense, its readiness to risk incomprehensibility, implausibility.

While Kincaid's position is authoritatively partial (she speaks as someone personally and deeply aware of a history of political disenfranchisements), Scarry's scholarship presents itself as impartial to political difference. Thus (while Kincaid is interested in the implications of her theorization of the distance between speech and pain for the throat of the colonized), the wounded body in Scarry's discussion of human creation has no gender, and no race. In the following excerpt from her chapter on torture, she is elaborating the politics at work between the infliction and recognition of pain: 'the denial [of the presence of pain] ... occurs in the translation of all the objectified elements of pain into the insignia of power, the conversion of the enlarged map of human suffering into an emblem of the regime's strength ... the act of disclaiming is as essential to the power as is the act of claiming. Blindness is his (the torturer's) power' (1985: 53). Scarry is interested in the political dynamics operative between a representative of a 'regime' – a torturer – and an anonymous, human, sufferer, but the connection she is drawing here between the 'regime's' infliction of violence and its simultaneous denial resonates deeply with recent feminist analyses of institutional alliances between social permission for rape and the difficulty survivors encounter in getting their narratives of assault believed.

It might be argued that Scarry's exploration of connections between pain, language and the structures of power are predicated upon the notion of pain as 'physical' – the sensation of a breaking limb, rather than a breaking heart, a referential coding of 'the body', rather than a metaphorical one. As such, perhaps her insistence that the wounded body creates the speech of the State should not be applied to the raped body – what kind of 'physical', referential pain is inflicted by rape? A body is visibly as 'whole' after rape as before. There are likely to be abrasions, bruises – perhaps worse if a 'weapon' was used – but these markings are mere witnesses to the presence of violence; they only hint at the 'wound' itself in a script that lends itself as easily to the description of an unfortunate accident as to the (sometimes) temporary annihilation of the semiotic process through which a woman may make sense of her self. For her own discussion, Scarry does need a notion of 'pure' pain, a pain of physical experience whose visibility can be directly exchanged into the invisible power of the war machines she explores. Can we think of the pain caused by rape – a pain whose parameters form the most dense interlocks between what are termed 'the physical' and 'the psychological'

– as quintessentially 'unrepresentable', as laced into the social production of power (and hence language) in an endless cycle of exchange between silence and narrative, 'the wound' and the regime, erasure and presence? The answer to this has much to do with the level at which one wants to define 'language'. At the level of ontology, I think one has to take very seriously the claim of Lacan (1985: 192): 'The use of the Word requires vastly more vigilance in the science of man than it does anywhere else, for it engages in it the very being of its object'; in this discourse, the very possibility of 'humanity' is a function of language, the 'Word,' i.e. the hypostacized process of symbolization. This is not, however, a discourse directly accessible by anything one could call a 'text' – it is legible only in terms of psychoanalytic algorithm. It may very well be the case that at this level, knowledge of pain and knowledge of language are – as Kincaid suggests – twin branches of one rooted struggle for any kind of psyche at all.

This is not the level, however, at which I wanted to think about the function of language in this facet of my interest in the experience of rape and its representation. In part, this has to do with the range of questions to which linguists, as opposed to psychoanalysts, are accountable. In part, it has to do with the salience of the term 'narrative' to my research. Another level at which language can be defined assumes a reality in which communication forms a surface of interactivity that indexes and reproduces the social. 'Narrative' in a Lacanian reading is not legible from utterance; 'narrative' for my research had to assume that texts – oral communication, newspapers, legal documents, fiction – are legible in ways that relate the concept of being human to a community via the representation of human experience. It is at this level that 'ideology' is produced – it is a world in which the effects of texts (language) are palpable, 'political'. It is at this level that 'belief', occurring between the recognition of alterity and the establishment of a contract, may be granted or refused to the teller of stories.

Narrative and 'plausibility'

The formal 'plausibility' of texts is widely held to rely on culturally powerful cohesion strategies, which are both endo- and exo-phoric (Halliday and Hasan, 1976). These strategies operate at levels that include the viability of the sentence, the paragraph, and collections of paragraphs. The cohesion strategies within narrative text are peculiarly reliant on culturally specific paradigms of 'knowledge' about reality, a knowledge often organized into causally bonded networks of information about people, divinities, life and perception, and frequently coded and protected as belief-systems that ensure and enhance a community's survival. Research on narrative structure among discourse analysts highlights both storytellers' use of 'formulae', schemas, or even 'text-grammars' as a linguistic means of ritualizing the representation of experience, and the fact that where cross-cultural difference precludes understanding of these formulae, the 'point' of the story gets lost to the listener. In his early work on the oral narratives of New York working-class teenagers, Labov cites the relation of cohesion to plausibility as integral to a story's success: 'credibility is seen to rest on a series of formal, causal relations that lead from the initial situation to the maximally reportable event ... and reportability is central to narrative "success"' (Labov, 1972: 229). In later research, he develops a model for the description of the way story-tellers accent the salient connections within their texts; strategies for 'evaluation' (both 'internal' and 'external') are revealed as crucial facets of a story-teller's expertise. Labov suggests that for the narrator to have their story laconically dismissed entails personal humiliation, and he conflates, in this connection of pride and 'plausibility', two notions that need to be separated.

Making a distinction between the 'plausibility' of a tale and the 'credibility' of its teller is important. The plausibility of a story in itself is a function of its hearer's readiness to make sense of its organization at multiple levels: the plausibility of narrative relies on the symbiotic relation of text organization (schemas) and cultural assumptions about the way the world works.

Not only does a storyteller's failure to use culturally appropriate metalingual moves announcing the story *qua* story risk its degradation, a story's success depends also on the cultural familiarity of its characters, their 'psychological' shape, and the range of their interactivity. There is, of course, vast imaginative space for idiosyncratic and unfamiliar narrative choreographies within any community; what is important to my argument, however, is the relation between the familiarity of a scenario and its hearer's readiness to find it 'plausible'.

Studies of juries' reactions to witnesses' (i.e. survivors') accounts of their rape have shown that the closer the account matches certain narrative expectations about rape culturally held and disseminated, the more likely it is that the perpetrator will be found guilty. Thus, a survivor who tells of being raped by a stranger, or a white woman who is assaulted by a black man, has a much stronger chance of a 'plausible' tale than a black woman raped by her acquaintances late at night (e.g. Estrich, 1987) in a bar.

This 'plausibility' is separable from the 'credibility' of someone who is telling the story of her own assault. Although the scholarship cited above speaks to the sympathy of jurors towards survivors whose tales match, in some respect, stereotypic scenarios, the fact that the tale becomes 'plausible' does not confer 'credibility' on the survivor in any simple way. It would be possible to substantiate this observation by referring to survivors' experiences of being 'told to cry' or 'asked ... to dress real conservative' on the witness stand. As attempts to arrange 'innocence' for the survivor who is a witness, such instructions reveal the noetic quagmire of a woman who has survived a sexual assault. The logic of a 'plausible' rape story involves either a strongly identifiable about-to-be rapist, or a woman who 'asked for it' in some way, perhaps by being a 'woman'. There is no guarantee that a survivor whose story evokes stereotypic plausibility earns her own 'credibility' from her listeners – in order to function fully as a 'victim' within the narrative of a crime, she has to be innocent of complicity with that crime. While there are myriad adventures pre-choreographed by cultural stereotypes about rape in which the survivor`s tale may carry 'plausibility' (e.g., her attacker was a complete stranger, or she was attacked by a man from whom she hitched a ride home late at night), a survivor's 'credibility' can be degraded by the very stereotypic semes that grant her tale independent validity. Most stereotypes about rape seek to accuse survivors of their own assault. The creation of her 'credibility' then, for the survivor, is an almost oxymoronic task – while the validity of her story (and thus, her right and ability to represent herself) does interact powerfully with widely held notions about men, women and sexual violence, to position herself as the narrative victim of a rape deeply risks her personal 'credibility' as a woman. A piece by Paul Drew (1987) which discusses the linguistic process of cross-examination of the witness in a British rape trial illustrates this. He tracks the cross-examiner's attempts to reveal the witness's knowledge that she was in a dangerous context prior to her assault, and describes the witness's in-sistence on a poor memory about certain contextual details as moves towards the establishment of her own innocence – 'such details may go unnoticed by people who have no reason to notice them, who have no suspicion of what is about to happen, and who are therefore innocent of the events to which they are witnesses ...' (Drew, 1987: 17). In other words, to be in a 'rape story' at all as the victim places a narrator in direct confrontation with stereotypes about gender and sexuality whose implica-tions may eviscerate both her 'credibility' as an innocent sufferer of a crime and her pragmatic right to authority over her experience.

The difficulty of a survivor's status in relation to 'plausible' scenarios about how rape occurs is one arena in which her 'credibility' gets chal-lenged. But 'credibility' is accumulated from more than simply the relation between familiar or stereotypic texts and a 'new' story; 'credibility' is also a function of a relation between a pragmatic voice and the narrative 'I' claimed for that voice in oral autobiography. There is no automatic identity between a speaking narrator and her autobiographical 'I' – the complex deictic plurality produced by this difference, and its implications for the recipient of the tale, form the arena of much modern literary criticism. Within oral narrative, the representation of a pragmatic 'I' interacts with the narrative subject across frames of time which effect stereophonic

resonance; the ambiguities, connections and contradictions of this resonance create the semantic field from which a hearer harmonizes the multiple
presence of the narrator (her physical voice, her pragmatic 'I', her narrative
'I') into integrity, or 'credibility'. In other words, although the construction
of the narrating 'I' is inherently involved with rapid deictic instabilities,
'credibility' refers to (fictive, temporary) stabilization of the storyteller's
identity, a stabilization that unifies her pragmatic and narrative selves under
conditions comfortable to the listener. Elaine Wachs (1985), in her analysis
of women telling one another 'New York horror stories' (experiences
both autobiographical and second-hand), suggests that crime victim stories
work as cautionary tales. They help to integrate the teller's experience
'back' into the context in which she needs to know how to survive, and
they insist on her intelligent connection to that context. To narrate the
story of violation is, then, interpersonal proof of the teller's continued
social existence. Thus, while the explicit terms of a hearer's conditions for
'stabilizing' multiple identities remain probably invisible to the storyteller,
her credibility – not merely as a storyteller, but as a viable human voice
– relies on her narrative control of time and subjectivity.

'The girl who lived up on the mountain'

This section provides an introduction to 'Barbara's' narrative. 'Barbara' is
the pseudonym for the woman with whom I worked during this part of
my research. She is a white, working-class, New York-born woman, whose
first language is English. I have her permission to quote from the audio-
tapes of her narrative.

In the following sections, the relationship between the various subject
'I's of the autobiographical story-teller is explored through an analysis of
the opening minutes of Barbara's autobiographical oral narrative of her
experiences concerning sexual assault. What follows are the opening
minutes of Barbara's story:

... okay um the first time I was like what I would consider now raped um was
when I was about seven or eight years old I don't remember exactly what year
it was um coz for a long time I didn't can I like analyse myself? like throw in
whatever I wanna say? /[JFB:] Sure, just/ Just talk, okay and I was sleeping
over a friend's house and er neighbor next door neighbor who was you know
was one of my friends and I remember lying in bed one night and she had
already fallen asleep and somebody came in the room and I don't know exactly
who it was even coz in the family there was the father and two brothers but
some male I was like lying on my back you know like like staring like the radio
was on you know and I used to like to lie in bed and listen to the radio when
I was a little girl so um and um he whoever that person was came and you
know with his hand I was like digitally raped I guess the term would be you
know that he like spread my legs and put his fingers up inside my vagina and

I was like really frozen and I didn't I knew something you know it's like I don't I knew something was going on I didn't scream I didn't do anything but um I just felt really like I was frozen like shocked and then he left and it was it all happened in a matter of minutes but I remember I remember feeling incredibly shocked and feeling I think that that was the first time I remember having a sense of irony about life you know like of um of of or kind of kind of thinking about what paranoia was although I wouldn't have defined it at that time as a seven or eight year old although I did read a lot in those days you know when I was younger and had a pretty sophisticated reading reading ability at that age but I that there was a song on the radio that was popular at the time about this girl who lived up on the mountain and how none of the boys would ever have her because none of them would ever dare to climb the mountain and I remember thinking how ironic that was that here I am like that some guy something is happening to me why aren't I up on the mountain or something or like you know [laughs] you know wait a minute it's really easy access or something you know I felt like it was kind of irony and er it's the first time I ever remember feeling reflective in that way you know kind of anyway so that was um that was that time ...

Barbara's opening words bifurcate her narrative voice across two frames:

(a) *the first* time I was raped
(b) what I would consider now raped
(a) was when I was about seven or eight years old

In the frame of (a), 'I' is positioned as a protagonist, securely bolted into the sense of story evoked by the almost formulaic deixis of a *first time*; (b) interrupts the verb at the syntactic onset of the passivization into which *was raped* will move 'I', and shifts the frame from what one could term 'direct narrative' into a pragmatic one acutely concerned with narrator agency. This is not the same frame Barbara uses in the words following: *I don't remember exactly what year it was*; here, she works in the frame more usually called 'pragmatic' in which a storyteller marks her consciousness of the split in time between the moment of her tale's 'real' occurrence and the moment in which she is in the process of relaying it as a tale. The frame of (b) is concerned not with memory, but with language (it could be referred to as 'analytic' or 'metalingual') and choreographs a minute, but complete, separation from the narrative 'I's experience by claiming the verb *raped* as one acknowledged or owned only by an 'I' constituted by a deictic *now*, a present which covers the ambiguity of the temporal frame in which Barbara marks herself as the architect of her story and the frame in which she comments upon the arbitrariness of her tools.

Narrative, pragmatic, analytic and reflective frames

The construction of 'frames' – text whose temporal, aspectual and attitudinal orientation toward their subject 'I' is cohesive – in Barbara's initial narration seemed significant. The design of the text operates across at least four frames, deictically separate but frequently (as in the opening sentence, via the verb *raped*) syntactically interlocked, or overlapped.

The classically 'narrative' frame positions the subject as a child within the experience of anonymous abuse; the classically 'pragmatic' frame notes the evidential relation of the storyteller to her storytelling. The other two frames involve more directive control of their subjects – one focuses intently on the moves of the pragmatic 'I' (as described above with the term 'metalingual' or 'analytic') and the other is reflective, not of the pragmatic 'I,' but of the meaning and identity of the narrative 'I' and her experience. This fourth frame is deeply complex, and turns out, as I will suggest, to bear much of the weight of Barbara's narration of her own 'intelligence', her right to social ontology. Barbara's opening 'time' is refracted through these four frames.

Narrative frame   In the Narrative frame, 'I' *was about seven or eight*, 'I' *was sleeping, lying, staring, raped, frozen*, and positioned within the immediate and local temporal context of the violation: *the radio was on* (which entails that 'I' could hear it), *there was a song … That was popular at the time* (here, not only the local detail about contemporary music, but the syntactic *'the'* – in contrast to *that* used in different frames (e.g. *I wouldn't have defined it at that time*) – roots *time* within a Narrative frame that contains both the occasion of the assault and its historical locale.

Pragmatic frame   In the Pragmatic frame, 'I' marks her mind as the resource for her narrative; 'I' *remember*(s), doesn't *know*, and *think*s about specific details within the story – her precise age, the identity of the perpetrator, and also (a point in which this Pragmatic 'I' overlaps with that created by the Reflective frame) about her reactions to this assault when it occurred – *I remember (feeling incredibly shocked)*; *I remember (thinking)*. 'I' here is a subject presented as both separate from the 'I' of the Narrative frame (who acts, or is acted upon, but who does not meditate), and in possession of the material which can produce that 'I'.

Analytic frame   The Analytic frame interrupts the material of other frames through 'I's concern with the language available for defining rape, and its 'participants'. This concern splits the 'I' of the Pragmatic frame, who marks her consciousness as her narrative source, into an 'I' who marks a distinction between consciousness and words. Within this frame, 'I' (both explicitly and indirectly) measures the match between the language convention offers and the experience in which both the 'I' of the Pragmatic frame and the 'I' of the Narrative frame are involved. An instance of the former would be: *can I like analyse myself?*; instances of the latter include (*like digitally raped*) *I guess the term would be* and *what I would consider now* *raped*. As far as I can read, most of the occasions on which Barbara selects this frame involve the memory of either the actual moments of her being bodily invaded, or the identity of the perpetrator. In the following words – *somebody came in the room and I don't know exactly who it was even coz in the family there was the father*, the 'I' of the Narrative frame 'in the room' is juxtaposed to the Pragmatic 'I' marking an imprecise detail, and *even* functions *analytically*, highlighting the degree to which the perpetrator is anonymous. This anonymity gets stressed by the next phrases – *there was the father and two brothers but um some male* – where *some male* operates within three frames. In the Narrative frame *some male* refers to the presence seen by 'I' 'in the room'; in the Analytic frame, *some male* functions as a metalingual summary over *the father and two brothers*; and, finally, *some male* refers to a conceptual conclusion about the typical identity of rapists 'I' reaches within the Reflective frame.

Reflective frame The 'I' of the Reflective frame explicitly ponders the meaning of the child's rape, which entails consideration both of the identity of the child and the analysis of what it was that happened to her. This is the only frame within which a relation between the 'I' of the narrative frame, and the 'I's of the Pragmatic and Analytic frames is sketched, and the sketch occurs by referring to the 'I' of the Narrative frame in the continuous imperfect (*and I used to like to lie in bed and listen to the radio when I was a little girl*) and to the cognitive, or metaphysical, effect of the rape. I use the term 'metaphysical' for the description of phrases such as *and feeling (I think) that was the first time um (I remember) having a sense of irony about life*, and *it's the first time (I) ever (remember) feeling reflective in that way*. In these words, an implicit 'I' (zero pronoun of the gerunds *feeling, having,* and so on; the verbalized 'I' is shared with that of the Pragmatic frame) hints at the creation of a metaphysics, a philosophy about the meaning of human destiny, which is directly caused by the 'revelations' of this form of violence. It is these words which (unlike those of other frames) suggest a connection between the 'I' telling the narrative and the 'I' who experienced rape as a child ('I' presents a mind, her intelligence, ranging across time and space to locate an overarching philosophical salience to what is remembered); it is through the span of this range that the 'I' of the Narrative frame is offered evaluation, and hence an existence beyond the moments of her violation, within the Reflective frame. Thus, descriptions of the child's reading ability (*when I was younger and had a pretty sophisticated um reading ... ability*) and her pleasure in the radio carry the tone of analytic reminiscence, which colours the phrases involving the reactions of the child to the fingers inside her: *I knew something was going on (I didn't scream I didn't do anything) but I just felt really like (I was frozen like shocked)*. Here, the parenthecized phrases resonate in both the Narrative and the Reflective frames – in the Narrative Frame,

'I' 'in the room' reacts to what is going on, and in the Reflective frame that reaction is scrutinized, simultaneously stated and evaluated. *I knew something was going on* is clearly Reflective – the combination of the a-specific *something* succeeding the explicit definition of what it was that was going on (*he like spread my legs*) suggests 'I' as an analyst, not a recipient. *I didn't scream I didn't do anything*, however, cohere both with the recipient 'I' and with the 'I' overseeing the meaning of a child's reaction. The last thing I want to note here about the Reflective frame is the way it announces some of the terms most important to Barbara's conceptual-ization of her history. The words *irony, paranoia, reflective* hint at a semantic paradigm deeply significant to Barbara; the 'I' of the Reflective frame is a philosopher, whose lexicon is marked as a product of experience and imagination.

It is important to stress that the four frames of subjectivity discussed above are heuristic prisms. In other words, although each one's boundaries can be motivated (in relation to the 'I's they choreograph, and sometimes in terms of their syntactic choices), it is not as though each one is a cloth of a different colour, out of which Barbara has deliberately cut and stitched a neat textual quilt. Not only are there different ways of reading her narrative's organization, but what matters about the variety of 'subjects' created by Barbara's opening story is their fluidity, their instability rather than their cohesion into a static autonomy. It may be possible to motivate reading this text through two frames, or six; the point is not so much the number nor their juxtaposition, it is rather their illumination of Barbara's strategy towards the performance of a mobile 'subjectivity' within her narrative. This mobility, coupled with the resonance of repetition that occurs (almost stereophonically) where the 'I's of two frames syntactically interlock or overlap, effects what I want to call *dimension* over the auto-biographical 'I'. The flexibility of Barbara's 'I's, and the speed of their transitions, has probably much more to do with the fact of her audience than with any independent narrative need.

As I suggested above, 'credibility' can be thought of as a function of a hearer's readiness to harmonize the variety of perspectives within an oral narrative about the storyteller into momentary 'steadiness'. This may, of course, be immediately challenged by the storyteller, but harmonization and steadiness are both required if the complex pragmatic attachment between the storyteller, her tale, and her audience is going to be woven into the *storyteller's* social credibility. The multiple subjectivities visible through 'framing' Barbara's text, as I have suggested above, offer her listener at least three things – first, the richness of the 'I's dimension (an assurance, perhaps, of the 'intelligence' of both the listener and the storyteller); second, the opportunity of hearing a graphic story of sexual violation, without ever being asked to participate aurally 'in the room' too long (only one of the frames is Narrative, all the others are more interested in an 'I' who thinks rather than an 'I' who experiences); and thirdly, the display of potential subjective dispersal – if the gift of 'credibility' is to be bestowed, perhaps the listener has to be offered the opportunity to refuse?

The politics of doubt

Michel de Certeau describes belief as occurring 'between the recognition of an alterity and the establishment of a contract'. (1985: 192). Such a location acknowledges the principles of *exchange* intrinsic to the hope of credibility and marks doubt as essential to the possibility of attention. The variety of subjectivities presented by the first minutes of Barbara's narrative, and the deftness with which they interrupt and complement one another, suggest complexity; as summarized above, this pragmatic complexity presents ambiguities for the audience. On the one hand, the rich fluidity of the subject 'I's may suggest autobiographical dexterity, or 'intelligence'; on the other hand, too much subjective shift may motivate a listener's doubt about the storyteller's integrity or conceptual coherence. The decision about 'credibility' belongs, pragmatically, to the hearer, which entails that she be offered the grounds from which to make it, to 'make sense' of the multiple 'I's Barbara's voice presents. Like Kincaid, Barbara proposes her imagination, her facility with thought, language and design, as the symptom of her visceral memory of invasion. The question of the specificities of *sexual* invasion's relationship to (or, with) the formation of 'mind' as it negotiates myriad ordinary violences and miracles remains open. What is clear, however, from these readings of Barbara's 'first time' of experiencing rape, is that her narrative strategizes subjectivity (the textual evidence of 'mind') as the minutely supple interplay of exchange among authorial agency, textual 'frames' of time and pragmatic attention, and the internal development of a lexicon (and philosophy) about the social fact of sexual violence. As suggested earlier, Barbara's narrative technologies cannot be claimed as unique to her experience as a survivor, nor to the fact that she is telling her own story of rape; neither (given the difficulty of establishing social integrity attested to by many survivors) can they be ignored. In a world sometimes too ready (the legal world is perhaps always too ready) to equate the oral autobiographer's 'I' with 'truth' *or* 'mendacity', it is crucial to acknowledge the critical deictic choreography involved within any autobiographical act, and to move from the recognition of that complexity into the exploration of the effect of subjectively experienced abuse on both story-telling and story-evaluation.

References

de Certeau, M. (1985) 'What do we do when we believe', in M. Blonsky (ed.), *On Signs*, Johns Hopkins University Press, Baltimore, MD.

Drew, P. (1987) 'A study of cross-examination techniques within rape trials', unpublished paper, Oxford University.

Estrich, S. (1987) *Real Rape*, Harvard University Press, Cambridge, MA.

Halliday, M. and Hasan, R. (1976) *Cohesion in English*, Longman, London.

Labov, W. (1972) *Language in the Inner City*, University of Pennsylvania Press, Philadelphia.

Lacan, J. (1985) *Speech and Language in Psychoanalysis*, Methuen, New York.

Ong, W. (1981) *Orality and Literacy*, Methuen, New York.

Scarry, E. (1985) *The Body in Pain: the Making and Unmaking of the World*, Oxford University Press, New York.

Wachs, E. (1985) *Crime Victim Stories: Urban Folklore in New York*, Indiana University Press, Bloomington, IN.

CHAPTER 8

Putting discourse analysis to work in AIDS prevention

Anna Strebel

There is widespread agreement among social scientists internationally that acquired immunodeficiency syndrome (AIDS) is much more than just a biomedical problem. The social constructionist approach to the problem of AIDS (Gilman, 1988; Sontag, 1988; Treichler, 1987) takes account of prevailing public depictions of the disease, their interaction with current social structures, and their impact on individual experience, public views and policy formation.

Plummer (1988) suggests that two central discourses organize much of what he calls 'AIDSspeak': one focuses on the medicalization and the other the stigmatization of AIDS. The medicalizing account depicts an epidemic; it draws on associations with death, disaster and other diseases like the plague, syphilis and cancer, and makes use of militaristic metaphors. Such notions serve to entrench the power of medicine and science in everyday life, leaving individuals disempowered to take responsibility for prevention or management of AIDS themselves (Sontag, 1988; Young, 1987). At the same time, stigmatization has occurred because the disease is associated with sexually transmitted disease, with gays, sex workers and intravenous drug-users; in other words AIDS is the result of what is generally perceived as deviant and promiscuous behaviour (Gilman, 1988; Patton 1990; Sontag, 1988). Responses of moral panic have meant that instead of receiving sympathy and support, people with AIDS (PWA) are blamed, feared and avoided. From this discourse a return to 'traditional values and lifestyle', and the control of seemingly deviant sexuality are seen as solutions to the AIDS problem (Watney, 1988).

Increased rates of infection among people of colour in the USA and sub-Saharan Africans have reinforced these stances and responses. As a result, the problem has been established as one belonging to 'others', so that the population at large can deny their own vulnerability and project their fears onto 'guilty' minorities (Sabatier, 1988; Treichler, 1987). In South Africa too such scapegoating has been a dominant theme of public responses (Sadie and van Aardt, 1992).

It is significant that most social constructionist research on AIDS has occurred at the macro-level, involving analysis of state responses to AIDS and national media campaigns: for example Ingstad's (1990) work on cultural constructions of AIDS in Botswana and Seidel's (1990) account of the changing discourse of AIDS in Uganda. There has been far less documented investigation of how individuals or groups engage with these representations of AIDS. Moreover, both internationally and in SA, possible interventions arising from a constructionist approach have not been clearly explored (Strebel, 1995).

Drawing on constructionist understandings, feminist work on gendered power relations and the political economy of sexual relations has, however, articulated the problems women face in the prevention of AIDS. From this perspective patriarchy is seen to exert substantial though inconsistent control over women in ways that have direct implications for their protection from HIV infection. Safe sex options (condoms, abstinence, monogamy) reflect acceptance of a male sex drive that women must counter, and also represent attempts to re-exert control over female sexuality. Feminists argue that AIDS needs alternative, more emancipatory, responses. These include fundamental changes in power relations between men and women, as well as different notions of sexuality (Holland et al., 1990; Juhasz, 1990; Kippax et al., 1990). Furthermore, because of their differential positioning in society, women often lack access to economic resources, which leads to financial dependence on men and so to difficulty in insisting on safe sex (Bassett and Mhloyi, 1991; Larson, 1990; Standing and Kisekka, 1989).

These feminist analyses provide rich contextualization of the problem of AIDS for women and emphasize the central need for a broad social transformatory perspective, both in understanding the issues and in suggesting meaningful responses. Yet they are less helpful in generating specific, realistic and strategic choices for women.

Researchers working directly on AIDS prevention have drawn largely on experience in the field of health education, in response to the 'crisis of AIDS'. Much of this work has been located within a traditional social psychological paradigm, which views safe sex as a matter of individual choice, and behaviour change as a result of objective information to adjust negative attitudes and alter misperceptions. At a practical level, research into the validity of approaches like the theory of reasoned action, the health belief and self-efficacy models has been inconclusive. Implementation of their principles has also not led to the expected changes in behaviour (Becker and Joseph, 1988; Freudenberg, 1990; Valdiserri, 1989).

Discourse analysis and AIDS

The gaps and contradictions in the frameworks discussed above indicated the need for another form of methodological enquiry. Discourse analysis appeared to offer a useful starting point for a differently focused approach. A number of writers have drawn broadly on discourse analytic notions in approaching AIDS (Juhasz, 1990; Treichler, 1987), or voiced the need for such analyses (Schoepf, 1993; Seidel, 1990). Also some work using a discourse analytic approach that has taken account of issues of gender and AIDS has been carried out both abroad (e.g. Kippax et al., 1990) and locally (e.g. Miles, 1992). However, it is notable that none of this has been translated into practical ideas for prevention of HIV infection.

Of potential relevance to AIDS work was the apparently dual character of discourses: they are the means through which the world emerges and action becomes possible, but they also constrain which meanings or knowledges become dominant. At different times, for different reasons, some versions of social reality are deemed legitimate, 'given voice' and reside in the hands of 'experts', while others are silenced. In this way power relations are produced and reproduced through ideological systems. So it is the gaps and silences – that which is not said – which can become a significant focus in this kind of analysis (Levett, 1988; Parker, 1992). Nevertheless, power is not an all-or-nothing process, nor is it merely oppressive. Power can be both positive and productive, is manifest in multiple sites and is always accompanied by resistances (Foucault, 1976; Macdonell, 1986; Young, 1987).

These ideas seemed to offer challenging spaces for perhaps finding ways of practically preventing HIV infection. However, questions about the extent to which discourse analysis promotes critical interventions and is socially transformatory were relevant (Abrams and Hogg, 1990; Burman, 1991; Parker, 1990). The 'how' of doing this in AIDS work also remained obscure. Burman (1991: 340) has argued that discourse analysis is not necessarily inherently politically transformatory but such interventions are possible. It:

> can (a) champion the cause of a particular discourse by elaborating the con-
> trasting consequences of each discursive framework, can (b) promote an existing
> (perhaps subordinate) discourse (as the 'empowerment', 'giving people a voice'
> model of research), can (c) intervene directly in clarifying consequences of
> discursive frameworks with speakers (as in training or action research, for
> example), as well as (d) commenting on the discursive-political consequences
> of discursive clashes and frameworks.

Hollway (1984a: 260), offering a possible explanation for why AIDS information has not changed risky behaviour, draws attention to the place of the unconscious in current psychological investments in specific behaviour, making them especially inaccessible to change. In what could be particularly relevant to the area of AIDS, she recognizes the complexity of the process and identifies how discursive shifts may occur:

Changes don't automatically eradicate what went before – neither in structures nor in the way that practices, powers and meanings have been produced historically. Consciousness-changing is not accomplished by new discourses replacing old ones. It is accomplished as the result of the contradictions in our positionings, desires and practices – and thus in our subjectivities – which result from the coexistence of the old and the new. Every relation and every practice to some extent articulates such contradictions and therefore is a site of potential change as much as it is a site of reproduction.

In the light of these considerations, my study aimed to explore how women saw the problem of AIDS and the range of discourses they utilized; to map their accounts in relation to prevailing depictions of the problem elsewhere; and to identify the consequent constraints and opportunities for action. If this analysis of discourses was to provide a meaningful challenge to traditional views of health education, the work would also need to feed concretely into debates about practical AIDS prevention activities. So, in order to explore Burman (1991) and Hollway's (1984a) ideas on social change through discourse analysis, a further intention was to actively pursue realistic and appropriate intervention options (Strebel, 1994). However, given the discussion above, this latter aim could be seen only as exploratory work.

Group discussions about AIDS

Fourteen focus group discussions were conducted. Two included men, while the rest were women-only groups. The ninety-five black participants were drawn from sexually transmitted disease and antenatal clinics, community nutrition centres, women's and youth groups of a political organization, domestic workers and students. Their ages ranged from fifteen to forty-seven years, with an average of twenty-six years. For two-thirds an African language was their mother tongue, while the rest were English or Afrikaans speaking. The majority were single with at least some secondary level education, although roughly half were unemployed.

The discussions, facilitated through the use of an AIDS-related vignette, were tape-recorded, transcribed verbatim and translated from Xhosa or Afrikaans into English where necessary. This process obviously raises questions relating to language and translation. Clearly many of the possible problems could be avoided by researchers who 'speak the language', but this is a complex notion, and subjectivity speaks in many voices. At the same time, these issues need to be seen in the light of suggestions that the language of AIDS is predominantly one of the developed world, mediated by Western media (Fortin, 1987) and that in South Africa the discourses of AIDS have overwhelmingly been in English.

First-stage analysis – sketching the landscape Potter and Wetherell's

(1987) conception of interpretative repertoires was used as an initial framework of analysis. Broad discursive themes were first drawn from the text, and the interplay between dominant, multiple and contradictory discourses explored. Two major repertoires of talk, relating to AIDS and to gender, were apparent. Those relating to AIDS were clearly identifiable and reflected the prevailing medicalization and stigmatization discourses described by Plummer (1988). Discourses of gender, while less clear-cut, centred principally around paradoxical notions of male power in gender relations on the one hand and women's responsibility for implementing safe sex on the other. However, while these discourses delineated and circumscribed understanding and options, they did not provide a seamless construction of the problem: women were invested in a variety of positions in relation to dominant discourses. They positioned and repositioned themselves within these discourses, they distanced themselves from them, they posed alternatives and they recognised the limits of particular positionings.

Second-stage analysis – meanings and discursive practices This overview of discursive positionings of women provided a powerful sense of the complexity of options avilable to them. Yet it lacked a focus on how such repertoires impacted on meanings and how this might be translated into possible action for participants. It also did not generate a language for communicating about practical interventions. So an attempt to pull things together, to consider the implications of analysis and develop a structure for communication and intervention, was needed. In doing this, I was guided by Hollway's interpretative discourse analysis approach, in which she defines discourse as 'a set of assumptions which cohere around a common logic and which confer particular meanings on the experiences and practices of people in a particular sphere' (Hollway, 1984b: 63).

The construction of AIDS as a silent and invisible disease A first step was to locate the initial findings historically and culturally; AIDS as constructed through and reflective of a dynamic interaction with particular social constellations. The present stage of the epidemic in South Africa is characterized by relatively few identified AIDS cases (7,289), estimations of a much larger number of those already HIV-infected (about 116,000) and more or less dire predictions of what the future holds (over 20 per cent of women HIV-positive by 2002) (DNHPD, 1995; Doyle, 1993). Together with reporting of these figures, much of the official and media response to AIDS has emphasized the need for testing, identification and control of those infected (Sadie and van Aardt, 1992).

This present situation contributes to AIDS readily being depicted as a silent and invisible disease, evidenced in a number of ways in the study. For many women AIDS was not yet part of their everyday experience, or much talked about. Also, they were not able to 'see' the disease, since those who were infected might show no symptoms. Moreover, it had not yet touched them directly, and very few people personally knew anyone infected.

Among women in the study, a further dimension to the 'invisible' problem, was the belief that HIV-infected people should keep silent about their condition, because of the consequences. It was said that 'having AIDS' would lead to isolation within the family and community, desertion by partner/s and family, and neglect by the medical profession. One participant said:

> She will be isolated, no one will want to have anything to do with her because people know that this sickness, it is infectious and it is incurable.

This apparently resulted from the sexual stigma attached to the disease, which leads to blame of the victim, rather than sympathy; and because the epidemic is associated with deviance and death. So the prudent strategy was to keep the condition hidden, which compounds the otherness and invisibility of the problem, as evidenced in the following statement by a participant:

> You know that's actually quite a serious problem, that people know that AIDS exists, but it doesn't affect them directly, so they're not really, I mean, they're not worried about the issue.

Thus we have the emergence of a strong discursive practice of silencing. The likely concomitant of this position is that of denial, leading to ideas that AIDS is not a tangible problem and there is no need to do anything. However, this response is not unchallenged since it provides a complicated and problematic 'solution'. The very silence and invisibility of the epidemic carries its own threats, as was evident in expressions of fear and uncertainty of women in the study.

The medicalizing discourse: the construction of individual powerlessness and dependence   The medicalizing discourse was central to much talk about AIDS and clearly contributes to the dilemma of prevention for women. While positioning within this discourse might offer some reassurances in the promise of scientific solutions, it also engenders feelings of powerlessness and dependence on professionals to identify and deal with the problem. In other words it suggests that the individual cannot do anything. Furthermore, the benefits of medical technology, in the form of treatment and vaccines, will not be available to the majority of black working-class women in SA. Hence the sense of fatalism of many of the women:

There is no way that she can protect herself because there is no cure for AIDS, there is no way out.

But, but, even if you go for testing, what are you going to do, because if you are HIV+, there is nothing that can be done.

There's the AZT tablet, now even that tablet is out of reach for us, and they tell us that we are the people who are prone to this AIDS, but still the only thing that can, um, at least give us some temporary relief is out of reach ... why can't they make it available for us? They keep it for the people who can afford it and the people who are not at, at risk of, um, contracting AIDS.

The stigmatizing discourse: the construction of blameworthy 'others'   At the same time, discourses of AIDS stigma were readily adopted, through associations with promiscuous sexuality, the deviant behaviour of the 'other', and, paradoxically, exposure to racist views of 'African AIDS', as evidenced in the following statements:

Many people associate AIDS with, um, sexual activities ... I think that's why some people distance themselves from AIDS.

I am talking from a black perspective. In the first place, there are a lot of people who actually feel it's a white thing, okay, and a gay thing, these two things are combined.

People say it's just the white man's way of taming the black man, so it's some form of, people just regard it as some form of indoctrination.

Investment in such positions with the help of denial increases the sense that personal risk is not great, that AIDS is not of immediate concern to black women who are not gay or promiscuous. As a result, the perception that the individuals or groups do not need to do anything, as in the silent disease discourse discussed above, is reinforced. Once again, however, the potential escape from discomfort which this route promises is challenged by the implications of alternative discourses like those outlined below, which evoke strong fear and the previously mentioned helplessness.

Gendered discourses: the paradox of responsibility and powerlessness   For many women in the study the complexity of the situation is compounded through gender repertoires. Here, a central contradiction was clearly demonstrated. On the one hand women are positioned and position themselves as responsible for prevention of infection:

A woman can control herself, if her man is sleeping around, she knows how to control herself, the important thing is that she should protect herself.

They are also by implication responsible for spreading the virus. As a result, they should do something, take action to curb spread of the virus and to care for those infected, as is happening internationally and especially

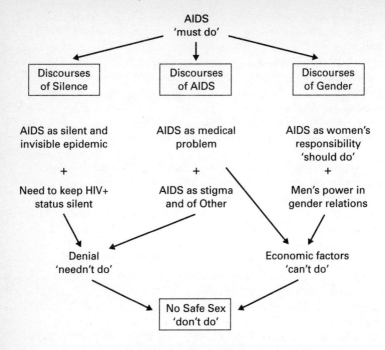

Figure 8.1 The big picture

in sub-Saharan Africa (ActUp, 1990; Kaleeba et al., 1991). However, positioned in discourses of gendered power relations, women are seen as dependent on men, lacking control over their lives, and so unable to insist on condom use, abstinence or monogamy of male partners: so they can't do anything. This is frequently made worse by their economic needs:

> She cannot tell him to use a condom because she hasn't got a job ... she is dependent, she has to think about her life.
>
> But it's difficult because if you refuse [sex] he will beat you.
>
> You'll find that your man sleeps around during the day, but when he comes to his wife he'll want to have sex with her too.

As a result of these conflicting stances, they feel both guilty and helpless. (See Figure 8.1 for this framework).

AIDS action: spaces for change

The above analysis provides a possible framework for understanding why AIDS-related behaviour change might not be regarded as a priority by many South Africans, nor be a viable option for those women who might wish to protect themselves. Yet it reflects a bleak picture, identifying tensions, constraints and complexity. However, drawing on notions of the dual nature of discourses (as discussed earlier), it seems that the very multiplicity of discourses, the softly stated alternatives and contestations, the detail and nuance all offer spaces for change and point to a key to a more positive response. Dominant discourses are neither static nor unchallenged. They are contrasted to alternative positions, to less dominant ones and to silences, and they are modified in interaction with discursive positionings. Thus the reflexive process of identifying the range of available repertoires and the investments associated with positioning in relation to them does seem to allow for movement, changes in response to and management of the problem.

Out of this comes the possibility of more direct intervention. Juhasz (1990: 43) proposes that what is needed is a challenge to the process of attempts to control women through depictions of AIDS, an active engagement to 'muster our representational forces to attempt to contribute to the social construction of women and AIDS'. In similar vein, Watney (1989: 71) suggests that there must be resistance to the dominant cultural agenda of AIDS, that the 'rhetoric of AIDS can be forced to speak new meanings', as has happened among gays (Becker and Joseph, 1988; Freudenberg, 1990). In this study there were some examples of this: of possible shifts in depictions of the problem, spaces for alternative responses, and positioning within previously silenced discourses.

Regarding medical depictions of AIDS, a shift within the medical paradigm might involve an alternative view of hopefulness for those infected, a sense of living with, rather than dying from, AIDS. As more becomes known and a better understanding is developed about what retards and what facilitates the progression of the disease, more treatment options will emerge. A sense that something can be done to reduce the agony of being HIV+ might make individuals feel that knowing their HIV status is worthwhile, as some participants recognized:

> There is a possibility that if you have, if you have, if you are HIV+ and you go for a test sooner, you stand a better chance of living longer than if you go later.

In the area of the stigmatizing of AIDS, there are a number of possibilities. A challenge to the discourses of 'the other' is likely, as AIDS statistics grow and the epidemic becomes more visible and therefore less silent. The virus may then be represented more strongly as everyone's problem (as in the rest of Africa). This could reduce denial and increase the likelihood of recognition of personal risk. We could expect more people positioned in an alternative, more positive discourse of dealing with AIDS, in which HIV infection is not a disgrace and those infected need acceptance and care, as suggested by one participant:

> It would be better if they did tell us, so that we know that they have AIDS, so
> that we can show them affection, so that a person does not feel shunned by
> other people ... he should be accepted so that he does not suffer.

Such a shift would need to include careful deconstruction of homophobic
and moralistic views that were evident in the study.

As political changes in South Africa better represent the interests of
the majority of the people, fewer people might be invested in positioning
themselves in racist discourses. Also, we could expect the development of
an indigenous discourse of AIDS, as the problem is constructed more in
terms of people's own experience in their own language, on the basis of
increased exposure to the disease and its ramifications. Such a process
may be facilitated by accentuating the intersection of traditional health
practices with the disease, and by engaging with notions of traditional
culture. However, the strength of the investment in discourses of sexual
stigma might not be easily tempered, especially if it is still black women
and men who are the majority of those infected in SA. Attempts by
AIDS workers to shift attention from ideas about high-risk groups to
notions of risky behaviour might help.

In gendered discourses there are also potential spaces. Notions of
male power may be countered by reinforcing perceptions of potential for
more power for women, and drawing on the strength of women's collective
action (as articulated in this study), although the entrenchedness of patriarchy and economic dependence makes this difficult:

> Women have always stood up for their rights in other issues, work-related issues,
> the home, domestic issues. I think they should stand up for AIDS exactly the
> same way they have for other issues.

Also, depictions of women's responsibility for AIDS can be shifted to
those of shared responsibility with men for a community and family
problem. And, importantly, spaces need to be opened around notions of
sexuality: to expand the realm of desire and sexual options, to include
alternatives to penetrative intercourse, to challenge views of prevention as
control of women's (or limitation of men's) sexuality, and to tackle issues
of sexual abuse.

Reflecting on the process

The above analysis offers some hope for creating a climate more conducive
to tackling the problem of HIV infection practically. Yet they are not
shifts that will automatically or necessarily occur, as Hollway (1984a) has
suggested. Even with the active commitment of AIDS workers and policy-
makers to such a task, dominant discourses will not easily shift, and
unintended or unexpected constructions and investments will remain.

Moreover, the realm of discourses is abstract and obtuse, and the above-mentioned alternatives can only be long-term, slow-impact contributions to what is an urgent crisis. Nevertheless, this mode of analysis has generated a conceptual framework and provided strategies for both broad-ranging and small-scale focused interventions: for example, through the media, in community work and also in individual counselling. The process of mapping the present discursive positions and practices has also suggested some more immediate and direct strategies at the level of 'political activism', in line perhaps with Burman's (1991) notion of empowerment.

Although the particulars of such an enterprise are inevitably context-specific and need to be negotiated, this research has raised some possibilities. To start with there was the muted voice of mobilization of women, broadly around related socio-economic issues (employment, education, health care), but also specifically regarding AIDS issues (female methods of protection, access to drug trials, home care of PWA). Although such rhetoric is not easily translated into the daily reality of women's lives, South African women have a long history of involvement in church groups and political organizations, like the Women's League of the African National Congress. And in this study they expressed their strong concern about AIDS as an urgent problem for themselves and their families. This energy needs to be harnassed for the development of collective responses from women. As one participant said: 'This problem requires that we should hold meetings as women and we gradually involve the men and the youth as well.'

Men also need to be brought directly into AIDS work at all levels. This requires the issues to be reframed to emphasize AIDS as a problem for everyone, to develop a model of collaborative action. This will increase the likelihood of effective strategies for women (Strebel, 1993). It also requires a specific focus on gender relations as a priority. To succeed, such a project needs to look at male sexuality, at gendered power relations and the investments involved in different discursive positioning for women and men. Overall, much more focus on getting AIDS on the political agenda in South Africa is required.

As both an AIDS researcher and an activist at the time, the central dilemma I faced in this work was trying to marry the complex and challenging theoretical language of discourse analysis to the 'hands-on' urgency of intervention, education and advocacy. I found the 'discourses of discourse analysis' frustratingly impermeable and encapsulated. While I was excited by the potential power of the approach in recognizing hegemony and acknowledging contradiction, I was struck by the relative silence about how this might transform practice. This became particularly telling within the context of a commitment to engaging in dialogue with research participants about outcomes. There were, however, some spaces offered for direct interventions.

Note

This work, which formed part of a doctoral thesis (see Strebel, 1994), was carried out with the aid of a grant from the International Development Research Centre, Ottawa, Canada.

References

Abrams, D. and Hogg, M. (1990) 'The context of discourse: let's not throw out the baby with the bathwater', *Philosophical Psychology*, 3 (2), 219–25.

ActUp (The ActUp/New York Women and AIDS Book Group) (1990) *Women, AIDS and activism*, South End Press, London.

Bassett, M. and Mhloyi, M. (1991) 'Women and AIDS in Zimbabwe: the making of an epidemic', *International Journal of Health Services*, 21 (1), 143–56.

Becker, M. and Joseph, J. (1988) 'AIDS and behavioral change to reduce risk: a review', *American Journal of Public Health*, 78 (4), 394–410.

Burman, E. (1991) 'What discourse is not', *Philosophical Psychology*, 4 (3), 325–42.

DNHPD (1995) 'Fifth national HIV survey in women attending antenatal clinics of the public health services in South Africa, October/November 1994', *Epidemiological Comments*, 22 (5), 90–100.

Doyle, P. (1993) 'Editorial: adult HIV prevalence for males and females', *AIDS Scan*, 5 (2), 3–4.

Fortin, A. (1987) 'The politics of AIDS in Kenya', *Third World Quarterly*, 9, 906–19.

Foucault, M. (1976) *The History of Sexuality, Volume 1: An Introduction*, Allen Lane, London.

Freudenberg, N. (1990) 'AIDS prevention in the United States: lessons from the first Decade', *International Journal of Health Services*, 20 (4), 589–99.

Gilman, S. (1988) *Disease and Representation: Images of Illness from Madness to AIDS*, Cornell University Press, Ithaca, NY.

Holland, J., Ramazanoglu, C., Scott, S., Sharpe, S. and Thomson, R. (1990) 'Sex, gender and power: young women's sexuality in the shadow of AIDS', *Sociology of Health and Illness*, 12 (3), 336–50.

Hollway, W. (1984a) 'Gender difference and the production of subjectivity', in J. Henriques, W. Hollway, C. Urwin, C. Venn and V. Walkerdine, *Changing the Subject: Psychology, Social Regulation and Subjectivity*, Methuen, London, 227–63.

Hollway, W. (1984b) 'Women's power in heterosexual sex', *Women's Studies International Forum*, 7 (1), 63–8.

Ingstad, B. (1990) 'The cultural construction of AIDS and its consequences for prevention in Botswana', *Medical Anthropology Quarterly*, 28–40.

Juhasz, A. (1990) 'The contained threat: women in mainstream AIDS documentary', *Journal of Sex Research*, 27 (1), 25–46.

Kaleeba, N., Ray, S. and Willmore, B. (1991) *We Miss You All. Noerine Kaleeba: AIDS in the Family*, Women and AIDS Support Network, Harare.

Kippax, S., Crawford, J., Walby, C. and Benton, P. (1990) 'Women negotiating heterosex: implications for AIDS prevention', *Women's Studies International Forum*, 13 (6), 533–42.

Larson, A. (1990) 'The social epidemiology of Africa's AIDS epidemic', *African Affairs*, 89 (354), 5–26.

Levett, A. (1988) 'Psychological trauma: discourses of childhood sexual abuse', unpublished doctoral thesis, University of Cape Town, Cape Town.

Macdonell, D. (1986) *Theories of Discourse: An Introduction*, Basil Blackwell, London.

Miles, L. (1992) 'Women, AIDS, power and heterosexual negotiation: a discourse analysis', *Agenda*, 15, 14–27.

Parker, I. (1990) 'Real things: discourse, context and practice', *Philosophical Psychology*, 3 (2), 227–33.

Parker, I. (1992) *Discourse Dynamics: Critical Analysis for Social and Individual Psychology*, Routledge, London.

Patton, C. (1990) *Inventing AIDS*, Routledge, New York.

Plummer, K. (1988) 'Organising AIDS', in P. Aggleton and H. Homans (eds), *Social Aspects of AIDS*, Falmer Press, London, 20–51.

Potter, J. and Wetherell, M. (1987) *Discourse and Social Psychology: Beyond Attitudes and Behaviour*, Sage Publications, London.

Sabatier, R. (1988) *Blaming Others: Prejudice, Race and Worldwide AIDS*, Panos Publications, London.

Sadie, Y. and van Aardt, M. (1992) 'Vigs-politiek in Suid-Afrika: 1987–1992', *Politikon: The South African Journal of Political Studies*, 19 (3), 81–100.

Schoepf, B. (1993) 'AIDS action research with women in Kinshasha, Zaire', *Social Science and Medicine*, 37 (11), 1401–13.

Seidel, G. (1990) 'Thank God I said no to AIDS: on the changing discourse of AIDS in Uganda', *Discourse and Society*, 1 (1), 61–84.

Sontag, S. (1988) *AIDS and its Metaphors*, Penguin, London.

Standing, H. and Kisekka, M. (1989) *Sexual Behaviour in Sub-Saharan Africa – A Review and Annotated Bibliography*, Overseas Development Administration, London.

Strebel, A. (1993) 'Good intentions, contradictory outcomes? AIDS prevention and care for South African women', *CHASA Journal of Comprehensive Health*, 4 (1), 22–5.

Strebel, A. (1994) 'Women and AIDS: a study of issues in the prevention of HIV infection', unpublished doctoral thesis, University of Cape Town, Cape Town.

Strebel, A. (1995) 'Whose epidemic is it? Reviewing the literature on women and AIDS', *South African Journal of Psychology*, 25 (1), 12–20.

Treichler, P. (1987) 'AIDS, homophobia and biomedical discourse: an epidemic of signification', *Cultural Studies*, 1 (3), 263–303.

Valdiserri, R. (1989) *Preventing AIDS: The Design of Effective Programs*, Rutgers University Press, New Brunswick.

Watney, S. (1988) 'AIDS, "moral panic" theory and homophobia', in P. Aggleton and H. Homans (eds), *Social Aspects of AIDS*, Falmer Press, London, 52–64.

Watney, S. (1989) 'The subject of AIDS', in P. Aggleton, G. Hart and P. Davis (eds), *AIDS: Social Representations, Social Practices*, Falmer Press, London, 64–73.

Young, A. (1987) 'How medicine tamed life: a review article', *Culture, Medicine and Psychiatry*, 11, 107–21.

PART THREE

Methodological Innovations and Directions

CHAPTER 9

Pieces of mind: traumatic effects of child sexual abuse among black South African women

Ann Levett and Amanda Kottler with
Nomfundo Walaza, Pindile Mabena, Natalie Leon
and Nomsa Ngqakayi-Motaung

Between 1981 and 1990 little of what psychologists term 'cross-cultural' research was published on child abuse; this came mainly from social anthropology (e.g. Korbin, 1981, 1987; Scheper-Hughes, 1987). There has been less on sexual abuse and the exploitation of children (Ennew, 1986; Mennen, 1995); no examination of such phenomena has been reported with the clear aim of clarifying differences in the way different discourses dominate in different communities. Notions of childhood, abuse and psychic trauma in different socio-cultural contexts are likely to differ (Ennew, 1986; Levett, 1988, 1994). Given the extent of interest in child sexual abuse in the last two decades, this puzzling gap might be understood as the overwhelming preoccupation of modernity social scientists who are interested in children, but only *particular* children – those who live in the northern hemisphere in more or less Westernized and mainly urbanized contexts (Burman, 1994).

The power of modernity discourses around child sexual abuse is evident in the unexamined assumption of universal similarities in constructions of abuse, trauma and psychological consequences of sexual abuse (e.g. Korbin, 1981, 1987, 1991). Implicit assumptions that take the view that positivist-based research is 'most scientific' and 'truthful' (because of claims to objective and quantifiable methods) are characteristic of empiricist psychological and psychiatric research (Bracken, 1993). An 'intellectualist' perspective grounded in such assumptions would take the view that, in different cultural contexts, any difference from modernity discourses can be understood as arising from ignorance or a lack of sophistication (Sperber, 1985). Although this form of relativist explanation of differences, and search for similarities, is generally based in genuine concern for, and humanist ideas about, providing expertise and education to 'the Other', it is deeply ethnocentric and constitutes a kind of colonialist imperialism not uncommon in social and psychological research.

Straightforward empiricism is likely to operate on the basis of universalist metropolitan assumptions – for instance, that it is possible to achieve equivalence of meaning in the translation of a questionnaire or checklist from English into an African language, or in translating an interview with an African language speaker into English. Such research is carried out in order to establish the extent and variation of attributed social or emotional phenomena that are actually based in modernity psychological constructs such as depression, abuse or trauma (Drennan and Levett, 1996).

Because of an implicit belief that human emotions are fundamentally biological, many psychologists have not yet recognized that what we term emotional experience and how we talk about it evolves through our development and positioning in particular social symbolic systems. In communities with a colonial history, where there has been a struggle to resist the dominance of alien groups, variously identified – and where part of the resistance is a pride in local languages and categories of identity, and hence in various traditions – complexities of experience are not readily tapped through direct questioning or interviews translated from English or other European languages associated with modernity systems of knowledge. Emotions may be differently constituted. For example, see recent critiques of attempts to translate questionnaire research into a black African language (Kortmann, 1987, 1990) and discussion of the subtle problems of interpretation in South African multilingual contexts (Drennan et al., 1991), where apparently straightforward arrangements between researchers and interpreters are far from simple. The extensive anthropological discussions concerning universalist assumptions (that similar-appearing social phenomena or human behaviour across different cultural contexts are experienced in the same way and will have similar causes and consequences) are relevant here (Sperber, 1985).

Hegemonic globalized discourses of child sexual abuse

There is a widespread set of ideas that have been produced and reproduced in the intellectual academic arena, and in professionalized health care and social work practices, which has come to constitute a regime of truth in middle-class discourses around child sexual abuse. This claims that any child who has any experience of what is termed sexual abuse will be psychologically affected, probably seriously, either at the time of abuse or (in the sense of latent damaging consequences, where some later incident or situation precipitates psychological disturbance because of its associated links with the early event) at some future time. On the one hand there is the problem of the wide range of phenomena that have been collapsed into the single category, child sexual abuse (Friedman, 1990); this category can vary on a continuum between violent rape, to a single or repeated experience of unfamiliar genital touching, or even 'dirty talk' by an adult to a child or young adolescent. On the other hand is the enormous list of 'traumatic effects' that have come to be understood as being related, in a simple cause-effect manner, to remembered (or suspected) experience of sexual abuse in childhood (Haugaard and Emery, 1989). These traumatic effects cover most forms of psychological disruption or distress, as widely covered in the literature (Browne and Finkelhor, 1986; Kendall-Tackett et al., 1993). These two over-inclusive and over-simplified metropolitan discourses (sexual abuse and trauma) have become part of conventional middle-class wisdom. They are used in various ways by clinicians, researchers, lobbyers, women in psychotherapy, media reports and features, and amongst the literate general public, as organizing anchors in a range of contexts, variously to justify measures, to explain problems, etc.

Little or no account is taken of the conceptual, definitional and even methodological problems involved in such claims and of accumulating evidence that there is no necessary, direct or simple connection between childhood experience that might be termed sexual abuse and problems of living (Levett, 1988; Wakefield and Underwager, 1988; Sullivan, 1992). Even more significant in a country such as South Africa, no account is taken of issues related to the local socio-cultural and class context, and the constitution of subjectivity in this context. We need to understand that it is a form of appropriation or neocolonization to 'name' a girl raised in this context as 'sexually abused' and 'damaged', and to hold that a set of traumatic consequences is to be expected, as has been claimed for the metropolitan youth of North America, the UK and elsewhere. Although potentially stigmatic, not all such experience is necessarily disruptive, even in modernity contexts. Furthermore, these discourses on the dangers of sexual abuse and damage have become significant factors in controlling the lives of children and women.

In contemporary 'Western' or metropolitan discourses concerning child-hood sexual abuse it emerges that the way one is identified as traumatized (and identifies oneself as such) results in some women being regarded and treated differently from others – it is a stigmatic process (Levett, 1995). Such women are liable to produce a sense of subjectivity as different, even though all women in South Africa – rural or urban – grow up with a pervasive sense of their potential to be sexually abused or assaulted (Levett, 1988). This in itself contributes to the construction of subjectivities, marked by gender-related vulnerabilities, which are different from men. Women learn in childhood and adolescence to avoid certain situations, self-presentation and types of men, entering and constituted within practices of self-surveillance that operate as controls restricting our choices and options as agents in the world. Women who have some degree of feminist consciousness have come to understand these aspects of their lives as manifestations of patriarchy since feminist writers of the 1970s and 1980s have exposed the links (e.g., Brownmiller, 1976; Russell, 1975, 1984). However, there is little exposure to feminist critiques of patriarchy amongst working-class and black communities in South Africa (Levett and Kottler, in press).

As has been argued elsewhere (Levett, 1988) both expectations of experiences of sexual abuse (based on current prevalence estimates) and actual experiences categorized in this way, and the search for 'traumatic effects', contribute in significant ways to the development of gendered subjectivity in modernity girls and women. These become part of self-identification as female, as damaged or potentially damaged (lesbian identity is often 'explained by' early experience of abuse). Paradoxically, certain forms of behaviour are produced and reproduced in relation to protective males and also in reaction against male control, as feminine or in need of protection.

We have no documentation of ethnographic-type studies of what the category we term 'sexual abuse' might mean to girls and women in differently developed and maintained socio-cultural communities (Levett, 1994). What are the other available discourses around childhood, sexuality and gender development? What are the concerns and feelings of a child or young woman when such events occur? And of her community and family, about her? Are categories of psychological damage (or pollution?) different in various respects? Having mapped out such differences, we would need to ask the question whether metropolitan discourses of abuse and psychological trauma would be more useful to the child, the family, and the community, in such circumstances.

For the socially concerned researcher, motivated by the wish to improve the position of all sexually exploited children and women, there is a tension between this political aim and the recognition of problems in applying naive empiricism to populations whose social and cultural matrices are different from modernity ones, embedded in languages and practices distinctive in many ways from those of Anglo-European and North American backgrounds where the hegemonic conventional wisdom of globalized middle-class and intellectual culture originated. Are there ways in which discourse analysis can be useful in tagging and highlighting the invisible shackles of our assumptions around child sexual abuse without doing an injustice to the political goals of activists working on behalf of women and children? Although there are no clear answers to these questions, the beginnings of some answers are attempted here, in a brief discussion of recent research among black South African urban women with minimal exposure to modernity education.

South African middle-class modernity discourses around child sexual abuse

In 1986–88 a discourse analytic study of texts on child sexual abuse was carried out. They were collected from undergraduate university students, thus termed middle-class (Levett, 1988). These texts were produced by English-speaking, South African women (white and coloured) who placed themselves and sexually abused children in various positions related to dominant discourses of psychological trauma; the dominant discourses largely reflected contemporary professional literature on child sexual abuse, i.e. conventional hegemonic wisdom.

The 1986 study evolved because of contradictory narratives that emerged in therapeutic work with middle-class women, many of whom reported they had been (or believed they had been) sexually abused as children. Many women describe a wide range of diverse painful experience in their childhood and current lives but seem to believe the sexual abuse experience to be the root of their problems. Through exposure to professional and media accounts, women fix on widely ranging incidents of sexual abuse (from molestation to incest) to 'explain' current difficulties. Many expect that through 'breaking the silence' and simply narrating accounts of this experience (sometimes clarifying confusion), current difficulties will rapidly improve or disappear. It was decided to explore middle-class women's discourse about trauma and child sexual abuse.

The texts about child sexual abuse were produced as described elsewhere (Levett, 1989). In brief, three vignettes based on commonplace accounts of molestation were presented to small groups asked to discuss the stories and to give their opinions about ways in which the girl depicted might (or might not) be affected at the time of the abuse and in later years. Discussions were tape-recorded and transcribed. Analysis of discourses was carried out drawing loosely on the method described by Hollway (1984).

Originating in North American feminist discussions of sexual violence, the discourses of professionals (psychologists, sociologists, social workers, child care workers) who publish material about child sexual abuse and its damaging consequences have spread through the popular media, newspapers and through contexts of formal education, which are accessible to middle-class women. These both underwrite their fears and, in some, contribute to a more militant feminism. Paradoxically, middle-class women learn that brothers, fathers and other authority figures, who feel obliged to protect and supervise girls and women, patrol them in relation to 'the Other' – and insist that they patrol themselves through self-surveillance – the boundaries of class and race. In South Africa, for middle-class women (white and coloured), fear of sexual abuse and assault is most commonly governed by fear of unfamiliar, often explicitly black, men (e.g. labourers or gardeners) (Levett, 1988).

The 1986 study demonstrated that women students largely reproduced dominant discourses about the traumatic effects of child sexual abuse found in the professional clinical and academic literature. There was fuzziness obscuring differences between molestation within the family and violent rape perpetrated by a stranger, and a general belief that any such experience would be psychologically 'damaging' for the child, at the time and also in later years. The discourses of trauma dominated the text; these included developmental disruptions (production of deviant behaviours such as precocious sexualized behaviour, 'promiscuity' and lesbianism, fear of men and difficulties with intimate relationships, sleep disturbances, eating disorders, depression, anxiety, scholastic problems, etc.). Thus institutional rhetoric and practice pervades middle-class wisdom (at least among psychology students), performing particular roles in the continuing colonization and subordination of middle-class girls and women.

At the same time, there was scattered evidence of anomalous discourses among the middle-class women, indicating what in Foucauldian terms is viewed as resistance: the understroke of power. In Foucault, power and surveillance are always associated with resistance. The dominating power of authority figures (professional and patriarchal) and hegemonic discourse is given authenticity and reproductive power through counter-discourse. Thus some middle-class women (including ourselves) do have access to alternative ways of viewing experience of child sexual abuse, and there are possible alternative reactions that are empowering in situations of child sexual abuse and in antagonistic relation to seeing oneself simply as a victim and powerless without the protection of men. Many middle-class women recognized clearly the paradox of needing male protection when it is frequently familiar male figures who are involved in sexual abuse and assault, and some spoke of using humour or karate as a way to retaliate.

Notes on a study of South African black women's discourses around child sexual abuse

Using brief vignettes concerning common situations of child sexual abuse as a focusing device, taped interviews with minimally educated African language-speaking, South African women were arranged to elicit 'local knowledge' about child sexual abuse and ideas about 'effects'. The aim was twofold: (i) to establish whether dominant discourses found in metropolitan modernity contexts had filtered into the day-to-day consciousness of these women; and (ii) to explore the kinds of problems that can be expected to arise in using translated material for discourse analysis (a postmodern enterprise that does not search for 'truth' but for variation in social phenomena).

The loosely structured interviews, in Xhosa, Zulu, Sotho and Afrikaans, were conducted in 1991 by fluent same-language speakers, all postgraduate psychology students. The participants were black women aged between eighteen and forty who identified themselves as Sotho, Zulu, Xhosa or Afrikaans language speakers, with up to six years of formal schooling. Two participants were interviewed at a time by one researcher, to facilitate the possibility of enhancing the range of the discussion. These tapes were translated into English by the original interviewers in a further, second-level interview situation with the second author (AK), where the process of interpretation was examined and various problems were documented.

The researchers met several times to discuss the background to the current study and to consult around the scenarios to present in the (translated) vignettes, the interview process, the purposes of the research and the matter of translation. It was agreed that interviewees would be paid for their participation and transport costs in order to reduce possible feelings of exploitation by their privileged, educated peers and the university. It was understood that this might result in bias to please the interviewers from the university – a hangover from positivist research conventions. However, this was felt to be potentially beneficial rather than biasing since the study aimed for richness and diversity, exploring the limits of discourse rather than a narrowly conceived focus.

Various methodological problems related to the study began to emerge at an early stage. Early on it was pointed out that regarding answers about 'home language' as definitive in black African township life would be misleading if there was any intention to compare the different groups. One researcher, who described herself as Zulu, said that both Zulu and Sotho (her language at school) were spoken in her home in Soweto, where she grew up; she thought that her upbringing was not especially linked with Zulu practices but that this might vary from one family to another and from one situation to another. This is common in Soweto, where many African languages are spoken. It was made clear that we would be tapping the discourses of urbanized black women, as expressed in their home languages.

Although almost every black South African will identify with a particular 'culture' with its own language (Zulu, Xhosa, Venda, etc.) the project was never planned as a comparison of discourses between different language groups. It was agreed that there would be more commonality than difference among little-educated women living in township conditions, particularly since many are second- and third-generation urban dwellers. It was also suggested that middle-class, educated South Africans (black and white) might hold largely similar sets of ideas but doubt was expressed about this; for instance, sexual behaviours and attitudes with regard to children might be different.

Following discussion, although this could be seen to compromise the (positivist empiricist) idea of comparison between middle-class and black underclass discourses, it was decided to make one vignette depict rape of

a child by a stranger, rather than the accounts of molestation that characterized the middle-class study. The black African researchers felt that no
useful discussion would come from talk about a child who had 'only been
molested'; the idea of molestation would be confusing and would be
received with puzzlement by participating black African women. This was
borne out in the texts collected and, in itself, is an interesting finding,
marking the discourse as different from that of middle-class women. In
the latter, the vignettes explicitly concerned molestation (repeated by a
familial figure or once-off situations involving a stranger); the whole range
of professional discourses of psychological trauma were produced in
relation to occasional and single-event hand/genital molestation.

All the interviewing researchers had been educated at the University of
Cape Town and were fluent in English. The black African researchers
were worried about finding women interviewees who would be prepared
to talk about sexual abuse at all – even in relation to vignettes. Taboos
about talk concerning sex and sexuality are governed by customs that
control limited contexts in which such talk is permitted. The coloured
Afrikaans-speaking researcher did not feel that this would prove a problem
in her community. The strength of taboos on sexual (and other areas of)
talk was difficult for some of us to comprehend. In acknowledging that
this might be a problem, it was felt that the monetary compensation for
the time involved might improve the chances of obtaining interviews,
given the conditions of high unemployment, poverty and need. In the
texts collected taboos were not evident in glaring ways but rather in the
widespread tendency to use terms such as 'these things', 'this thing he
did', 'this problem', 'that thing' for events depicted explicitly in the
vignettes; this was also true in many Afrikaans texts. Of course, in English
too there is a lack of language to denote many sexual behaviours except
through detailed descriptions.

Discourse analysis: issues

All the researchers had difficulty in disengaging from conventional psychological methods, e.g. a pressure to collect a large body of taped interviews.
We had to keep reminding ourselves that we were looking not for some
notion of a representative sample, but rather for rich material.

An aspect difficult to modify was the way in which the study was
actually framed in terms of modernity discourses: we depicted certain
narratives as examples of child sexual abuse in the vignettes. We asked
open-ended questions that arose out of our own internalized discourses
of abuse and signs and symptoms of trauma (for example, how would
the mother know that this had happened to the child? Would the teacher
know? How would her friends know?). In actuality, interviewees seemed
initially to understand these questions to concern *talk about* such experience

– for instance, in what circumstances would the child find it possible to tell about her experience. Responses ranged between the kind of mother she had (a 'good mother' would be told), the family's material problems, the child's age and understanding of sex (or moral values).

> If it's a child who doesn't know anything she will be able to talk but if it's a child who *knows something* she will keep quiet.

In general, there was not much similarity in these texts when compared with dominant middle-class discourses on trauma. Problems emerged concerning translation, especially of concepts of emotion and their exact meaning where they were introduced. Neither the meaning of 'ill' nor that of 'emotionally' could be more specifically translated.

> The child will be *quite ill*. Even *emotionally/spiritually* [*moeng* – Sotho] she will feel quite different.

Most common was an idea of embarrassment:

> It will be difficult for the child to talk to the friends about this. *This thing* is quite *embarrassing*. All that needs to happen is that she must just tell the mother and as a mother I will be able to handle it and see that she gets better. If a child discusses *this thing* with friends it becomes an issue for everyone to talk about.

> The child will feel *embarrassed* [*dihlong* – Sotho] she will be puzzled.

It is unclear what the subjective state is in the terms used. Is this shame or humiliation, and is the feeling related to 'not knowing' what was happening and what was expected of her, or to a sense of devaluation? In doing a more detailed interpretation one would need to return to the participant who expressed this idea in order to clarify what she intended to convey. (This of course is the sort of problem one is as likely to encounter in interviewing English-speaking participants as in translated material – it is often assumed that we know what a same-language speaker intends to communicate when we do not necessarily know at all.)

The difficulties in organizing around unfamiliar discourses in a study with a generalized bias of looking for modernity discourses of trauma were potent inhibitors in the later stages of the research. If the researcher does not have a clear picture of prevailing power structures within which meaning is constructed, ironically one resorts to something like a frequency estimate in order to systematize dominant discourse. This makes analysis tentative. As work on this material continues, the analyses and interpretations will be discussed repeatedly with the black research assistants (who, it must be noted, have had less exposure to the critiques that inform deconstructionist studies than the authors, but whose understanding of the language and local conditions will be better).

In relation to the rape vignette there was much talk about *physical pain and injury*. This was the main emphasis of the effects discourse – others would know what had happened because of a (temporary, injury-related) change in the way the child would walk. The dominant discourses that emerged in regard to the rape vignette concerned how best to deal with the physical injuries. 'Take her to the doctor/clinic/hospital' was a widespread view; there was no mention of traditional healers (perhaps because the interviewers came from a university) although it has been claimed that 80 per cent of black South Africans prefer traditional healers (*Argus*, 22 January 1996). There was very little about how the child might feel – 'frightened' or 'sore' were fairly common responses.

There was a significant discourse concerning the age of the child; for example, if the child was young (around five) she would quickly forget an experience of rape.

> [After a few months] it will be different. You see, each and everything does come to an end. The child will get over the experience … the child will forget about it … but if she experiences *other difficulties* then she won't forget.

It is unclear whether 'other difficulties' means similar experiences or a range of problems, such as sexually transmitted disease or pregnancy.

> If we as a family are able to encourage and console her she will get over it. Parents are supposed to tell her 'you know, this is just something that happened to you, it's a mistake, but you know it's not what life is all about'.

Once the physical injuries heal, there would be no memory and there was no discussion around emotional consequences other than a possible (transient) fear of men. Temporarily she might feel different (it was usually unclear what this denotes) and she might be withdrawn. However, if the child is an adolescent, the ideas of consequences were different:

> Well at fourteen or fifteen they know everything, they are older … and they know the difference between good and bad. So what happens, even if she was raped, you will find her *very much alive* [not like the other one]. You won't even see that this thing has happened. They even end up being in love with the rapist … She won't forget.

An occasional theme of devaluation, as in the following extract, suggests stigmatic effects:

> What will this child do with her life that lies ahead when/if he … breaks her virginity or makes her something that no one else will ever look at?

One participant introduced a different aspect of 'knowing'. This concerned what we might term a 'loss of innocence'. She said:

In her [spirit] she will still have that thing. Even if a person talks nicely to her she will still be torn in two that there are some people who are good and some who are bad. So that thing destroys her [?optimistic attitude to] life because in life you should only know one thing – but this is the way things are.

When molestation was discussed most participants spoke of the varying circumstances in which the child would tell someone (the mother, the teacher, a friend) what had happened. Dominant discourses around molestation related to the age of the child and 'knowing', i.e. whether or not she would 'know' what 'this thing' was about.

Concerning the vignette depicting incestuous molestation:

If it was a stranger then you will think it was *just the devil going past, you won't take it seriously*. But this thing happened within the house, within the family ... she will hate this uncle and his family and *when she is getting more mature mentally* she will even hate her mother.

And concerning what can be done to help the child:

She needs lots of love. The family must give her love – especially if it is something from the family it must not be known. *Give her love and not say anything* to other people.

You need to guide the child ... that *in life there are difficult things such as these things*; there are good and bad things.

At the end of the interview participants were asked to say why they thought some men might initiate sexual interactions with children. The following were typical responses:

A person who does these things is just very naughty. He made himself used to this evil thing ... *in fact I don't know why these people do this – there are so many women around.*

I think what is wrong is that *the devil has got into them*. You know, when the devil has got into you he makes you do anything.

Conclusion

As remarked, numerous complications are to be found at different levels of abstraction in the methodology and the practical aspects of inter-pretation when a modernity-inspired study is carried out to explore psycho-logical issues in a different socio-cultural context.

We have discussed the problems of assumption of a common core of meaning and experience in the term 'abuse' in distinctive language and cultural groups, or in the idea that dominant metropolitan ideas about psychological trauma will exist and will be found to have a parallel among people who have minimal modernity education, little access to professional health care, and little exposure to the media because of poverty and social circumstances. Furthermore, as we can see, the notion that practices of translation and back-translation will eliminate the opacities of language and the bias of metropolitan discourse, or that equivalence can be achieved through the employment of educated other-language-speakers in a simple and straightforward way is dubious, to say the least, as is the idea of unbiased and a-subjective researchers and informants.

Some of the problems likely to arise in an oversimplified approach to document 'traumatic effects of child sexual abuse' in translated and interpreted texts are clearly illustrated where a discourse analytic study of local knowledge is attempted. What we can learn from this is that careful research exploring depths of social life and human experience must pay attention to all such issues. We need ways to disrupt or elasticize our conceptual grids.

Systematic research, a fundamentally modernity-based intellectual exercise, has ramifications for shaping policy; it also has implications for the perpetuation of existing power structures. Honest and open self-interrogation must highlight the biases and assumptions (the master discourses) we take with us, as intellectuals, into our fields of study. We do not believe that such research should not be done because of these problems, however. Answers to oppression and exploitation are not to be found through oversimplified neocolonialist research or by passive withdrawal, but rather through active and energetic critical engagement with such material as is available. Frank discussion of both similarities and differences between communities of people is needed in order to achieve a sounder basis for the evaluation and redistribution of valuable resources.

While criticizing the master discourses used in research in postcolonial societies as the tools of contemporary intellectual life – including deconstruction, and discourse analysis is one offshoot from this – Gayatri Spivak comments favourably on the work of Derrida. She remarks how he is always willing to examine how exactly, as an intellectual, he responds to requests to behave as an intellectual – i.e., we must examine our positions, our definitions and methods as though they are foreign bodies. 'He [Derrida] will not allow us to forget the fact that the production of theory is in fact a very important practice that is worlding the world in a certain way' (Spivak, 1990: 7).

Black working-class women, although located in South African cities, are not colonized or constituted as subjects in the same ways as the metropolitan elite. Gendered subjectivity in this position is produced and maintained in somewhat different terms in relation to power and knowledge. We do not know much about exactly how gender and other authority systems are produced and reproduced, even within modernity contexts. If the gaps in our understanding are ignored by researchers, filling them up with our assumptions will distort our understanding of the day-to-day experience and needs of women who, after all, constitute the greater majority in South Africa today. It is important to map out the details of social life through identifying and examining 'pieces of minds' and our practices. Comparing these with hegemonic ideas and social practices that dominate in our middle-class and intellectual communities will provide a diverse but better overview of the rich patchworks of social life, and suggest new avenues for less exploitative practices.

Note

Acknowledgements and thanks are due to the Centre for Scientific Development (CSD) for funding for this research. The views expressed are those of the authors and are not to be attributed to the CSD.

References

Argus, 22 January 1996.

Bracken, P. J. (1993) 'Post-empiricism and psychiatry: meaning and methodology in cross-cultural research', *Social Science and Medicine*, 36 (3), 265–72.

Browne, A. and Finkelhor, D. (1986) 'Impact of child sexual abuse: a review of the research', *Psychological Bulletin*, 99, 66–77.

Brownmiller, S. (1976) *Against our Will*, Penguin, Harmondsworth.

Burman, E. (1994) *Deconstructing Developmental Psychology*, Routledge, London.

Drennan, G. and Levett, A. (1996) 'Translation in psychological research: theoretical and conceptual aspects', unpublished paper, University of Cape Town.

Drennan, G., Levett, A. and Swartz, L. (1991) 'Hidden dimensions of power and resistance in the translation process: a South African study', *Culture, Medicine and Psychiatry*, 15, 361–81.

Ennew, J. (1986) *The Sexual Exploitation of Children*, Polity Press, Cambridge

Friedman, S. R. (1990) 'What is child sexual abuse?', *Journal of Clinical Psychology*, 46 (3), 372–5.

Haugaard, J. J. and Emery, R. E. (1989) 'Methodological issues in child sexual abuse research', *Child Abuse and Neglect*, 13, 89–100.

Hollway, W. (1984) 'Gender difference and the production of subjectivity', in J. Henriques, W. Hollway, C. Urwin, C. Venn and V. Walkerdine (1984), *Changing the Subject: Psychology, Social Regulation and Subjectivity*, Methuen, London, 227–63.

Kendall-Tackett, K. A., Williams, L. M. and Finkelhor, D. (1993) 'Impact of sexual abuse on children: a review and synthesis of recent empirical studies', *Psychological Bulletin*, 113 (1), 164–80.

Korbin, J. E. (ed) (1981) *Child Abuse and Neglect: Cross Cultural Perspectives*, University of California Press, Berkeley, CA.

Korbin, J. E. (1987) 'Child sexual abuse: implications from the cross cultural record', in Scheper Hughes (ed.), *Child Survival*, D. Reidel, Dordrecht.

Korbin, J. E. (1991) 'Cross-cultural perspectives and research directions for the 21st century', *Child Abuse and Neglect*, 15 (Sup. 1), 67–77.

Kortmann, F. (1987) 'Problems in communication in transcultural psychiatry', *Acta Psychiatrica Scandinavica*, 75, 563–70.

Kortmann, F. (1990) 'Psychiatric case finding in Ethiopia: shortcomings of the self-reporting questionnaire', *Culture, Medicine and Psychiatry*, 14, 381–92.

Levett, A. (1988) 'Psychological trauma: discourses on childhood sexual abuse', unpublished doctoral dissertation, University of Cape Town.

Levett, A. (1989) 'A study of childhood sexual abuse among South African university women students', *South African Journal of Psychology*, 19 (3), 122–9.

Levett, A. (1994) 'Problems of cultural imperialism in the study of childhood sexual abuse', in A. Dawes and D. Donald (eds), *Childhood and Adversity: Psychological perspectives from South African Research*, David Philip, Cape Town.

Levett, A. (1995) 'Stigmatic factors in sexual abuse and the violence of representation', *Psychology in Society*, 20, 4–12.

Levett, A. and Kottler, A. (in press) '"She's not a feminist!": through a lens, darkly', in Burman, E. (ed.) *Deconstructing Feminist Psychology*, Sage, London.

Mennen, F. E. (1995) 'The relationship of race/ethnicity to symptoms in childhood sexual abuse', *Child Abuse and Neglect*, 19 (1), 115–24.

Russell, D. E. H. (1975) *The Politics of Rape: The Victim's Perspective*, New York, Stein & Day.

Russell, D. E. H. (1984) *Sexual Exploitation*, Sage, Beverly Hills, CA.

Scheper Hughes, N. (1987) (ed.) *Child Survival*, D. Reidel, Dordrecht.

Sperber, D. (1985) 'Apparently irrational beliefs', in *On Anthropological Knowledge*, Cambridge University Press, Cambridge.

Spivak, G. C. (1990) 'Criticism, feminism and the institution – with Elizabeth Grosz', in S. Harasym (ed.) *The Post-Colonial Critic: Interviews, Strategies, Dialogues*, Routledge, London.

Sullivan, T. (1992) *Sexual Abuse and the Rights of Children: Reforming Canadian Law*, University of Toronto Press, Toronto.

Wakefield, H. and Underwager, R. C. (1988) *Accusations of Child Sexual Abuse*, Charles C. Thomas, Springfield, IL.

CHAPTER 10

'The knowledge that one seeks to disinter': psychiatry and the discourse of discourse analysis

Martin Terre Blanche

In this chapter I critique two very different disciplines, institutional psychiatry and discourse analysis, which work to define the space between university-trained professionals and other South Africans. In each case I base my critique on an incipient scandal – recidivism in psychiatry and reification in discourse analysis – which seems perpetually about to engulf those who sustain and are sustained by these disciplines. I first review the function of the scandals as necessary for the continuation of the disciplines, then demonstrate their operation in the analysis of a particular text and finally comment on possible future directions for critical work in South African psychiatry and discourse analysis.

Psychiatry and the recidivism scandal

An article in the Johannesburg *Star*, by health writer David Robbins (1994) features the work of South African psychiatric reformer professor Carllo Gagiano. (Another version of these events, as presented for scientific consumption, can be found in Fourie and Gagiano, 1987.) Gagiano has been credited with reducing the in-patient census at the Oranje hospital in Bloemfontein by more than a thousand per cent in ten years – from 1,250 in 1984 to 108 in 1994. When he first arrived at the hospital, as chief of psychiatry, he found patients crowding at the bars, pleading to be released; his response was to order the bars cut away. This is how Robbins has him describe what happened:

> As the hacksaws were busy at the main entrance to one of the wards the patients began to scream and rave inside. I told the warden to unlock the outer door. He demurred. I told him that I would take the consequences. When the door was flung open, most patients in the ward surged out and disappeared. The staff wanted to give chase. I said let them go (Robbins, 1994: 11).

'Amazingly,' Robbins continues the story, 'Gagiano's gamble paid off. Within 30 minutes all the patients had returned' (ibid.).

Without detracting from the immediacy of this account it is easy to recognize in it a re-enactment of countless similar dramas, performed over the past two hundred years, in which the mad are set free so that they may present themselves voluntarily for readmission. Such tales of madness rendered tractable through the paradox of liberation have spread across the world together with the more overt institutional practices of Western psychiatry. Histories of psychiatry the world over are filled with similar stories of great men who sweep aside institutional barriers to accord the insane their true measure of freedom: Pinel in France, Langermann in Germany, Pisani in Italy, Guislain in Belgium, Sabler in Russia, Viszánik in Vienna, Conolly in England, Cotton in the United States, Hyed in Thailand, Gagiano in South Africa. (Perhaps the best known South African example before Gagiano is that of doctor James Barry, who was the first to expose the inhumane conditions in which lunatics were kept at the Old Somerset Hospital in the Cape and who was herself later the subject of scandal when it was discovered after her death that she was a woman.)

Psychiatry's liberation narrative has two forms. The first, as exemplified in the Pinel and Gagiano stories, celebrates the liberation of the insane while binding them ever more tightly into moral and psychological dependency; the second, as exemplified in the voluminous literature on psychiatric recidivism, relapse, rehospitalization, readmission or the 'revolving door' problem (e.g., Daniel and Freeman, 1983; Kastrup, 1987; Rosenblatt and Mayer, 1974), turns on this dependency as a sign of the essential hopelessness of mental illness.

In the United States and much of the Western world the heroic form of the narrative was in the ascendant from the early 1800s until the 1850s, when a cult of curability reigned, and again in the 1960s and 1970s, when large numbers of psychiatric patients were deinstitutionalized. The second, despondent, form became hegemonic in the second half of the nineteenth century, and again in the decades since the 1970s. Both forms function to reinscribe psychiatry and mental illness as existing in the space between freedom and incarceration.

These oscillations also occurred in South Africa, although often delayed and in unequal measure for different race groups. As in Europe and America, a large-scale 'liberation' of the insane occurred from the second half of the 1960s, with in-patient admissions declining by 27 per cent, while out-patient visits went up by 834 per cent between 1964 and 1976 (Visser et al., 1989). However, at the Oranje Hospital and similar facilities catering mainly for black patients a similar heroic transformation in the pattern of psychiatric dependency has either been achieved only since 1985, or has not occurred at all.

As in Europe and America, there has locally also been a despondent inflection to this tale. When the South African Medical Research Council

(MRC) established its Clinical Psychiatry Research Unit in 1980, de-institutionalization's initial successes were already being transcribed into the minor key. Gillis, who was appointed as first head of the unit, summarized the unit's research agenda as follows: 'The areas which were selected as being of greatest concern were mental illness in the aged, the high readmission rate to South African psychiatric hospitals (approaching 50% overall and rising), and substance abuse' (1987: 797). The importance of the readmission question was later endorsed in an official statement by the Society of Psychiatrists of South Africa (Ben-Arie and Nash, 1986). Gillis and his colleagues (Gillis et al., 1986; Gillis, 1987; Gillis et al., 1987; Sandler and Jakoet, 1985) have since conducted extensive research to try to account for the high readmission rate, while others have investigated the nature and extent of the burden placed on the families of deinstitutionalized psychiatric patients (Hamber, 1992, 1994, 1995; Landman, 1994; Ngcobo, 1995) and the dangers of over-enthusiastic deinstitutionalization (Freeman et al., 1994; Hamber and Rock, 1993).

Although South African psychiatry can obviously not be understood purely in terms of globally replicated narratives around liberation and incarceration (for instance, racial inequities in resource provision, reviewed in Dommisse, 1987, and overt and covert racist ideologies, reviewed in Swartz, 1989, play a much larger role in this country than elsewhere), such narratives clearly do shape the actions and understandings of those involved in the South African psychiatric system and a more detailed analysis of how these discourses are played out in the South African context would appear to be useful.

Discourse analysis and the reification scandal

Extensive guidelines on how to proceed with the kind of analysis of South African psychiatry I have started here can be found in the academic literature on discourse analysis. However, like psychiatry, discourse analysis is itself held together by a set of frequently repeated but inadequately explicated narratives, some of which I shall attempt to outline below.

Arguably the central 'scandal' constituting the discipline of discourse analysis is that of 'reification' (i.e. treating an idea as an object). According to Parker (1992: 5) a discourse is 'a system of statements which constructs an object', a formulation that leaves discourse analysis open to definition as being itself a system of statements that constructs the object of discourses. This is the reification scandal.

Discourse analysts not infrequently point out how other analysts are guilty of reifying the process of analysis (e.g. Potter et al., 1990; Parker, 1990; Burman, 1991) and it has become almost a canon of discourse analytic writing to declare pre-emptively that one does not intend one's particular brand of analysis to be mistaken for a mere methodology that can be applied unthinkingly to whatever discursive emergency comes to hand. As an alternate defence, discourse analytic theorists may flit rapidly from one formulation to the next in the hope that the fly-swatter of reification will always land on a discursive methodology that has already been vacated.

Even Foucault (1980: 86), so adept at fabricating a certain kind of inscrutable coherence, seems fearful that he may fall prey to reification:

> And after all, is it not perhaps the case that these fragments of genealogies are no sooner brought to light, that the particular elements of the knowledge that one seeks to disinter are no sooner accredited and put into circulation, than they run the risk of re-codification, re-colonisation?

Of all these strategies for ensuring that the reification scandal never quite breaks, or ever quite goes away, that of styling discourse analysis as a form of 'qualitative research' is perhaps the most common. Presenting results in quantitative form would imply that social facts can be definitively identified and enumerated, and when discourse analysts do venture into quantitative domains they therefore appear to do so almost apologetically, tacking on a couple of frequency tabulations as an afterthought (e.g. Van Dijk, 1987; Wetherell and Potter, 1992; Levett, 1988). However, it can be argued that by appealing to the quantitative–qualitative dichotomy, and by aligning itself with the subjugated term, discourse analysis simply rein-scribes a scientific master-narrative that assumes the existence of objective, quantitative knowledge, while carefully preserving a space for subjective, qualitative exploration that may precede serious quantitative enquiry.

To disrupt this positioning of discourse analysis as an exploratory qualitative technique, I therefore propose a form of discourse analysis that relies heavily on quantification – not to summarize or confirm qualita-tively derived themes, categories or discourses, but to provide an initial overview before the serious work of qualitative enquiry commences. This is demonstrated below.

'Apparently a known schizophrenic': a case study in psychiatric discourse

Among the many mechanisms used to prop up the apartheid state there was until the early 1990s a system of conscription for those classified white and male. In my case I elected to do community rather than military service and was assigned to a mental hospital as a clerk. Having an academic background, I also assisted psychiatrists with research work and in this way gained access to a collection of case records entered on a computer data base over a five-year period. I use these records here to explore simultaneously the recidivism and reification scandals as they are reproduced in South African psychiatry and discourse analysis. I focus in particular on an open-ended section of each record headed '*evaluation/ initial history: leading up to this admission*', which contains a brief description of the presenting complaint, similar to the following (all case material in this chapter has been changed to ensure anonymity):

> 29 year old unmarried female, no children, staying with parents in X, presenting in a psychotic state with tactile hallucinations, sexual delusions and delusions of misinterpretation, delusions of influence, that started 1 m ago and got progressively worse over last week. Delusions are directed towards father. Father is transmitting his 'lust' to her. Hypomanic features. Marked conduct disorder with substance abuse as child. 4 previous admissions. Defaulted meds.

While the ostensible purpose of a vignette such as this is informational, it is also, in Anspach's (1988: 357) words, 'an arena in which claims to knowledge are made and epistemological assumptions are displayed, a linguistic ritual in which physicians learn and enact fundamental beliefs and values of the medical world'. For example, at least five epistemological strands, explanatory schemas, discourses, can be reconstructed from the little vignette quoted above:

1. *The old maid discourse.* Having violated the 'normal' developmental path for a woman (getting married and having children), the patient is now sexually frustrated and projects her frustration onto the nearest male figure.
2. *The rotten apple discourse.* Even as a child the patient was a delinquent who took drugs. Maybe she's fried her brains.
3. *The noncompliant patient discourse.* She stopped taking her medication. That's why she's gone off the rails again.
4. *The schizophrenia discourse.* She is deluded and has hallucinations. If I'm pressed for a diagnosis I'd say schizophrenia. But then on the other hand maybe it's mania.
5. *The recidivist discourse.* She's been here 4 times before. Are you surprised she's back?

While it is easy to imagine a similar qualitative analysis of ten or even a hundred such vignettes, it obviously becomes increasingly difficult to sustain as the numbers increase. Given that the data available to me, which I shall call the Initial History Text, consisted of 1,880 vignettes (66,041 words or 357 pages of double-spaced typescript), I thought that some form of quantitative analysis was called for.

Numerous quantitative indices have been applied to such texts. A simple frequency count of the words used in the Initial History Text (Figure 10.1), shows that, unsurprisingly, the most frequent words are *history* and *patient*. Somewhat more interesting is the prominence of *depression* and depression-related words (*suicidal, depressed, suicide, bipolar*), confirming earlier studies involving psychiatric patients in the same city (Strong, 1987; Terre

history
patient
depression
year admitted
2 old no years
admission
previous not
suicidal 3 abuse
known depressed
months alcohol
poor ago weeks
suicide family OD
behaviour paranoid

Figure 10.1 Words used in the Initial History Text

problems features
disorder treated Tara
well since
ward
hallucinations
ideation delusions
admissions
bipolar presented
psychotic past 4
week last
previously referred
aggressive prior sleep
appetite X one
vegitative 6 month
hospital manicpsych
treatment auditoryhome
Dr husband mood5
999 episode days
brought Sterkfontein
now query casualty
psychiatric became

Note: Font size is relative to word frequency.

substance episodes
diagnosed schizophrenic
following symptoms
personality energy
chronic over long recently
ECT social agitated attempts
decreased work insomnia
feeling loss started before
day wife stressors
few mother attempt 10anxiety
functioning multiple affective
took discharged major thought
lithium medical increased feelstwodue
transferred medication schizophreniafather
children severe meds anxiouslow
all seen sleeping overdose
psychosis stopped positive womanage
problem out time depressivefirst
job daughter financial boyfriend
concentration left thoughts downsonbizarre
male unable numerous female1990
withdrawal OPD apparently foundclinicvisual
cannabis 8 man eatingwherepost
felt drinking child 1988died

Figure 10.1 cont

Blanche, 1993), which showed that patients themselves most commonly invoke depression to account for their hospitalization. However, another finding from these studies, namely that patients also make extensive use of the discourse of social stress to explain their circumstances, at first glance appears absent from the text, with only *stressors* occurring with sufficient frequency to be included in the table.

Frequency counts such as that given in Figure 10.1 provide some indication of the lexical content of texts, but are obviously limited in their usefulness. As an example, one of the more prominent, *abuse*, is a case of homonymy and could (among other possibilities) refer either to substance/alcohol abuse perpetrated by the patient or to child/sexual abuse perpetrated upon the patient.

One of the techniques used in corpus linguistics to overcome the difficulties that arise when terms such as *abuse* are listed out of context is to identify target word collocations (cf. Miall, 1992) – words that occur with statistical regularity in the vicinity of selected key words. While frequency counts could be compared to trawling for fish and using the catch to estimate the variety and number of species present in a particular area, target word collocations represent an attempt to describe the kinds of ecological interdependencies that exist among the different species.

As an example, the collocations of *sin* in the Bible are all those words that occur within a span of a certain number of words of *sin*. In effect collocations are multiple word-frequency lists, with a separate list computed for each key word. The list of collocates for *sin* may for instance include *fathers*, *deadly*, and *repent* as relatively high-frequency items, while *fish* is most likely a low-frequency collocate, or not a collocate at all.

The assumption behind the idea of collocation is that words are not evenly distributed through semantic space, but clump together in more or less distinct constellations separated by lesser or greater tracks of meaninglessness (or unsaid meaning), and furthermore that the force with which words attract and repel is reflected in their relative distance in spoken or written language. Unlike the stars, however, which (as the King James Bible tells us) have been 'set in the firmament' (Genesis 1.17), the ways in which words are constellated may vary from one text to another. The sorts of results obtained from a collocational study will also, amongst other things, depend on the distance allowed between collocates (e.g. adjacent words only or all words within a span of say fifteen words) as well as on the boundaries which are set (e.g. all collocates, or only those occurring in the same sentence or paragraph).

Target-word collocations are based on some indicator of the strength of association between words. The statistical index most commonly used is the z-score (Miall, 1992; Bradley, 1990). Given the total number of words in a text, the 'span' of words considered to be a target word's typical context (e.g. five words on either side), the frequency with which the target word occurs in the text, and the frequency with which another word (or 'collocate') occurs within the target word's context, the z-score returns a coefficient of collocation that is significant at the 1 per cent probability level when it reaches 2.57 or above. The score is computed as follows:

$$ z = \frac{C - (P \times L)}{\mathrm{sqrt}((P \times L \times (1-P))} $$

where C = the frequency with which a collocate occurs in the same context as a target word type, L = the total number of word tokens in the same context as the target word (at most the span × the total frequency of the target word), and P = the frequency with which the collocate

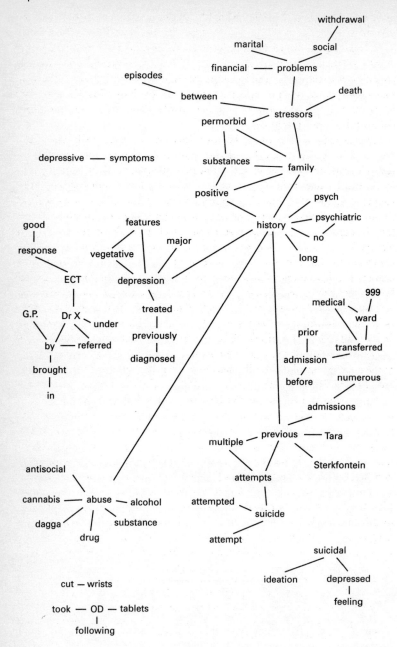

Figure 10.2 Lexical nets for Initial History Text

occurs in the text as a whole divided by the total number of tokens in the text as a whole.

To analyse the Initial History Text I have invented a version of target word collocation termed *lexical nets*. This differs from conventional collocational studies (as used in corpus linguistics and literary studies) in that target words are not selected on an a-priori basis. Instead a z-score is calculated for *each pair* of unique words in a text, and significant collocations visually plotted.

Lexical nets for the Initial History Text are displayed in Figures 10.2, 10.3 and 10.4, which are based on z-scores computed using a span of seven words on either side and truncated at vignette boundaries.

As can be seen from Figure 10.2, the word *history* is not only the most frequent in the text, but also appears to be at the centre of a web of signification. Patients are portrayed as having a history of *depression* (to the left of Figure 10.2), a *family* history of psychiatric illness (to the top), a history of substance *abuse* (to the bottom left) or a history of *previous admissions* (to the bottom right). Several of these themes contain further branches. For example: *Family history* is linked to a discussion of stressful life events such as *financial and family problems* (at the top); *History of depression* is linked to *ECT* treatment (to which patients are ritualistically described as having shown a *good response*) and to having been *under, referred by* or *brought in by Dr X* (I replaced all surnames in the text with X); and *History of previous admissions* is linked to the issue of *(multiple) previous suicide attempts*. Some smaller nets thematically (but not statistically) related to these themes are also shown in Figure 10.1.

As a distillation of the Initial History Text, Figure 10.1 can be read in many different ways – as a map of the pathways open to the (recidivist) psychiatric patient, as a table of accounting practices used by psychiatric registrars to confirm the patient status of those they have been asked to treat, and so on. However, whatever reading is imposed on the figure it is hard to escape the impression that what is shown is a peculiar kind of self-referential epistemology: A patient is a patient because s/he is a patient (has been previously treated/diagnosed/admitted), or because members of her/his family have previously attained patient status. This is particularly evident in the almost ceremonial reference made to previous admissions, with phrases such as the following occurring in numerous vignettes:

Previous admission 1982 and 1983 for paranoid psychosis;
8 previous admissions for Bipolar Affective Disorder;
40 year old unmarried male previously diagnosed as schizophrenic;
Two previous admissions – X-clinic 5 weeks and Weskoppies 6 months;
Multiple admissions to nearly all hospitals in Witwatersrand, Cape Town, Pretoria.

The idea that previous encounters (of patients or their families) with

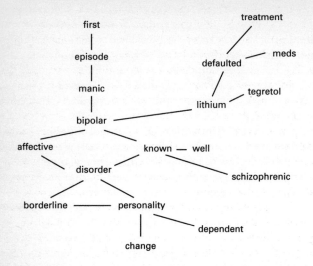

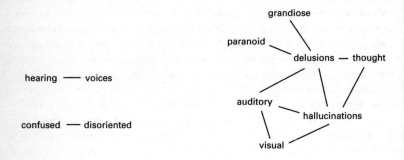

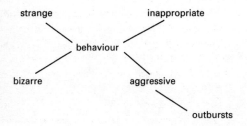

Figure 10.3 Lexical nets for Initial History Text

psychiatry explain their current status does not exclude the use of more substantial explanatory strategies, but appears to be quite central to making a case for why any particular person qualifies as a true patient, as in the following examples:

> 38 year old woman with 3 weeks history of manic symptoms with disinhibition, promiscuity and grandiose delusions. *Multiple previous admissions to other psychiatric hospitals and diagnosed as rapid cycler bipolar disorder.* Substance abuse – poppers, cannabis, alcohol. Stressors – bad relationship with boyfriend, moved to X, new job, financial, divorce, parents' deaths, infertility.

> 43 year old woman who presented with nine month history of depression, getting worse over last 3 weeks with negative thinking and suicidal ideation. *Two previous admissions to sanatoria for depression. Treated with ect.* Between episodes patient was functioning well off medication. Stressors – financial, lost her job, husband resigned from his job, legal problems.

> Patient presented with paranoid delusions, concerning black men who wanted to kill her. At time of admission was agitated and reported auditory hallucinations. *Long prior psychiatric history of similar problem, strong history of alcohol abuse for 15 years,* but had stopped drinking one month previously.

This emphasis on previous encounters with authority is reminiscent of Spencer's (1988) studies of probation officers' reports, in which previous criminal convictions (analogous to previous brushes with institutional psychiatry) are always carefully reported, although much else may be selectively left out.

Figures 10.3 and 10.4 show other lexical nets present in the Initial History Text, but not linked to the key word *history*. The net shown at the top of Figure 10.3 may be termed the *bipolar affective disorder* net, which is linked (by sharing the word *disorder*) to a *personality disorder* net, and (through the phrase *well known*) to the word *schizophrenic*. Interestingly, terms usually associated with schizophrenia and also shown in Figure 10.3, such as *delusions*, *hallucinations* and *inappropriate behaviour*, are not statistically linked to *schizophrenic*, suggesting that if a person is already *well known* as a *schizophrenic*, further evidence regarding schizophrenic symptoms are considered superfluous, as in the following vignette:

> Patient referred from X-hospital, where he has been for three and a half years – apparently a known schizophrenic. Sent for treatment and management of aggression which is not possible at X-hospital.

By contrast, details of the symptomatology are required where the registrar is unable to state categorically that the patient is already known to the medical authorities as a schizophrenic or some other category of mental illness:

> Sudden onset, auditory hallucinations, paranoid delusions, delusions of control.

Inappropriate, disinhibition, insomnia. According to husband she gets these episodes up to three times a year. Includes bizarre behaviour and disorganised speech.

Again, the language is reminiscent of the criminal justice system, where offenders' accounts and those of their families have to be treated with studied scepticism, while previous convictions instantly qualify a person as a 'known house-breaker', a 'well-known child molester' and so on. The contrast between stammered and incoherent lay accounts on the one hand and the certainty provided by previous diagnosis on the other is illustrated in the following phrases culled from randomly selected vignettes:

> According to wife patient has had aggressive outbursts
> Well known bipolar disorder
> According to wife, alcoholic habits in past
> Known alcoholic
> According to parents patient has been totally irrational
> Well known bipolar patient
> Change in personality according to husband
> Well known schizophrenic

Additional lexical nets are shown in Figure 10.4. In the box at the bottom right of the figure are two- and three-word phrases which are statistically related, but not linked to any of the larger nets. The small net above represents a stereotypical opening sentence stating various biographical details, which occurs in many of the vignettes and which will not be further discussed here.

Finally, the net at the top of Figure 10.4, which resembles a spider's web, may be thought of as a *vegetative features* net. It is remarkable both for its extreme enmeshment and for its isolation from the rest of the discursive structure. If the initial history is like a pinball game, the *vegetative features* net represents an area where the ball bounces rapidly from side to side, setting lights flashing and bells ringing, before finally resuming a more linear, but not necessarily related, trajectory:

> Problems started about one month after stepson moved into home. Unable to handle situation. Feels neglected and ignored. Feels stepson is encroaching the previous family life pattern. Doesn't see solution to problem of stepson. *Also – increased sleep pattern. No energy or libido. No weight loss.* Bulimic.

If space were available a more detailed analysis of the various tributaries of the psychiatric discourse present in the Initial History Text would obviously be possible, but it should be clear that the lexical nets do provide a context within which more detailed exploration can proceed. Unlike some discourse analytic studies, which quote selected illustrative examples in corroboration of whatever inferences are made, lexical nets are explicitly

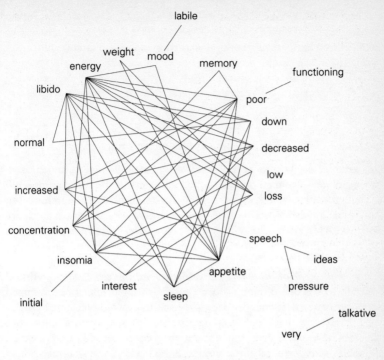

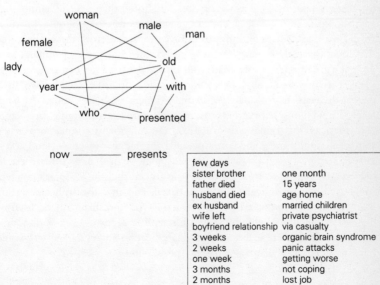

Figure 10.4 Lexical nets for Initial History Text

concerned with systematically parsing the entire text, and presenting results in the context of their frequency in the text as a whole. In this case they reveal to us a Kafkaesque world, governed by an insane circularity forever predicated upon itself, where admission explains readmission, where categories of madness are always already known, and where well-rehearsed symptom checklists are recited over and over again with no necessary relation to actuality.

Critique and future directions

This chapter set out to be polemical – in methodology as much as in subject matter. The methodological polemic was intended to disrupt a too easy identification of discourse work with safe qualitative research, and to propagate an inversion of the conventional qualitative–quantitative sequence. This attempt may have had some success, but inevitably gives rise to a further set of difficulties. I discuss five of these below.

The enchantment of numbers Lexical nets are the result of a statistical projection of word distances on a one-dimensional line to a presumed many-dimensional discursive space and back to a two-dimensional printed page. Assuming that one accepted the notion that average inter-word distances have some deep significance, the process of double projection is fraught with technical uncertainties. Should word types, as they occur in ordinary text, be used as data points, or should they first be lemmatized (e.g. should *I, me, my, mine* be coded as a single word type)? Should 'function words' such as articles and prepositions be excluded from the analysis (for the most part they were)? How should the many dimensional space represented by the z-score matrix be resolved back into two dimensions? (Rather than the manual projection I relied on, one could have used cluster analysis, factor analysis, or multi-dimensional unfolding.) At what level should links between words be considered 'significant'? In a large text such as the Initial History Text, far too many connections reach statistical significance, and I simply used the highest z-scores, stopping – at a z-score of 13.36 – when the resultant lexical nets threatened to became too unwieldy. It could equally be argued that the strongest connections are also semantically the most trivial, and that the truly interesting connections emerge at a level *below* 13.36. Quantification can be used to disguise subjectivity behind a gloss of scientific accuracy, and if discourse work is to draw more extensively on quantification strategies analysts would have to become vigilant against this possibility.

The insignificance of numbers Setting aside such technical quibbles, diagrams such as those used in this chapter invite ridicule for the extreme literal-mindedness with which they interpret the idea of *repetitive patterns*, displaying as they do connections between mere words, while it seems more probable that God would have stocked our linguistic aquaria with larger, more shadowy creatures (phrases, sentences, natural meaning units), and that it is in the elaborate mating rituals that occur between these higher-level elements that we may witness the spawning of human subjectivity. Lexical nets are too fine-grained and too flimsy to catch anything bigger than the amorphous plankton of the discursive ocean. The idea of a mechanical device of any sort being useful in making sense of language is in itself already suspect.

The cartography of numbers   Lexical nets purport to be no more than a backdrop to the serious work of *qualitative* discourse analysis. However, in the analysis presented in this chapter, talk relating to the nets takes up so much space that there is little left for any kind of qualitative work. In fact, perhaps the most interesting analysis is of a single vignette, done near the start and entirely without the benefit of quantitative information. The rationalization given for constructing lexical nets is that they give an overview of the entire text and thus provide a context for qualitative analysis. However, this disguises the arbitrary nature of the Initial History Text. Maybe the text should have been larger. Maybe I should have included similar vignettes from other hospitals, thrown in a couple of standard psychiatric texts, some transcripts of interviews with staff and patients and so on. Conversely, maybe the text is too large. Maybe I should have segmented the sample in terms of admitting physician, sex, diagnostic category, date of admission, and constructed separate nets for each cell. As Hicks and Potter (1991) have demonstrated in their attempt to relate discourse work to quantification strategies, any kind of quantitative analysis works only for as long as one accepts the sampling frame within which it operates. It could of course be argued that the same is true for qualitative analyses, but it seems likely that in a straight qualitative study other kinds of perhaps more useful contextual information would have had a greater chance of being included – information such as that for the greater part of the period during which the data was collected the hospital in question was reserved for white patients only.

The salt-flats of abstraction   Sooner or later discourse analysts all seem to end up with wanting to find repetitive patterns in texts. These they then call 'repertoires' (Potter and Wetherell, 1987), 'devices' (Gilbert and Mulkay, 1984), 'maps' (Wetherell and Potter, 1992) or 'discourses' (Parker, 1990, 1992). This chapter tried to take this idea to its logical (numerical) conclusion. The result is, in Cox's (1989) words, 'salt-flats of abstraction' from which all the 'beautiful specifics of culture' have been stripped. We are left with no way of knowing that patient #378 has in the past three weeks shown a tendency to fall over his own feet, that patient #1018 believes that Satan has taken over her boyfriend's personality, that patient #1465 is a political detainee who suffers from echolalia and suicidal thoughts and has been tearing holes in his clothes. Maybe meaning is contained not in frequent words and stereotypical formulations, but in everything that is infrequent, atypical and silent.

Doing things with words   Although I have in some sense tried to describe what the vignettes do (rather than what they claim to describe), I have been strangely silent on how they are actually used. What is their exact function in the sequence of admission, treatment and discharge to which each patient is exposed? When are they referred to (if at all), and to what purpose? More seriously – what do I intend to do with the parasitic text which I have created from them? Do I intend using it to mobilize resistance among potential and actual psychiatric patients (since completing the first draft of this chapter I have become involved with a psychiatric service users activist group, but have not been able to imagine a way of making this work useful to the group)? Will I attempt to have it published in psychiatric journals to sensitize psychiatrists to the ways in which the language they use describes as well as constructs illness? Or are these words to be confined to the world of discourse about discourse?

References

Anspach, R. R. (1988) 'Notes on the sociology of medical discourse: the language of case presentation', *Journal of Health and Social Behaviour*, 29, 357–75.

Ben-Arie, O. and Nash, E. S. (1986) 'Deficiencies and inequalities in psychiatric services', *South African Medical Journal*, 69, 343–4.

Bradley, J. (1990) *TACT User's Guide*, University of Toronto, Toronto.

Burman, E. (1991) 'What discourse is not', *Philosophical Psychology*, 4 (3), 325–42.

Cox, S. (1989) 'Devices of deconstruction', *Critical Review*, 3 (1), 56–76.

Daniel, G. R. and Freeman, H. L. (1983) *The Treatment of Mental Disorders in the Community*, Bailliere, Tindall & Cassell, London.

Dommisse, J. (1987) 'The state of psychiatry in South Africa today', *Social Science and Medicine*, 24 (9), 749–61.

Foucault, M. (1980) *Power/Knowledge, Selected Interviews and Other Writing 1972–1977*, Harvester Press, Hassocks, Sussex.

Fourie, J. and Gagiano, C. A. (1987) ''n Moderne psigiatriese gemeenskapsdiens in die Oranje-Vrystaat', *South African Medical Journal*, 73, 427–9.

Freeman, M., Lee, T. and Vivian, W. (1994) *Evaluation of Mental Health Services in the OFS*, Centre for Health Policy, University of the Witwatersrand Medical School, Johannesburg.

Gilbert, G. N. and Mulkay, M. (1984) *Opening Pandora's Box: A Sociological Analysis of Scientists' Discourse*, Routledge, London.

Gillis, L. S. (1987) 'Psychiatric research – a new tomorrow', *South African Medical Journal*, 72 (5), 797–9.

Gillis, L. S., Sandler, R., Jakoet, A. and Elk, R. (1986) 'Readmissions to a psychiatric hospital: outcome on follow-up', *South African Medical Journal*, 70 (12), 735–9.

Gillis, L. S., Trollip, D., Jakoet, A. and Holden, T. (1987) 'Non-compliance with psychotropic medication', *South African Medical Journal*, 72 (9), 602–6.

Hamber, B. E. (1992) 'The quality of life of the South African psychiatric outpatient', unpublished honours dissertation, University of the Witwatersrand.

Hamber, B. E. (1994) 'Community psychiatric care … moving towards effective community services in South Africa', paper presented at the psychology and societal transformation conference, University of the Western Cape, January 1994.

Hamber, B. E. (1995) 'The burden of care: an analysis of the burden of care on the caregivers of psychiatric outpatients', unpublished masters dissertation, University of the Witwatersrand.

Hamber, B. E. and Rock, B. M. (1993) 'Mental illness and human rights: in search of context, consequence and effective care,' *Rethinking Rights*, 1, 72–91.

Hicks, D. and Potter, J. (1991) 'Sociology of scientific knowledge: a reflexive citation analysis of science disciplines and disciplining science', *Social Studies of Science*, 21 (3), 459–501.

Kastrup, M. (1987) 'The use of a psychiatric register in predicting the outcome "revolving door patient": a nation-wide cohort of first time admitted patients', *Acta Psychiatrica Scandinavica*, 76 (5), 552–60.

Landman, M. (1994) 'Mobilisation of social support for state patients in Lebowa', unpublished PhD dissertation, University of South Africa.

Levett, A. (1988) 'Psychological trauma: discourses of childhood sexual abuse', unpublished doctoral dissertation, University of Cape Town.

Miall, D. S. (1992) 'Estimating changes in collocations of key words across a large text: a case study of Coleridge's notebooks', *Computers and the Humanities*, 26, 1–12.

Ngcobo, A. (1995) 'The Durban alliance for the mentally ill', paper presented at the international launch of the report on world mental health and regional conference on mental health policy, Cape Town, October.

Parker, I. (1990) 'Real things: discourse, context and practice', *Philosophical Psychology*, 3 (2), 227–33.

Parker, I. (1992) *Discourse Dynamics: Critical Analysis for Social and Individual Psychology*, Routledge, London.

Potter, J. and Wetherell, M. (1987) *Discourse and Social Psychology: Beyond Attitudes and Behaviour*, London, Sage.

Potter, J., Wetherell, N., Gill, R. and Edwards, D. (1990) 'Discourse: noun, verb or social practice?', *Philosophical Psychology*, 3 (2), 205–17.

Robbins, D. (1994) 'Changing the face of mental hospitals', *Star*, 5 September 1994, 11.

Rosenblatt, A. and Mayer, J. E. (1974) 'The recidivism of mental patients: a review of past studies', *American Journal of Orthopsychiatry*, 44 (5), 697–706.

Sandler, R. and Jakoet, A. (1985) 'Outcome after discharge from a psychiatric hospital', *South African Medical Journal*, 68, 470–4.

Spencer, J. W. (1988) 'The role of text in the processing of people in organizations', *Discourse Processes*, 11, 61–78.

Strong, T. L. (1987) 'Psychiatric relapse: a comparative study of potential contributing factors', unpublished BSw (Hons) dissertation, University of the Witwatersrand, Johannesburg.

Swartz, L. (1989) 'Aspects of culture in South African psychiatry', unpublished doctoral dissertation, University of Cape Town.

Terre Blanche, M. J. (1993) 'Depressed in, stressed out: PD ward patients at Tara Hospital', unpublished manuscript.

Van Dijk, T. A. (1987) *Communicating Racism: Ethnic Prejudice in Thought and Talk*, Sage, London.

Visser, M. J., Haasbroek, C. P. and Bodemer, W. (1989) *Psigiatriese Hospitale in Suider-Afrika*, Verslag P-100 Instituut vir Psigologiese en Edumetriese Navorsing, Human Sciences Research Council, Pretoria.

Wetherell, M. and Potter, J. (1992) *Mapping the Language of Racism: Discourse and the Legitimation of Exploitation*, Harvester Wheatsheaf, Hemel Hempstead.

CHAPTER 11

Dialogue, inter-subjectivity and the analysis of discourse

Kevin Kelly and Hilde Van Vlaenderen

This study was conceived in the context of a broader study (Kelly and Van Vlaenderen, 1996), the purpose of which was to explore the relational dynamics of participation in a community health development project. The present chapter explores one of the findings of this broader study; namely, that there were systematic discrepancies between participants' descriptions of their own participation in the project, and the description of their participation by others. We attempt to understand the discourse dynamics implied by such discrepancies in the context of community development work.

Participation and dialogue in community health development

In the following section we discuss the concepts of 'participation' and 'dialogue'. These are the primary concepts that have been used to describe discursive processes in community health development.

The term 'participation' has come to prominence in the field of health through the emergence of the 'primary health care' (PHC) movement. Kasege (1991) suggests that what is 'primary' in PHC is not the vision of health for all, not the emphasis on basic services, nor is it the emphasis on 'care' as opposed to 'cure', but the implementation strategy of community involvement in health matters and in the functioning of the health system as a whole.

Bennett (1992) points out that participation has come to mean different things in different contexts. He emphasizes the need to understand that there are different forms of community involvement and these should be distinguished rather than as they presently are, lumped together as if participation refers to a clearly definable process. This contention is supported by Rifkin (1986) in a review of over two hundred PHC projects.

'Participation' is also a key concept in the 'people-centred' approach to development (Brown, 1985; Erasmus, 1992; Cohen and Uphoff, 1977;

Korten, 1990; Moulik, 1987; Santhanam et al., 1982; UNRISD, 1979) and in the 'participatory research movement', which emerged alongside the people-centred development approach (Brown, 1985; Van Vlaenderen and Nkwinti, 1993). Here, as in the PHC movement, the term has been applied in such a diversity of ways that its explanatory value has been compromised. A considerable degree of confusion seems to prevail amongst policy-makers, social scientists, development workers and local people involved in development, as to its definition and implications (Rahnema, 1990). There is a need to clarify the meaning of the term 'participation', which seems to have become something of a 'buzz-word' used to legitimize any and all community development projects, at least in the South African context.

Several authors in the field of participatory development have stressed the relationship between the concepts of participation and dialogue (cf. Boeren, 1992; Gengaje and Setty, 1991; Rajakutty, 1991). The Bhoomi Sena project in India (Oakley and Marsden, 1985), often thought of as a model of participatory development, has taken dialogue as a guiding principle. Dialogue is thought of as a kind of communicative context that enables participatory development to take place. Through dialogue a commonality of individual perceptions is facilitated and this is used as a basis for social action that represents the common good.

Schrijvers (1991) is somewhat more pessimistic than are the above authors about the possibility of dialogue in development contexts. She outlines the difficulties involved in bringing about dialogue in the context of two participants wielding different degrees of power in a research situation. She suggests that dialogical forms of communication can be established most easily if there are only small power differentials in the research situation, a condition she describes as 'studying sideways' as opposed to 'studying down' or 'studying up'.

Habermas's (1984) 'theory of communicative action' outlines the 'speech conditions' of ideal dialogue. These conditions refer to communicative contexts where there is no domination of the dialogue by one of the participants or by one of the perspectives represented and there is an equality of discursive opportunity between participants. However, it seems that even if micro-contexts are created in which power dynamics are minimized, dialogue does not necessarily take place. In a case study Ellsworth (1989) shows that the dialogical dynamics of marginalization continued to operate even where communicative ethics were explicitly designed to overcome marginalization.

It is exactly in those situations where dialogue is not possible that the need for participation is usually most strongly asserted. If dialogue is not possible because of inequality of discursive opportunity and imbalances of discursive power, development work is left without a *modus operandi*. Development work requires joint action and decision-making between partners who differ in their degree of familiarity with and access to dominant modes of discourse.

Brazilian pedagogue Paulo Freire (1972) sees dialogue both as a means of communication and as a goal towards which communication strives. His work consists of a sustained reflection upon the socio-political and cultural processes that militate against 'intersubjectivity' – i.e. co-constituted understanding – and are found in the relationship 'oppressor–oppressed'. His dialogical methodology has been widely applied in 'community-building', but it seems to be rather less applicable in transition situations, where 'partners' meet in a discursive environment where the structurally powerful are advantaged in terms of access to legitimate and dominant modes of discourse.

In contemporary South Africa in almost all spheres of public service there is an acknowledgement of the need for the transformation of existing services. There is a widespread recognition that this process requires 'community participation' in the planning and implementation of new services. The planners of such services (including those in need of the services and service providers) would typically meet under adverse 'speech conditions'. The situation of transition necessitates the meeting of parties who are grossly different in terms of access to resources, education, power and the sense that their efforts can make a difference. Very often 'democratic procedures' are regarded as a sufficient safeguard of community interests, but we believe that in the community development arena the superficial application of ostensibly democratic procedures all too often serves to legitimize relations of domination under the guise of correct procedure. Rahnema (1990) suggests that the use of the concept of participation in development sometimes obscures real power differentials between 'change agents' and those on the 'receiving end' of the development relationship, and sometimes serves as a disguise for manipulation.

We believe that there is a need to study development processes that claim to involve community participation, and to develop ways of thinking about different types of participation and their interaction. We see the need to develop a critical understanding of the communicative processes involved. We have found little evidence of in-depth, evaluative research that examines communicative ethics in context; i.e. through case study. For these reasons we undertook a study of a community health development project, with a view to articulating some of the micro-processes and problematics involved in fostering dialogue. The aim of this empirico-interpretative research was to articulate the process of the project in terms of participation and dialogue, to explore this process at the level of theory that can be applied in other contexts, and to develop a useful methodology for the assessment of communicative interactions in participatory endeavours. An extended account of this research is provided by Kelly and Van Vlaenderen (1996).

The specific aim of the present study was to develop ways of thinking about the discrepancy between the way in which people described their own participation and the way in which others described their participation; i.e. in the subject's self-discourse and the discourse about the subject from the point of view of 'the other'. We were intrigued by the relation between these two forms of discourse about the subject, which seemed to be central to the communicative culture of the project as a whole, and important for understanding dialogical processes in the context of the project.

The context of the study was a community health development initiative that attempted to bring together a range of 'partners' in drawing up a proposal in a health development project, which was to be sponsored by an international donor organization if it fulfilled certain criteria determined by them. The partnership was supposed to take place between health services, training institutions and under-resourced communities and was to be aimed at addressing health issues identified by people in those communities as being critical to them. The following participants were involved: a university; local community-based organizations and political organizations; local development and welfare non-governmental organizations; local health institutions (including a psychiatric hospital; a general hospital and a number of community health clinics); individuals from various communities within the town of 90,000 people; and the donor agency represented by evaluators.

After many meetings a 200-page proposal, representing ten sub-projects and a management structure, was presented to the funders. The proposal did not receive funding because in various ways it did not meet the funders' expectations. The rejection of the proposal resulted in the abortion of the whole initiative, although certain of the sub-projects continued to develop without funding.

Those representing the disempowered communities in the town realized that there needed to be a transformation of the health sector and that they needed to be part of the transformation process. Professional health workers (and allied disciplines) recognized that a process of community participation was necessary. At this level at least, there was a degree of common purpose; i.e. agreement that there needed to be some form of cooperative action. In spite of the expressed commitments towards working in a cooperative manner, and a great deal of effort on the part of most participants, the project gradually became a site of conflict that overshadowed the cooperative intentions. As researchers we were interested in understanding this.

Analysing the discourse of self and other

Thirteen participants in the project were interviewed. An attempt was made to select participants who represented a broad range of what the researchers anticipated were the different ways of participating in the project. Because it began to emerge that the modes of participating with which participants were identified were not always what the researchers had anticipated, the choice of participants targeted for interviewing was deliberated upon and changed as we proceeded.

A semi-structured interview format with a twelve-question interview schedule was used to obtain descriptions of the project and its outcome, descriptions of personal involvement and of the involvement of others in the project, and descriptions of the meetings attended. The interviews were audio-recorded and transcribed.

Our interpretative approach was strongly influenced by 'grounded hermeneutic research' methodology (Addison, 1992). In particular we held the idea that research questions should be allowed to develop during the course of the research. A hermeneutical model is exploratory, discovery-oriented and theory-generating rather than hypothesis-testing (Elliot, 1989) and involves a reflective process of engaging with the data, during which the questions guiding the research are re-examined and reformulated (Brown et al., 1989). The process of asking more perspicacious, better-defined questions leads to richer knowing.

The 'reading guide' method used by Brown et al. (1989) was adapted for use with the interview material. The development of a reading guide begins with the generation of a set of questions based on an initial understanding, through which the textual material is to be read. As the reading proceeds the questions are refined and new questions emerge, leading to the need to develop a new reading guide. Development of the reading guide or the development of second- and third-order reading guides facilitates further and deeper exploration of the material. In this context the reading guides assisted the researchers to analyse the discourse of participation beyond the subjective accounts of participation, and this led to the idea of 'discourse analysis through alterity', which will presently be discussed.

Stage One: reading guide for individual interviews The following reading guide was used:

1. How did the participant see his/her own participation in the project?
2. How did the participant see the grouping of other actors in the project?
3. How did the participant see the participation of other actors in the project?
4. What was the participant's understanding of the process of the project and its problematics?

The reading guide was then applied to the transcriptions. The researchers underlined with different coloured pens any material that related, even in an oblique way, to each of the questions of the reading guide. Subsequently the material relating to each question was clustered together and summarized. Thus we obtained responses to each question from the perspective of each respondent's experience.

The researchers used both the content of what participants spoke about and the discursive strategies which they used in order to develop these responses. The analysis of discursive strategies was important in identifying and picking through the contradictions within the accounts given. Looking to identify modes of participating we were especially sensitive to ways of speaking about self and others that reflected the 'actual' constructions of identity and difference between participants. By actual we mean the identifications that were created in the context of what was done in the project and reflected the effective (as opposed to putative) modes of participation in the project. This meant that we were cautious in accepting the claimed self-identifications of the participants. This was facilitated by attunement to the identifications that emerged in talking about 'the community', 'community needs', 'organizers', 'management committee', 'university', 'whites', 'blacks'. These were key words in establishing actual identifications and the discursive justifications packed around these terms led us more and more to set aside the claimed identifications, such as identification of self as a participant representing the municipal health clinic.

We became increasingly aware of how participants established their own function and identity in the project in relation to other participants; some they identified with and others 'against whom' they were set. The use of the term 'they' was useful in distinguishing the ways in which identifications operated by a kind of exclusion; i.e. I am this through not being that. This became central to our analysis and the second-order reading guide was developed to explore this further.

Stage Two: reading guide for describing common modes of participation To obtain a general account of the dynamics of participation in the project as a whole, which would elucidate how the different forms of participation interacted, and specifically how self- and other descriptions related, a second reading guide was developed and applied to the descriptions obtained in Stage One. At this level the researchers sought out the common ways in which people experienced 'participating', and set about defining these common ways by using the following two questions to read 'across' the individual accounts.

1. What common modes of participating can be identified from the perspective of self-identification? (It was deemed possible that an actor may have participated in a number of modes.)
2. From the point of view of each of the common modes of participating how are the other modes understood? (In the case of a participant having participated in a number of modes the interviews were re-read so that their experience and understanding of the roles of others could

be understood from the point of view of each mode of participation engaged in.)

This analysis involved a circular movement between the emerging general account and the thirteen particular accounts, and we attempted to retain the meaning of the descriptions at the individual case level, yet to present them without the contextual detail in which they were embedded at the individual level. A summarized description was written for each specific mode of participation from the point of view of a person identifying with that mode of participation, and second, from the perspective of not identifying with that mode of participation; i.e. from the point of view of the other modes of participation.

Initially we attained twelve modes of participation, but as we worked with the material we reduced this to four major modes.

Modes of participation and their interaction

The following modes of participation were identified:

1. Participating from the perspective of having organizational resources and special project skills.
2. Participating as a representative of a non-community-based institution motivated to participate in the project.
3. Participating from the perspective of identifying with the sector of the community which the project defined as having the needs to be met.
4. Participating from the perspective of trying to coordinate the process and to bring coherence to the project as a whole.

For purposes of illustration a central feature of each mode will be presented, first from the point of view of adopting the particular mode, and then from the perspective of the 'others' not identifying with it. The authors termed the latter mode of participation the 'alterior' perspective (from Latin *alter*, other). More comprehensive and general descriptions of each of these modes can be found in Kelly and Van Vlaenderen (1996).

Mode One: having organizational resources and special project skills
Mode One participants saw themselves as having to take stronger initiative and responsibility as funder-imposed deadlines approached, when others appeared to them not to be taking appropriate initiatives. They felt that they had sufficient knowledge of community needs, in relation to the resources available (of which they had first-hand knowledge), to enable them to translate community needs into projects in the course of drafting sub-project proposals.

An alterior view Those identified with the disempowered community (Mode

Three) felt that in the course of interpreting needs into interventions, there was a tendency on the part of those with skills and specialist knowledge to dominate. At a point where the project seemed to be going nowhere Mode One participants took over the process and proceeded with project formulation on their own. They were seen to have interpreted community needs into programmes of action according to their own prejudicial interpretations of what was most expedient and in ways that favoured and imposed professional and institutional interests upon the needs of the community.

Mode Two: as a representative of a non-community-based institution motivated to participate in the project Mode Two participants felt a need to develop their own institutions through the project and saw their institutions benefiting from involvement, both materially and in terms of credibility in the 'new South Africa'. They believed the project would give them resources to work out programmes that they thought were good for both the community and their institutions. They experienced their own interests as needs. They felt the need to extend existing institutional programmes in a community-oriented direction, but felt threatened when-ever encouraged to participate in ways which did not coincide with pre-existing institutional programmes and plans.

An alterior view Mode Three participants saw Mode Two participants as competitors in the quest for funds who masked their wish to dominate behind a veneer of community interest. They were seen as foisting institutional agendas upon the community, and their participation was regarded with suspicion because it lacked a commitment to institutional transformation. They were regarded as arrogantly thinking that they knew what was good for 'black people'. The funders were categorized as Mode Two participants because they were seen by all participants as responsible for imposing preconceived ideas and requirements upon the process of health services development.

Mode Three: identifying with the sector of the community that the project defined as having needs to be met Mode Three participants felt ambi-valent about participating because the project threatened to be 'white' dominated and this meant that it would probably perpetuate the power dynamics of South African society by serving the interests of the powerful above the interests of the disempowered. Yet they participated because any opportunity to develop community resources was better than none, and they were committed to serving the interests of the disempowered community the project was supposed to serve. However, their ambivalence gave rise to a response of passivity in relation to participation. Finally it led to resistance to the entire process.

An alterior view The more active participants identifying with Mode Three were seen, from the perspective of Mode Two (institutional/professional) participation, as needing to bring their own political aspirations and personal needs for power to bear through the project. Mode Two participants felt that the participatory needs analysis was a sufficient measure of community needs and that Mode Three participants were being overly sensitive in saying that the project did not address community needs, which in their interpretation it clearly did. Mode One participants felt that certain Mode Three participants were being destructive towards the entire process, to the extent that they were critical without making explicit and constructive contributions towards the development of alternatives.

Mode Four: trying to coordinate the project as a whole Participants in this mode saw themselves as initiative-takers who directed and guided the projected from its inception. They saw themselves as mediating between the funders and the project, and between the interests of the different participants.

An alterior view Both Mode Two and Three participants saw themselves as not sufficiently supported by Mode Four participants, who were seen as being aligned with conflicting interests to their own. Mode Three participants saw coordinators as siding with Mode Two interests and Mode Two participants saw coordinators as siding with Mode Three interests. Perception of the coordinators as having been aligned with a particular group precluded them, in the eyes of other participants, from playing the role of mediators and promoters of dialogue.

Theoretical reflection

The alterior view was mostly unseen from within the perspective of each mode, and alterior views remained largely undisclosed in the context of the project. Alterior perspectives might be thought of as 'blind spots' in the self-understanding of each mode of participation; i.e. if we take self-understanding to refer to the social rather than purely subjective meaning of the mode of participation. The dialogical process occurred in a context in which each subjectivity was understood differently by the subjectivity with which it attempted to communicate, as compared to the way it understood itself. This impeded the development of dialogue. The impetus created by the physical activities of the project – such as attendance of meetings, the promise of resources and a discursive framework that smoothed over conflicts of understanding – allowed participants to continue in their supposed dialogue, in spite of this state of affairs.

A's understanding of B's social actions might be considered from the point of view of B to be an excess or a misunderstanding, to the extent that this understanding does not coincide with B's own self-understanding. It appears to be a kind of first loyalty of psychological life to believe that one's intuitive self-understanding is the most true or real understanding. We cannot, however, fully know how we participate in social processes until we attain some measure of 'distanciation' from our self-identifications as actors in social processes. Ultimately there can be no appreciation of social discourse within the context of that discourse, before actors understand the reconstituting discourses they expose themselves to through engaging with others who bring their own meanings to the encounter.

To illustrate, it can be said that those representing institutions were not intuitively inclined to appreciate that their mode of participation was viewed by other participants as bound up with interests that were self-serving and opposed to the interests of the community. Whereas Mode Three participants had understood the discourse of participation to imply institutional transformation and greater community control over health resources, the institutional constituency were for the most part motivated by a model of community service that left institutional power largely intact. Mode Three participants viewed institutional participation (Mode Two) as an attempt to entrench institutional power rather than to transform the power structures of the health services in the direction of community control. In the difference between these two modes of understanding Mode Two participation, we have a significant tension that was not disclosed or overcome in the course of the project, and gradually undermined the will to participate on the part of both Modes Two and Three. Perhaps if these conflicting discourses had been exposed too early, the project would have become a site of unmanageable conflict with nothing to bind it together. However, because the communicative process never addressed these tensions the coherence of the project never developed beyond being a relatively superficial plan for joint action.

The Habermasian ideal seeks 'intersubjectivity'. This refers to an understanding that surpasses and transcends the subjective understanding of individual participants, and can be agreed upon by all and used as the basis for social action. But the assumption of there being an existent 'intersubjectivity' – i.e. a shared ground of understanding – was a central problem in this project which, in our opinion, prevented participants from seeing the discursive conflicts within and between participants; unrecognized discursive tensions between self and alterior perspectives. The discourse of 'common interest' which began with the initial offer of funding, initiated and motivated the project. Yet because the discursive process did not facilitate the recognition of the alterior discourses that redefined the actual groupings in the project, and redefined the meaning of each mode of participation, the discursive process lost touch with the real dialogical dynamics of the project.

We suggest that the interaction of contrasting discourses is appropriately described by the term 'inter-subjectivity'. In contrast to the term 'intersubjectivity' (common ground of understanding) the idea of inter-subjectivity recognizes the differences that lie between differently positioned subjects (subject–subject: hence inter-subjectivity) who are bound together by a structural process of communication. The analysis thereof begins with recognition of conflicts of interpretation. In relation to this project our understanding of these conflicts was only attained by virtue of the research methodology we applied, which specifically looked at the differences between how participants saw themselves and how others saw them. We will now go on to discuss the need for such 'distanciated' perspectives that represent inter-subjective reality, within the context of development projects.

Kelly and Van Vlaenderen (1996) make five general suggestions about measures that might assist the creation of a discursive environment conducive to dialogue in development projects. In summary these are:

1. greater transparency of the interests at play, which might be achieved through a process of needs analysis in respect of all groups of participants, and not only the disempowered;
2. open-ended assessment of needs, which does not end with the choice of intervention strategies; and a dynamic relation between needs and strategies, which at the outset and throughout should not be considered apart;
3. educational preparation of service providers to assist the transition from provider to dialogical partner and capacity-building within the community towards enhancement of the ability to participate in the dominant modes of discourse in the project;
4. the need to take into account the influence of the socio-political context in which the project is situated;
5. the need for a greater degree of reflection upon dialogical processes in the context of the project. It is this last need that is particularly salient to our present interest in the relation between dialogue, discourse analysis and inter-subjectivity.

We might say that point 5 above refers to the need for meta-communication; i.e. dialogue about ongoing discursive interactions. Ellsworth (1989), in attempting to engage marginalized minority-group participants in a group pedagogical process, initially understood the exercise to have failed because the discursive dynamics of marginalization precluded participants from engaging fully in the process. But when such participants were invited to reflect upon dialogical processes they reported that it assisted them to overcome, for example, reticence about contributing to the discussion. We know of at least one work within the field of discourse analysis that expresses an interest in the strategic use of reflexivity to interrupt existing discourses (Marks, 1993) and this seems to be a promising direction to take; i.e. to develop discourse analysis as intervention. Promotion of consciousness of inter-subjective dynamics in development projects is a move in this direction.

Reflection upon dialogical processes requires a sensitivity on the part of participants to how they are being seen by other participants. A number of respondents in our study said that they would be curious to know how others had experienced them. It seems quite remarkable that participants can engage in such an extensive dialogical process and not emerge with a better understanding of how they are constituted in the eyes of other participants. Yet it can safely be said that if there was any change in this respect, it was in the direction of greater entrenchment and isolation of subjective perspectives.

It is suggested that only by understanding the entire network of modes of participation are we able to reach a comprehensive account of how we participate in social processes. Openness to having self-understanding enhanced by what is brought to that understanding from the point of view of the other begins with an openness towards recognizing the horizonality (perspectivity) of one's own understanding; an openness to knowing oneself 'otherwise'. The encounter of the subject with itself constituted in the eyes of the other interpreting subject, and the mediation of the understanding of oneself in this social context, is an embodiment of what has been referred to as inter-subjectivity. In our view this is essentially a discourse analytic process, which throws into relief the limited horizons of subjective self-understanding and brings about an understanding of the social reality of the subject's participation in discursive processes. But when power is at stake, and where the possibility of dialogue is compromised by inequality in the degree of familiarity with dominant modes of discourse, the tensions of interpretation (inter-subjectivity) may all too easily be glossed over in the interest of unity and coherence. The project studied shows us that when they are not addressed they tend to resurface and exert a destructive influence on nascent intersubjectivity (proper common ground).

We believe that it is valuable to begin critical analysis of communicative events by looking at the conflicts of interpretation and seeing how these are managed in their context. This gives an insight into how power is managed in these situations and this in turn gives a good indication of whether or not the participatory endeavour is likely to succeed. However, it is quite possible that relationships of domination might not show as conflicts of interpretation. A particular discursive mode might be so dominant that any form of opposition to it, or any alternative, would have no place in the development initiative. The parameters of the development project might exclude certain discourses – for example, the participation discourses of those with little formal education. So there may be forms of domination that never show as conflicts of interpretation and, as we have stated above, the need to communicate directly about the conflict of interpretations is but one of a number of interventions needed to enable dialogue in development.

The tendency not to take into account the fact that the reality of who we are and what we represent is constructed not only here where we are, but there where they are, is an impediment to dialogue even under relatively favourable speech conditions. It is the impediment of subjectivity. Analysis of the tensions of interpretation between subjectivities (inter-subjectivity) and the way they are managed is critical to the understanding of the workings of power in development and fundamental to the creation of discursive environments conducive to dialogue.

References

Addison, R. B. (1992) 'Grounded hermeneutic research', in B. F. Crabtree and W. L. Miller (eds), *Doing Qualitative Research: Research Methods for Primary Care*, Vol. 3, Sage, London.

Bennett, F. J. (1992) 'Community participation in primary health care', paper presented at Institute for Social and Economic Research, Rhodes University, Grahamstown.

Boeren, A. (1992) 'Getting involved: communication for participatory development', *Community Development Journal*, 27, 259–71.

Brown, L. D. (1985) 'People centred development and participatory research', *Harvard Educational Review*, 55, 69–75.

Brown, L. M., Tappan, M. B., Gilligan, C., Miller, B. A. and Argyris, D. E. (1989) 'Reading for self and moral voice: a method for interpreting narratives of real-life moral conflict and choice', in M. J. Packer and R. B. Addison (eds), *Entering the Circle: Hermeneutic Investigations in Psychology*, State University of New York Press, Albany.

Cohen, J. M. and Uphoff, N. T. (1977) *Rural Development. Participation: Concepts and Measures for Project Design, Implementation and Evaluation*, Rural Development Committee, New York.

Elliot, R. (1989) 'Comprehensive process analysis: understanding the change process in significant therapy events', in M. J. Packer and R. B. Addison (eds), *Entering the Circle: Hermeneutic Investigations in Psychology*, State University of New York Press, Albany.

Ellsworth, E. (1989) 'Why doesn't this feel empowering? Working through the repressive myths of critical pedagogy', *Harvard Educational Review*, 59, 297–324.

Erasmus, K. (1992) 'Saints or sinners: NGOs in development', paper presented at the biennial conference of the Development Society of Southern Africa, Grahamstown.

Freire, P. (1972) *Pedagogy of the Oppressed*, Penguin, Harmondsworth.

Gengaje, R. K. and Setty, E. D. (1991) 'People's image of development: development implications', *Journal of Rural Development*, 10, 311–32.

Habermas, J. (1984) *Theory of Communicative Action*, Vol. 1, Beacon, Boston, MA.

Kasege, D. C. O. (1991) 'Community empowerment: the key to health for all', keynote address at Namibian National Primary Health Care Workshop, 16–28 February.

Kelly, K. J. and Van Vlaenderen, H. (1996) 'Dynamics of participation in a community health project', *Social Science and Medicine*, 42 (9), 1235–46.

Korten, D. (1990) *Getting to the 21st Century: Voluntary Action and the Global Agenda*, Kumarian Press, Connecticut.

Marks, D. (1993) 'Case-conference analysis and action research', in E. Burman and I.Parker (eds), *Discourse Analytic Research*, Routledge, London.

Moulik, T. K. (1987) 'Techniques of mobilising rural people to support rural development programmes', *Rural Development: Training to Meet New Challenges*, 4, APDAC, Kuala Lumpur.

Oakley, P. and Marsden, D. (1985) *Approaches to Participation in Rural Development*, International Labour Organization, Geneva.

Rahnema, M. (1990) 'Participatory action research: the last temptation of Saint Development', *Alternatives*, 15, 199–226.

Rajakutty, S. (1991) 'People's participation in monitoring and evaluation of rural development programmes: concepts and approaches', *Journal of Rural Development*, 10, 35–53.

Rifkin, S. B. (1986) 'Lessons from community participation in health programmes', *Health Policy and Planning*, 1, 240–9.

Santhanam, M. L., Sastry, Y. and Vijayakumar, S. (1982) 'Human and social factors in people's participation', *Journal of Rural Development*, 1, 770–831.

Schrijvers, J. (1991) 'Dialectics of a dialogical ideal: studying down, studying sideways and studying up', in L. Nencel and P. Pels (eds), *Constructing Knowledge: Authority and Critique in Social Science*, Sage, London.

UNRISD (1979) *Dialogue About Participation*, Part 1, UNRISD, Geneva.

Van Vlaenderen, H. and Nkwinti, G. (1993) 'Participatory research as a tool for community development', *Development Southern Africa*, 10, 211–28.

CHAPTER 12

A trip to Utopia: discourse/post-modernism/nowhere

Anthony Collins and Trevor Mulder

A note on method: The problem is, when you start deconstructing one thing, you end up deconstructing everything else.

In the beginning was the Word

Overture Beginnings involve commitment. Once embarked upon, the voyage assumes a certain inevitability. For a stranger in a strange land, there is no going home: the old familiar can never be the same. This map documents an exploration on the continent of post-structuralism. Moulded from the ground of that continent, it desires you to breathe into it and give it life. The text kills the author, celebrates the reader and converts the distance between us into intertextual webs of ~~meaning~~. Your frontal cortex is exploding in electrical activity as you turn your vision to the vistas dimly lit beneath the fireworks.

Derrida's writing Derrida (cf. 1973, 1976, 1981) claims that in the beginning was writing, not speech. He takes serious issue with Saussure and the other semiological structuralists (like Lévi-Strauss) who prescribe for linguistics the study of speech alone. This phonocentricism, the priority given to speech over writing, assumes a metaphysics of presence. Derrida argues that there can be no privileged 'present', denying the immediately accessible realm of thought or experience that forms the springboard of the majority of Western philosophers' thought.

By arguing that signifiers and signifieds are arbitrarily assigned ('kind', English; 'pie', Latin; 'milder', German; all point to benevolence), that signifiers and signifieds have no separate existence (opening a dictionary will show that signifiers are related to each other in an infinite, circular relay with no ultimate signified), and that humans are unable to escape this system of signifiers, Derrida concludes that meaning can never be immediately present in a sign. No privileged present exists compared to the uncertainty of the past and future. He resorts to the technique *sous rature* to illustrate this. A sign is put *under erasure* to show that, although inadequate it is still necessary, '[s]ince the meaning of a sign is a matter of what the sign is not, this meaning is always in some sense absent from it too' (Sarup, 1988: 35). A graphic example of this would be: ~~meaning~~.

This theory maps out a territory completely different from the traditional realms of both phenomenology and positivism. Linked to these older theories and inherent in phonocentrism is an implied logocentrism of which writing is the scapegoat. Logocentrism posits a belief in the logos, what Descartes would have called the ultimate cause, the Mind that philosophers since have assumed their self-conscious audiences of having. Derrida is derisive of this yearning for the foundational sign, the signifier that would give meaning to all other signifiers, the centrism that posits a core alpha and omega.

Derrida's elevation of writing is indicative of his deconstructionist technique as a whole, of the inversion of binary oppositions. Mining land superficially covered by the structuralists, he unearths binary oppositions as crucial to both the acquisition of language and the perpetuation of logocentricism. Examples are:

> nature/culture
> health/disease
> subject/object
> male/female
> heterosexual/homosexual
> rational/irrational
> master/slave
> speech/writing

Derrida points out that not only is the former preferred over the latter but the latter gives the former its meaning by virtue of what it is not. It is the scapegoat of meaning. His technique inverts the bipolar opposition (e.g. speech/writing becomes writing/speech, i.e. the dominant term's dependence on the subordinate term is highlighted) and then puts the opposition 'under erasure' (e.g. writing becomes ~~writing~~, i.e. not to be accepted at face value as notated symbols but rather to be seen as forestructures inhabited by the traces of meaning metaphorically, like the dream-symbols of the unconscious psyche).

Derrida thus paves the way for a powerful methodology that looks for the underlying contradictions in a text and uses these exposed paradoxes to undermine the author's conceptual distinctions on which he or she originally relied. The above discussion of the metaphysics of presence was the tool used to dismantle Husserl's preoccupation with 'expression' and 'indication', but Derrida used others to similarly deconstruct writers like Freud, Saussure, Rousseau and Plato.

I really don't think I can go along with this. The stuff of Derrida is only comprehensible to people who already understand it, and they don't need to hear it again. What you're really trying to say is very simple: ideas are not simply tools for people to express themselves, but things that come before them, that shape how they can think, and most importantly how they can think about themselves. Listen to your own argument: the style you're using limits what you can say – it forces you to speak in highly specific ways and prevents you from speaking about certain things, in this case possibly the very things which are crucial. From the opening (Derrida cf. 1973, 1976, 1981 ...) you're lapsing into all sorts of legitimation stategies (latinisms, weighty references, pompous impenetrable style) which are just a form of intellectual intimidation – an attempt to impose your account by making it monolithic and unassailable by anyone who isn't already on the inside. The style of academic neutrality and authority is specifically designed to consolidate certain kinds of power to exclude those people and experiences outside itself. Remember Innocent, who could not speak back to stories that trapped him. This is not about theory, it's about creating alternative spaces, it's about someone in pain because of the stories that told him about himself. Let's try something completely different.

Prelude in A minor Well,' said Alice indignantly as their hot-air balloon finally took off, 'that will show the gravity of things a thing or two!'

'Humph,' muttered the Mad Hatter. 'Have you noticed how atrociously He mixes His metaphors: biblical, musical, geographical and now fictional? Soon we will be *pillars* of the *superstructure, built* on the *foundation* of a *materialistic argument*!'

'Nonsense!' exclaimed Alice, almost spilling her tea. 'Haven't you been watching? We left behind the Land of Fundamentals, not that we stayed there long. But, Mr Hatter, you sound to me like you've been once too often to Marx's Marshes. Oh, I hope we don't end up there like everyone else seems to do.' The Mad Hatter couldn't bear to see Alice wring her hands so, and besides he wanted some tea too, so he said patronizingly (hoping that 'He' wouldn't hear as well), 'There, there, there, Alice, I'm sure He knows what He is doing. I must agree with you though, we certainly are not in Kansas any more.'

'Not in Kansas any more!' shrieked ~~Alice~~ in alarm. 'That is not one of Lewis's metaphors. Oh no, what is happening to us!'

It was unfortunate that in the tussle some of the tea got spilt but the two occupants of the hot-air balloon soon settled down to their adventure again, the fracture in their discourse rippling quietly into the wind's stream. 'Here, would you like some too?' asked Dorothy rhetorically as she poured some tea into a saucer for Toto. Looking up again, she smoothed out the wrinkles in her frock and surveyed the new territory they were moving over. 'No,' she said to herself again, 'we certainly are not in Kansas any more.'

Foucault's discourse Foucault claims that in the beginning there is discourse. In *The Archaeology of Knowledge* (1969) he argues that discourse actually precedes the 'subject' (to use a term that avoids the assumptions of autonomy, rationality and freedom implicit in words like 'individual' or even 'person'), and thus constitutes the subject by making socially meaningful positions available to him, her or it. Foucault made explicit the rules of discourse and the unity of statements, however, he failed to link these discursive practices in their interplay with non-discursive practices such as institutions, political events, socio-economic processes and the human body.

It was in his next major work, *Discipline and Punish* (1975) that, according to a number of analysts (cf. Cousins and Hussain, 1984; Dreyfus and Rabinow, 1982; Smart, 1985), Foucault's work was radicalized to deal with themes of power and knowledge in the emergence of the human sciences and sexuality. The apparent difference in these two periods was related to the revolutionary events in France, 'May '68', in which the Communist Party was largely discredited in the eyes of workers and students. French intellectuals sought creative alternatives to the current philosophies of Marxism, existentialism, phenomenology and structuralism. Like Derrida, Foucault returned to Nietzsche for inspiration. From Nietzsche's will to power Derrida discovered the disguised use of metaphor as intrinsic to language, and Foucault discovered the link between power and knowledge.

Foucault divorced power from its locality in institutions like the state and claimed that it could be neither acquired nor seized like a commodity. Power was a strategy, not a possession of the dominant class or sovereign. Shifting from his former linguistic determinism, he claimed that relations producing power on micro and not macro levels were the ultimate principle of social reality. He describes his methodology and analytic work in *Discipline and Punish* (1975) and *The History of Sexuality: Volume 1* (1976) as a genealogy of difference. Instead of positing 'great men' and seminal events as the backbone of erudite historical knowledge, the genealogist focuses on local, complex, often illegitimate and disqualified knowledges, which reveal the contingencies that erudite historical knowledge later covers up with the evolutionary myth that progress is inevitable.

The *History of Sexuality: Volume 1* (1976) criticizes the repressive notion of power, the idea that oppressive social forces curtail some inner drive towards self-actualization. The traditional 'domination–repression' hypothesis neglects the positive and productive features of power. Against Freud's notion that society represses sexual drives, for example, the twentieth century has seen an explosion of discourses on the topic of human sexuality rather than, as would be posited by the repressive notion of power, fewer discourses. Thus power-knowledge are intimately connected: the exercise of power creates territories where knowledge may be found, it constructs and circulates 'apparatuses' of knowledge like methods of observation and control, procedures for documentation and surveillance;

knowledge, in turn, is never without discursive power – there is no objective 'scientific' truth as the discovery of atomic power has shown us, instead new networks of meaning come into existence/resistance in relation to existing discourse. A specific example of Foucault's thought:

> If sexuality was constituted as an area of investigation, this was only because relations of power had established it as a possible object; and conversely, if power was able to take it as a target, this was because techniques of knowledge and procedures of discourse were capable of investing it. Between techniques of knowledge and strategies of power, there is no exteriority, even if they have specific roles and are linked together on the basis of their difference (1976: 98).

It was Foucault's contention that analysis should be specific, not general; it should be linked to the particular rather than the spectacular. It is with this in mind that Derrida's and Foucault's thought will next be applied to a specific case bridging the (bipolar) gap between academic discourse and practical application. In a physical human being the interplay of power and knowledge is incarnated to construct both a subject of power and an object of knowledge.

Fugue in C 'Well, the grass is definitely not greener in the Emerald City,' said Dorothy in disgust as their balloon took flight again.

'Bye-bye Munchkins,' called the Tin Man cheerfully back to the citizens of Oz, who looked a bit like exploding popcorn beneath them now. He turned to the young girl beside him in the basket. 'Oh come on Dorothy, why so glum? You found out what you needed to know. Come on, be happy.' The Tin Man gingerly stepped over the *dog* and held out a velvet-gloved handful of daisies to the petulant child.

'Mind you don't step on Toto,' she snapped, but took the daisies anyway and began absent-mindedly to make a garland out of them. After a while she said to either the *hond* or the Tin Man, 'You don't understand at all. If the great wizard of Oz is not great or even a wizard but', she spat the words out, 'a scared little man, where does that leave us?' Both the *chien* and the Tin Man were confused so they scratched their heads in unison. 'I don't believe any more,' she said adamantly to herself and then scratched her head too, for she did not know what that meant – all she knew was that it felt good saying it. The *hund* looked at Dorothy and then at the Tin Man and then back at Dorothy again as she drew herself up to her full height and jutted out her chin. 'I don't believe in Him either!'

'Hush,' whispered the Lion, who had been cowering in the corner of the basket all this time. 'He may overhear you,' he cautioned.

The Tin Man looked apprehensively out of the basket onto the swirling sea far beneath them and then upwards towards the gathering clouds, 'Uh oh, it looks like we're in for a storm and I didn't bring my oil can along,' he said quietly.

And the Word became flesh and dwelt among us

Jacques Lacan (1968) came to the fore after the events in France of May
'68. People then were interested in Marcuse's notions of sexuality, desire
and forms of political self-expression, the links between Eros and civiliza-
tion (cf. Marcuse, 1955). Lacan's writing offered an analysis of the social
and linguistic construction of the subject by accepting no separation
between self and society, no reductionistic and prior biological-anatomical
basis that posited the 'body' before the 'language'. He undermined the
notion that the self (and sexuality) came before culture and language, and
investigated instead how discourses produces certain subjectivities.

Weaving this and Derrida's thought in with Foucault's idea of how the
human turns him or herself into a subject by techniques of power-
knowledge like sexual confessions and self-reflections we present a case
study: 'Innocent' (his own chosen pseudonym) is a nineteen-year-old
Afrikaans clerical worker, previously a successful student at a conservative
university, who decided to drop out for a year in order 'to sort my life
out'. Very worried about his 'excessive femininity' and previous desire to
'become a transsexual, but I don't have enough money' and 'what if I am
a failure as a woman', *Innocent* now self-labels 'homosexual'.

Foucault traces the modern category of the homosexual to Westphal's
article on 'contrary sexual sensations' in 1870, showing that whereas
previously '[t]he sodomite had been a temporary aberration; the homosexual was now a species' (1976: 43). This species was created by the very
psychological, psychiatric and medical discourses which had sought to
examine it in the first place, making mere acts of sodomy into a her-
maphrodism of the soul. Thus a new subjectivity was created, a new
possible identity within the discursive structures. The following extract
from a taped interview explores some implications of this discourse/
identity. 'Inn' stands for 'Innocent', the interviewee; 'Int' stands for the
interviewer.

Inn: Ya, I've become more aware of Christianity and stuff even though I have
not been practising that much, you know, I'm more aware. Well positively, it
showed me the right way and I know exactly what you have to do if you want
to go to heaven but negatively it's guilt, guilty not to.

Int: Ya there's quite a lot in that. I mean for saying yourself, you know, of
committing your life to the Lord and then, sort of, backsliding whatever and
falling, that whole thing and yet …

Inn: Like the reason for not reading my Bible tonight is because I know what
will be in there is the truth and so I want to avoid the truth for a while?

Int: Ya, well what I kind of found is, is, you place a lot of authority on it. You
know what I'm saying, you say that it doesn't matter what books say or what
other people say, this is what the truth is.

Inn: Ya.

Int: And what I am trying to find out is where does this conviction come that is truth within. Like it seems that your personal truth is that 'I'm gay' and this is saying, 'No, your truth is falsehood.'

Inn: Well, why I believe so strongly in it is because I have seen that the Lord is actually alive and that he is very much in touch, like speaking in tongues and people praying from things and they get it ... And, because I know this, I know that the Lord lives, that whatever he says must be true – that's why I believe in it so firmly. He is someone that exists, he is someone that is alive ... But actually through other people's lives I've seen that there is actually a God. My mother always says to me, '[Innocent], I don't know what it is with you because you know that there is a God and you are sort of like on the verge of committing, of committing yourself, but, but what is it?' And I say, 'I actually don't know, I don't know what's holding me back,' actually I know, I lie, it is my homosexuality because I am so like scared that when I become a full Christian I have to be straight because I can't say, 'I'm a Christian and I'm gay.' I realize that if I were to be a full Christian I would have to be straight and perhaps through the help of the Lord, whatever, I could become straight. But I'm just so, I'm too scared to take the risk.

Int: Because it will mean you dying basically?

Inn: Because, I mean, what happens, what happens if I, if I do become a full, a full Christian and still feel I am gay, then I am not really a Christian. I ... I ... I don't really understand ...

Int: A performance, a show?

Inn: Well perhaps I could become a Christian and not say I'm gay whatever but not marrying either, so that I don't have to have a heterosexual relationship.

Int: And ... [Interrupted]

Inn: But I can't do that because that would be like smearing it up – there's nothing there but just don't start scratching.

Int: Ya.

Inn: But actually if you scrape the butter away you are going to find something, it will be there the whole the time.

Int: Ya, no, especially if you push it down. So you kind of, you played a song yesterday called, 'I'm trapped' [both laugh] and said, 'this is my favourite song!' 'I'm just so confused, I'm trapped, I can't get out.' Is that how you feel because, from the way that you've been talking, it sounds like you really are trapped in believing the right way but not saying you're a Christian but your mother is and she is a very important part of your life as well. She's obviously praying for you as well, you know she is part of your whole desire to become straight. Your father's removed. Where do you sit? I was wondering if you could imagine anything, if you could ask God and he would give it and he would say, 'Fine, my child.'

Inn: To be a heterosexual.

A deconstruction of this text would reveal in the foundationalist framework 'one thing that sums it all up', a clash between the binary oppositions that make up fundamentalist Christian discourse, the statements (in a Foucauldian sense) of which could be arranged as follows (à la Derrida):

Good	Evil
God	Satan
Heaven	Hell
Truth	Falsehood
Heterosexual	Homosexual

Elsewhere in the interview Innocent had denied the biological/genetic theory of psychosexual orientation, asserting rather the influence of Satan as the cause of homosexuality. There is a clear contradiction between being 'good' and being 'homosexual', and an essentail crisis in Innocent being unable to situate himself positively with respect to both of them at the same time.

His discourse further reveals the following oppositions:

Full Gospel church	NG Kerk
Adult baptism	Infant baptism
Full Christian	Superficial Christian/backslider
Mother	Father

Innocent's father is an alcoholic, his mother is very devout. Their co-dependent relationship (his mother is dependent on his father's dependency on alcohol as that positions her as the 'stronger' partner and a martyr deserving attention at prayer meetings) illustrates Derrida's idea that the dominant term in the binary opposition relies on the subordinate term for meaning.

Derrida directs deconstruction towards metaphors, and one that will invert these oppositions is the 'smearing up'. 'Innocent' suggests a way out of this painful contradiction through satisfying his social circle and mother by becoming a Christian but not marrying, yet immediately disqualifies this 'solution' saying, 'But actually if you scrape the butter away you are going to find something, it will be there the whole time.' This metaphor presupposes some ground (perhaps bread or toast) over which his 'solution' of nominal heterosexuality is 'spread'. This seems to be saying that his ground, his authenticity, his 'truth', expressed in his anti-heterosexual homosexual discourse, is what is preventing him from becoming a 'full Christian'. This is the hidden discourse beneath the 'correct' discourse of Christian belief. Innocent's homosexuality serves as resistance to his mother's attempt to define him, and towards the dominant social definitions of masculinity in general. This embodies Foucault's notion that resistance exits wherever power occurs.

The underlying discourse of 'I'm really a homosexual' gives power to the dominant Christian discourse – it manifests in 'Innocent's failed bid

for autonomy', he is 'trapped' and 'confused', very intelligent yet suspend-
ing his studies until he can find his way again. Unable to plot a future, he
lives from moment to moment more than from day to day, and has begun
to rely on narcotics for 'escape'. Other people's testimonies of answered
prayer are internalized in a self-policing form of behaviour suggestive of
Foucault's (1975) account of Bentham's Panopticon. (The Panopticon was
an architecturally round prison in which the prisoners gradually monitored
their own behaviour because they never knew when they were being
watched from the central tower.)

Innocent's homosexual identity is thus not simply resistance, it is also
imprisonment. The intersection of the Christian discourses on goodness,
truthfulness and homosexuality is an empty set. Innocent cannot attain a
viable coherent subjectivity, he occupies a void of psychic pain, attempting
to extinguish himself through narcotics and possible suicide.

To complete this analysis homosexuality has to come under erasure. A
traditional psychoanalysis of Innocent would perhaps describe him as
evidencing ego-dystonic homosexuality or, in the latest DSM IV classification, a cognitive-behaviourist approach would define his problem as a
form of cognitive-dissonance. A post-structuralist analysis does not accept
this reification of homosexuality but looks at ~~homosexuality~~. In an interview regarding gay identity Foucault said:

> if identity becomes the problem of sexual existence and if people think that
> they have to 'uncover' their 'own identity,' and that their own identity has to
> become the law, the principle, the code of their existence; if the perennial
> question they ask is, 'Does this thing conform to my identity?' then, I think,
> they will turn back to a kind of ethics very close to the old heterosexual virility
> (Foucault, quoted by Gallagher and Wilson, 1987: 31).

Innocent's only experience of sexual behaviour with another male was a
failed attempt at fellatio. In his fantasies Innocent is totally passive, he
derives pleasure from giving pleasure and does not want to ejaculate thus
ruining the illusion: he is female. If Sartre is right, if '[t]he caress is not
a simple stroking, it is a shaping. In caressing the Other I cause her [sic]
flesh to be born beneath my caress, under my fingers ... Desire is
expressed by the caress as thought is by language' (quoted by Selkirk,
1988: 80), then what Innocent is saying/incarnating is, 'This is how I am
powerful. I can only know myself in relation to the hegemonic discourse.
I can only construct myself as a resistance.' Perhaps he has begun pre-
consciously to acknowledge that by naming himself Innocent, a term that
would subversively fit under the bipolar oppositions of Good/Evil as
innocent/guilty. Or perhaps he has begun to 'self'-destruct by answering
my final question in the segment without the sentence's subject: '[I want]
to be heterosexual'.

Serenade for Winds 'Hold on dearest, hold on,' shouted Tess against the wind.

Angel Clare attempted one more time to pull the balloon back down to the island but, although he was a hardy man, again it was to no avail. The basket with a lonesome Tess d'Urberville in it hovered too high above the ground for her to jump out. He shouted back to her over the storm, 'Jump, Tessy, I canna hold 'er any 'onger. I will catch you.'

'Oh Angel I canna, oh this happiness could not have lasted,' cried Tess.

'If I lose you I lose all,' replied Clare.

For one brief moment their eyes met and it was like before, then as the thunder crashed around the lovers, Tess let her side of the rope go. Slowly Angel and the island became a crimson patch on the sultry sea.

After a while the rain stopped and Tess wiped the tears from her eyes. Looking around the basket she found a daisy chain, scattered tea crockery and a stuffed dog. 'How odd,' she thought to herself as she picked a daisy from the chain. The sun was breaking through the clouds now and Tess thought dreamily of beautiful Liza-Lu again. Slowly she began to pick the petals off the flower: 'She loves me, she loves me not ...'

But we received him not

Once begun a voyage assumes a certain inevitability. To subvert that and the predictability of this academic paper you now have choice of multiple endings. Please choose and then turn to the number of your option:

1. The Marxist critique
2. The critical angle
3. The post-structuralist self-analysis
4. The balloon landed
5. The Monique Wittig invocation
6. The References (for the really brave)

*1. **The Marxist critique*** Post-structuralism is critical of Marxist thought. Foucault in particular emphasizes the historicity of Marx's analysis, preformed as it was by Ricardian economics. Against the inhibiting effect of general theories and a totalitarian view of ideology (as a false consciousness belonging to 'them' and truth as belonging to 'us'), Foucault leaves the Marxist with no one to blame and no powerful state to seize.

In its turn, Marxist critique of post-structuralism highlights some of the latter's weaknesses. Foucault's notion of power without a subject and the Panopticon as an anonymous centralization of internalized supervision undermines his own concept of the omnipresence of resistance, a underdeveloped theme in his later work. Thus Foucault appears to offer no encouragement for resistance or struggle, the revolution has failed and all that is left is token micro-revolts with enough media attention to warrant a space on the evening news.

Derrida's weakness is that he uses the system of 'truth' and 'logic' to demonstrate the truth of his own arguments against these – ironically he cuts off the branch he is sitting on. A Marxist critique would point out that this appears to support the status quo, become another form of bourgeois domination and, because his work is ahistorical and evasive of politics (there is no reference to Marxist thought), it is ultimately hostile to the Marxist dialectic. Instead of synthesis – a new idealized state – it posits a dissolution of the very dialectic itself: in Derrida's metaphor bourgeoisie/proletariat ultimately becomes ~~proletariat~~.

Ultimately, it is claimed by Marxists like Sarup (1988), the avant-gardes like Deleuze and Guattari offer no grand action, only advising the individual to let him or herself go against the grain of common sense. As a focused and materially based doctrine, Marxism is thus justified in saying that fascism and capitalism must be named and collectively fought against both in civil society and the state. However, I feel that post-structuralism's polite consignment of Marxist thought to the museum is something that needs to be noted: in a fractured and subject-less world culture perhaps the best critique is *cultural* (surreal art and protest theatre, for instance) rather than political game-playing.

2. The critical angle Critical theory might argue that social analysis works much like psychoanalysis. By showing what has been hidden, one can offer interpretations that can facilitate insight and thus bring about transformation. In the same way that psychoanalysis looks below the surface and uncovers hidden unconscious determinants in order to free us from them, so a critical examination of our assumptions about self and society can reveal unseen social forces that act on us. Foucault, Lacan and Derrida can help us understand these hidden relations between society, language and ourselves in a way that may provide us with wider reflexive space in which to exist, facilitating insight and transformation.

By providing Innocent with an understanding of his positioning within the historical discourses, we may be able to help him move beyond his trappedness. Instead of actualizing his discursive impossibility, his non-existence, through narcotics, denial, suicide, he may be able to use the contradictions within the discourses against each other to negotiate reflexively a viable space for himself.

3. The post-structuralist self-analysis Steele (1989: 223–37) borrows the proposition from Ricoeur 'that a person is like a text is metaphorically transitive because a text is also like a person' (1989: 227). He claims that consciousness and text have nearly identical structures as regards the schizons and fractures which reveal, 'unresolved but covered-over cultural and personal conflicts, distortions, repressions and omissions' (1989: 227). Under apparently objective language hides the subjective; under the sober and rational discourse emerges the poetic and playful, the propaganda of every text.

If I were to deconstruct my own text now it would take longer than this chapter to do and will only reveal/hide my continued unconscious issues. However, to return to the sane Mad Hatter's observation of the major metaphors in the text – the chapter is divided up with a paraphrased text from the Gospel of John; Foucault's geospatial metaphor is used – *territories* of knowledge rather than a foundation-based *building* of knowledge or a conflict-based *argument* in which one side is set up for a fall; and finally, we chose a whimsical poetry of literature characters, puns and musical innuendos to contrast and anticipate the academic discourse.

Highlighting these metaphors with their shadows, their antitheses that appear in the text, it would appear that we are preoccupied with the apparent contradiction between homosexuality and Christian theology. The text from John carrying tragic tones is ironized within the paradoxical/ incarnational womb of the essay – Innocent's dilemma, the central problem (for me) of post-structuralism being, 'How does discourse connect with non-discourse, the human body?' My emotional reaction to Innocent, my feelings of impotence at being unable to help him and a fear of yet another suicide, is trapped within the margins of the essay, in the literary character's crisis of faith in their author. Use of the geospatial metaphor fails me at precisely the weak point of my analysis: how is Innocent, the non-subject, ~~saved~~? How do I help him? I allude to Marxist foundationalism by positioning Innocent within words like 'hostile dialectic' and 'synthesis' and end the analysis with an unresolved 'maybe he will, maybe he won't' ambiguity myself.

In the end then, the reason why I have been devouring books, been physically ill and overly argumentative this last week or so is because the I that is not-I doesn't just want to understand intellectually a phenomenon like Innocent – I want somewhere (a geospatial metaphor) to express my frustration, rage and hope – and understanding is all post-structuralism can give me at the moment.

4. The balloon landed   The moon was bitter when the balloon landed. At first no one noticed and life continued on very much like before. But then slowly and gradually people realized that they didn't have faces any more, in fact they realized that they weren't people after all – they were electronic blips on a gigantic tv screen. No one was particularly worried about this state of affairs. No one was particularly worried, that is, until someone was foolish enough to point it out to them again. 'We are free, they *always* replied, 'at least we are free enough not to listen to what you have to say.'

As the programmes changed from documentaries on 'Do-it-yourself witch-burning' (recommended for all ages) and 'How to be come' (which was, thankfully, age-restricted) to the 'Closing thoughts for the day' (everyone really enjoyed that one, it made them feel safe somehow) no one realized that it was over. It really was the end. And the end wasn't that spectacular either – just a test pattern.

5. The Monique Wittig invocation

INVOCATION

There was a time when you were not a slave, remember that.
You say you have lost all recollection of it, remember ...
You say there are no words to describe it.
You say it does not exist.
But remember. Make an effort to remember.
Or, failing that, invent.

(Monique Wittig, quoted in Don Kilhefner, 1987: 123)

Note

With special thanks to everyone in the Honours Seminar in Critical Psychology, Rhodes University, 1989–93.

References

Cousins, M. and Hussain, A. (1984) *Michel Foucault*, Macmillan Education, Hampshire.

Derrida, J. (1973) *Speech and Phenomena, and Other Essays on Husserl's Theory of Signs*, Northwestern University Press, Evanston, IL.

Derrida, J. (1976) *Of Grammatology*, Johns Hopkins University Press, Baltimore, MD.

Derrida, J. (1981) *Writing and Difference*, Routledge & Kegan Paul, London.

Dreyfus, H. L. and Rabinow, P. (1982) *Michel Foucault, Beyond Structuralism and Hermeneutics*, University of Chicago, Sussex.

Foucault, M. (1969) *The Archaeology of Knowledge*, Tavistock, London.

Foucault, M. (1975) *Discipline and Punish: The Birth of the Prison*, Penguin, Harmondsworth.

Foucault, M. (1976) *The History of Sexuality: Volume 1: An Introduction*, Penguin Books, London.

Gallagher, B. and Wilson, A. (1987) 'Sex and the politics of identity, an interview with Michel Foucault', in M. Thompson (ed.), *Gay Spirit, Myth and Meaning*, New York, St. Martin's Press.

Kilhefner, D. (1987) 'Gay people at a critical crossroad, assimilation or affirmation?', in M. Thompson (ed.), *Gay Spirit, Myth and Meaning*, New York, St. Martin's Press.

Lacan, J. (1968) *The Language of the Self, the Function of Language in Psychoanalysis*, Johns Hopkins University Press, Baltimore, MD.

Marcuse, H. (1955) *Eros and Civilisation, A Philosophical Inquiry into Freud*, Beacon Press, Boston.

Sarup, M. (1988) *An Introductory Guide to Post-Structuralism and Postmodernism*, Harvester Wheatsheaf, Hemel Hempstead.

Selkirk, E. (1988) *Sex for Beginners*, Writers and Readers Publishing, New York.

Smart, B. (1985) *Michel Foucault*, Tavistock and Ellis Horwood, New York.

Steele, R. S. (1989) 'A critical hermeneutics for psychology, beyond positivism to an exploration of the textual unconscious', in D. Packer and M. Addison (eds), *Entering the Circle, Hermeneutic Investigation in Psychology*, State University of New York Press, Albany.

PART FOUR

Methodological and Political Reflections

CHAPTER 13

On political activism and discourse analysis in South Africa

Cheryl de la Rey

After participating in the first Discourse Analysis Workshop in South Africa, Erica Burman made the following observation: 'Fortunately the academics I met were appropriately suspicious about subsuming their politics within discourse analysis' (Burman, 1994: 481). But this comment is preceded by another observation that: 'As in Britain, discourse analysis is proving a useful vehicle for doing politically informed and useful research within South Africa' (Burman, 1994: 481). Does the latter not beg the question: if this approach is politically informed and useful, as suggested, then why are some of us 'suspicious', and how appropriate is this suspicion?

This chapter is about some of the 'suspicions' or questions that I pondered while listening to the various presentations in the workshop. In short, most of my reflections are encapsulated in the more general question suggested by Burman, namely, is discourse analysis an appropriate tool for South African researchers who aim to conduct studies that are both politically informed and useful? Before I attempt to explore this question in any direct way, I will briefly sketch the political context in which I locate this discussion.

Politics and psychological research in South Africa

The question of what is 'politically informed and useful research' has been debated in some depth in the recent history of South African psychology. This has frequently been talked about as 'the relevance debate'. The course of this debate about how psychology could become more relevant brought to the fore the historical role of psychology in supporting and maintaining the apartheid system of oppression. In January 1994 at the Psychology and Transformation Conference this culminated in a public acknowledgement by the president of the now defunct Psychological Association of South Africa (PASA) of the collusion of psychology with apartheid. Consequently, the image of psychology in South Africa as apolitical has been firmly debunked.

Thus, it would seem that several South African academics would have no qualms about rejecting the central assumptions of positivism, specifically the assumption of the political neutrality of scientific knowledge. This, then, should fit comfortably with the assumptions behind qualitative methods such as discourse analysis. In his introduction to the book *Knowledge and Power in South Africa*, the editor, Jonathan Jansen, pointed out that an underlying basis for a growing discontent within academic disciplines was the notion that the 'formation, content and methods of disciplines are profoundly political events' (1991: 3).

The acknowledgement of the political nature of psychology led to an ongoing discussion amongst some psychologists about the need to develop a liberatory psychology. In 1990 the Apartheid and the Crisis in Psychology Conference at the University of the Western Cape dealt with this question in some depth. But what is a liberatory psychology?

Liberatory psychology

The writings of Hussain Bulhan were influential in the discussions that grappled with definitions of a liberatory psychology for South Africa. Bulhan (1993: 28) argued that 'scientific African psychology embraces its revolutionary task of not only interpreting the African world but of *changing* it'. The imperative for psychology not only to interpret society but also to change it was explicitly stated by Saths Cooper in an earlier publication: 'To be a psychologist and a political activist in the public good ... seems to be what a new South Africa will require' (1990: 64).

The view that the research should both advance the status of knowledge and bring about transformation within a social system of oppression was first espoused by Stavenhagen (1971). The contemporary significance of this argument is evident in that it has recently been reprinted as the opening chapter in a section on the politics of research in the book *Social Research: Philosophy, Politics and Practice* (Hammersley, 1993). Here it is argued that the researcher should conduct research in ways that combine political and research activities so that there will be a joint furthering of knowledge and a contribution to change in favour of the powerless within any society.

Such a notion of 'knowledge for liberation' gave many academic activists the opportunity to align their broader political engagement with formal academic pursuits, and it is within this critical-emancipatory framework that many politically active psychologists subsumed their work. Hence, a question to be considered is: how does the more recent interest in discourse analysis resonate with this political context?

On politics and discourse analysis

Discourse analysis can be firmly placed within the framework of qualitative methodology. Henwood and Pidgeon (1994) identified three epistemological strands within qualitative methodology: empiricism, contextualism and constructivism. The first strand acknowledges the gains offered in employing qualitative methods, but maintains a concern for empirical notions of reliability and validity. The defining feature of the second strand is identified as the construction of intersubjective meanings. Discourse analysis is presented as the exemplar of the third strand, constructivism. Henwood and Pidgeon (ibid.: 233) argue that discourse analysis 'breaks most completely and explicitly with the empirical model'.

At the most general level the break may be marked by the explicit acknowledgement that politics is at the centre of social research. But the break is not merely a matter of method, but also one of epistemological position (assumptions about the bases for knowledge). Parker (1994: 92) spells it out: 'Discourse analysis treats the social world as a text, or rather as a system of texts.' Here lies the pith of the debate: is a discursively constructed world congruent with the critical-emancipatory aims of many politically active South African psychologists?

An observation by Hennessy (1993: 5), although made in relation to feminism, is germane here, namely that: 'taking a system of knowledge and putting it at the service of some other project', like liberation, 'means confronting the materiality of that system.' Some researchers would have problems with the privileged position given to discourses over other material constraints on action. As Parker (1992) has noted, discourse analysis may be seen by some as a means for academics to dodge the material basis of oppression. Perhaps this is the primary source of suspicion voiced by some South African psychologists whose politics favour materialist epistemologies (Whittaker, 1991, is an example). Potter and Wetherell (1987: 180) in addressing this very criticism remarked that discussions about contrasts between the material world and language open what they termed 'a veritable snake-pit of philosophical and political issues'.

Notwithstanding the significance of the philosophical issues, in South Africa – where the most pressing social problems have been identified as access to housing, water and jobs – an emphasis on discourse in the research done by psychologists may seem politically inappropriate. Holding on to a distinction between physical reality and meaning may well be politically necessary. Further debates among South African psychologists on the question of how language is related to the social may, perhaps, be a key to exploring the political usefulness of discourse analysis.

However, Parker (1992: 21) proposes that a focus on discourse may be 'part of the cure'. The potential political impact of discourse analysis is tied to the three auxiliary criteria that he proposes for research. These additional criteria for discourse methodology support the necessity of going beyond description to include an analysis of the role discourses play in the life of institutions, power and the transmission of ideology. The political usefulness of the methodology in South Africa may rest on this. Hence, when the researcher analyses a text dominant conceptions are revealed, taken-for-granted meanings are disrupted and the ways in which these discourses support or challenge institutions and the distribution of power in a society may be exposed. Particularly useful are the suggestions that discourse analysts should identify categories of persons who would gain and lose from the use of the discourse.

This extension of the steps of discourse analysis fits well with the outlines proposed by Nkomo (1991) for a post-apartheid epistemology that would reconceptualize the knowledge-power relation. In a chapter on epistemological and disciplinary transformations for a post-apartheid South Africa, Nkomo (1991: 310) appealed for an epistemology that would permit the disruption of 'the obscene falsehoods, ignorance and bigotry of the past'. The use of discourse analysis could draw attention to the politicized nature of what has often been taken as the norm or has been invisible.

Parker makes a further point of particular significance to South Africans in this transitional period in the history of our society. Since April 1994, when the first-ever democratically elected government took office, all spheres of South African society have been caught up in a process of rapid change. 'When progress and change are notions built into contemporary political discourse, and things are changing so fast, it is hardly surprising that this dynamic should be reflected in our everyday experience of language' (Parker, 1992: 22). The dynamic referred to here is that between history and the contemporary political discourse. Showing the contradictions is important when in times of change one discourse takes over from another. Discourse analysis may be usefully employed to draw attention to the direction in which history is being pushed and whose interests are being served.

Democracy and power in the research process

One of the consequences of taking a critical-emancipatory stance is that it compels reflection on how knowledge systems and the processes surrounding knowledge production may be supportive of privilege, including our own as researchers (Hennessy, 1993). Whether discourse analysis contributes to the goal of producing knowledge for liberation in South Africa depends on two further criteria: first, how power is dealt with in the research process, and second, the dissemination of the knowledge produced through research.

The issue of power relations between the researcher and the researched is crucial in the South African context given the demographics of academics in the country. Within psychology, for example, most of the research that has been published has been authored by white males. Little has changed since Seedat (1990) published an analysis of trends and silences in South African psychology which showed a marginalization of black males and women. Levett and Kottler (in press) confirm that the bias against women and women's issues in psychology has continued without much interruption. What does this mean for knowledge production?

It is within feminist politics in South Africa that the issue of differences in identity between the researcher and the researched has been most fiercely debated. This debate first became public at the Women and Gender In Southern Africa Conference in Durban in January 1991. Francie Lund, a social science researcher, made the following observation: 'The legacy of gendered apartheid – where gender, race and class intersect – was addressed in many of the papers; the same legacy was played out on the Conference floor. We were all trapped in different languages' (1991: 20). One of the issues that angered black women was the observation that most of the papers were researched accounts of the lives of black women analysed by white women, thus rendering black women the objects of study under the gaze of white privilege. The subsequent debate among feminist researchers pivoted on the question of the political and methodological validity of having researchers situated in a position of socio-political privilege analyse the lives of the oppressed.

This debate has particular relevance for discourse analysis as a method. There seems to be an assumption inherent in the process of analysing a text that the psychologist as researcher controls the bag of tricks. The researcher seems to act as a magician with powers to reveal what really lays hidden in the text. What are the implications for using this method in a country like South Africa, where most researchers are English-speaking in a multilingual population, not to mention the skewed demography of researchers as a group as mentioned earlier? Reicher (1994) has argued that it is important that we theorize our own position in the research process. Too often the positioning of the researcher is reduced to the acknowledgement of an identity – for example, owning a label such as white, middle-class and male. This is much too simplistic for, as Hennessy (1993) points out, the relationship between identities and social analytics is a complex one.

The issue of the positioning of the researcher is implicated in the notion of reflexivity. Reflexivity is of central importance in qualitative methodology, and discourse analysis in particular takes account of the reflexive character of research. But as Henwood and Pidgeon point out (1994: 24–25), the 'term 'reflexivity' is, of course, a complex one and has, over the years, acquired many and varied usages. In most applications of discourse analysis reflexivity refers to how talk is understood. Talk is understood not merely as description but as also formulating the nature of the action and situation (Potter and Wetherell, 1987). The dilemmas raised by Parker (1992) are most instructive for South African researchers wanting to use this method. First, he points out that a single conception of reflexivity is insufficient. Second, he argues that in order to determine how to use the notion of reflexivity, we need other criteria, and here he specifically points to the need for a moral position and a political position. In the South African context it is important that researchers place the reflexive focus on both the researcher and the participant; no matter what the method, we need to be conscious of our own positioning in relation to the researched and the social and political context in which the research occurs.

But, once we acknowledge that the researcher's account of other people's language is itself constructed, we are then free to examine the consequences of the researcher's discursive organization. The implications of this are significant when one considers that here is a method that does not hold itself up as 'scientific fact' above the scrutiny of the public gaze. This can make an impact on the potential for research to meet the criteria of democracy, empowerment and accountability that have frequently been argued for in relation to the research process in recent writings about social research. One example is the reference made by Nkomo (1991: 313) to a democratic epistemology. He argues that democracy should inform 'all practices in all sites'. But this call to democratize knowledge is not exclusively South African, since Wetherell (1994: 306), in commenting on a paper by Smith (1994), also refers to 'a powerful pull to democratize the research process'. The paper by Smith argues for the possibility of respondents becoming co-researchers where the process of interpretation becomes one of negotiation. This is, however, not always possible, for as Beall (1991) points out, participatory and consultative approaches are not feasible within all research methodologies and this should not render them illegitimate a priori. In commenting on the idea of co-research, Wetherell correctly points out that research always involves an 'appropriation of the other', since it is the researcher who directly benefits, publishing articles, presenting papers, etc.

Politics is not simply a matter of method

We may take cognizance of Reicher's (1994: 303) observation that: 'It is probably wrong to think that issues of politics in psychology can be resolved on a methodological level.' Indeed, several of the proponents of discourse analysis have agreed that there is no method that may be inherently progressive (Burman and Parker, 1993; Wetherell, 1994). Rather they adopt a pragmatic view that the political impact of research depends on how it is taken up in specific contexts. Reicher favours the view that if research is to be liberatory it should be undertaken in terms as defined by 'organizations of the oppressed'. This seems to locate liberatory research rather narrowly, especially when we consider that many of the oppressed are not organized into readily accessible social groups as he implies.

While there may not be any method that is in itself politically progressive, this does not mean that the choice of method is simply a technical issue. Griffin and Phoenix (1994) have drawn our attention to the politics of choosing a research method. Politics can be seen not only in the choices surrounding theory and method, but also in the crucial question of how the knowledge is disseminated and used. In this transitional period in South African history where we have a government of national unity, a key focus has been on the development of social policies to replace the apartheid policies of the past. Indeed, many psychologists who have had a history of political activism have turned to policy-relevant research but still within an emancipatory agenda.

As a qualitative method, there may be limitations to the use of discourse analysis in policy-relevant research studies. Finch (1986) and Griffin and Phoenix (1994) have pointed to difficulties in trying to convince authorities to take qualitative research seriously. Finch (1986) has argued that quantitative data provided by social researchers have been politically useful to governments in providing them with the 'facts' necessary for the management of industrialized societies. In South Africa the Human Sciences Research Council conducted numerous quantitative studies, which were either released or kept secret depending on whether the findings supported the apartheid policies of the white minority government (see Louw and Foster, 1991). As Finch argues, quantitative methods with an emphasis on objectivity and statistics derived from classifying people fitted more comfortably than qualitative data with the demand by policy-makers for 'facts' that could be controlled and manipulated. This conception of research based within a quantitative paradigm has become the dominant and acceptable form of research amongst policy-makers and laypeople alike. Thus researchers who use qualitative methods have difficulties in obtaining credibility for their work, and this ultimately limits its potential political impact. Whether research derived from qualitative methods becomes politically useful in the policy-making arena of contemporary South Africa to a large extent depends on whether 'those who use research have a more sophisticated awareness of the nature of social science knowledge than that which supported the dominant tradition' (Finch, 1986: 226).

The accessibility of research findings to the general population has been of concern, especially amongst South African feminists. One of the lines of division at the Women and Gender in Southern Africa Conference alluded to earlier was the division between academics and activists. There was an angry complaint from the activists that the research was generally incomprehensible. We need to be aware that research can be seen as disempowering if we understand disempowerment to include not understanding and being excluded from knowledge (Beall, 1991). If discourse analysis is to have an impact beyond the intellectual-academic sphere, there is a need to make it available in a more accessible form free from the mystification of jargon, so that it is not experienced as disempowering.

Conclusion

Ultimately, the political usefulness of discourse analysis to political activists may be in its potential to go beneath the surface, to disrupt what may seen as taken for granted and natural, to reveal contradictions and to show connections between that which may seem distinct. But it is important to note that political usefulness is not simply a matter of which method, rather it is about the entire process of doing research, for as Warwick (1993: 315) noted: 'Politics in one form or another impinges on a study from the initial choice of topic to the final interpretations made of the results.' To this may be added that politics may also decide whether research is undertaken or not, who becomes the researcher and the researched and what becomes of the findings.

References

Beall, J. (1991) 'Thinking aloud on differences amongst women: the case of researchers and activists in South Africa', paper presented at the Conference on Women on the Frontline, North Western University, Chicago, IL.

Bulhan, H. A. (1993) 'Imperialism in studies of the psyche: a critique of African psychological research', in L. Nicholas (ed.), *Psychology and Oppression: Critiques and Proposals*, Skotaville, Johannesburg.

Burman, E. (1994) 'Transforming psychology in South Africa', *Feminism and Psychology*, 4 (3), 479–82.

Burman, E. and Parker, I. (eds) (1993) *Discourse Analytic Research: Repertoires and Readings of Texts In Action*, Routledge, London.

Cooper, S. (1990) 'Social control or social empowerment? The psychologist as political activist', in L. J. Nicholas and S. Cooper (eds), *Psychology and Apartheid: Essays on the Struggle for Psychology and the Mind in South Africa*, Vision/Madiba, Johannesburg.

Finch, J. (1986) *Research and Policy: The Uses of Qualitative Methods In Social and Educational Research*, Falmer Press, London.

Griffin, C. and Phoenix, A. (1994) 'The relationship between qualitative and quantitative research: lessons from feminist psychology', *Journal of Community and Applied Social Psychology*, 4, 287–98.

Hammersley, M. (ed.) (1993) *Social Research: Philosophy, Politics and Practice*, Sage, London.

Hennessy, R. (1993) *Materialist Feminism and the Politics of Discourse*, Routledge, London.

Henwood, K. and Pidgeon, N. (1994) 'Beyond the qualitative paradigm: a framework for introducing diversity within qualitative psychology', *Journal of Community and Applied Social Psychology*, 4, 225–38.

Jansen, J. D. (1991) 'Knowledge and power in South Africa: an overview and orientation', in J. D. Jansen (ed.), *Knowledge and Power in South Africa: Critical Perspectives Across the Disciplines*, Skotaville, Johannesburg.

Levett, A. and Kottler, A. (in press) '"She's not a feminist!": through a lens, darkly', in E. Burman (ed.), *Deconstructing Feminist Psychology*, Sage, London.

Louw, J. and Foster, D. (1991) 'Historical perspective: psychology and group relations in South Africa', in D. Foster and J. Louw-Potgieter (eds), *Social Psychology in South Africa*, Lexicon, Johannesburg.

Lund, F. (1991) 'Impressions of a conference on women and gender in Southern Africa', *Agenda: A Journal about Women and Gender*, 9, 20–3.

Nkomo, N. (1991) 'Epistemological and disciplinary transformations in a post-apartheid South Africa', in J. D. Jansen (ed.), *Knowledge and Power in South Africa: Critical Perspectives Across the Disciplines*, Skotaville, Johannesburg.

Parker, I. (1992) *Discourse Dynamics: Critical Analysis for Social and Individual Psychology*, Routledge, London.

Parker, I. (1994) 'Discourse analysis', in P. Banister, E. Burman, I. Parker, M. Taylor and C. Tindall, *Qualitative Methods in Psychology*, Open University Press, Buckingham.

Potter, J. and Wetherell, M. (1987) *Discourse and Social Psychology: Beyond Attitudes and Behaviour*, Sage, London.

Reicher, S. (1994) 'Particular methods and general assumptions', *Journal of Community and Applied Social Psychology*, 4, 299–303.

Seedat, M. (1990) 'Programmes, trends, and silences in South African psychology 1983–1988', in L. J. Nicholas and S. Cooper (eds), *Psychology and Apartheid: Essays on the Struggle for Psychology and the Mind in South Africa*, Vision/Madiba, Johannesburg.

Smith, J. A. (1994) 'Towards reflexive practice: engaging participants as co-researchers or co-analysts in psychological inquiry', *Journal of Community and Applied Social Psychology*, 4, 253–60.

Stavenhagen, R. (1971) 'Decolonializing applied social sciences', in M. Hammersley (ed.), (1993) *Social Research: Philosophy, Politics and Practice*, Sage, London.

Warwick, D. P. (1993) 'On methodological integration in social research', in M. Blumer and D. P. Warwick (eds), *Social Research in Developing Countries: Surveys and Censuses in the Third World*, UCL Press, London.

Wetherell, M. (1994) 'The knots of power and negotiation, blank and complex subjectivities', *Journal of Community and Applied Social Psychology*, 4, 305–8.

Whittaker, S. (1991) 'A critical historical perspective on psychology in Azania/South Africa', in J. D. Jansen (ed.), *Knowledge and Power in South Africa: Critical Perspectives Across the Disciplines*, Skotaville, Johannesburg.

CHAPTER 14

On discourse, power, culture and change

*Ian Parker, Ann Levett, Amanda Kottler
and Erica Burman*

Look back over this book and you will find a variety of texts being read
with a critical eye and a variety of different theoretical frameworks being
brought to bear on discourse to draw out patterns of meaning and power.
Newspaper reports, television advertisements, magazine advice columns,
audio-taped interviews and group discussions as well as professional policy
documents each specify how power should be distributed, and the language
that is used in these texts sets up positions for their readers. In everyday
life these texts set out positions that can have devastating practical effects
on peoples' lives. We have been concerned with patterns of language in
this book not because we think those patterns are more important than
'real' political processes, but precisely because language locks people into
place as it encourages them to think about themselves in certain ways and
to place them in particular relations of power. But our contributors have
also been readers of these texts, and now you are readers too, so it is time
to step back and look at how relations of power are distributed in the
research process and how methods in social research connect with politics.

Methods, strategies and tactics in research

One way of describing what has been done in this book is to say that
discourse analysis has been applied to texts, but there is a paradox at work
here. Even though researchers, students and teachers of discursive approaches have to set out a method, there is really no method as such,
there is no one thing called discourse analysis. Discourse analysis is not
a set of methodological techniques that only carefully trained experts
understand and are able to use, and that can be taken out of the cupboard
and applied to each and every text. If discourse analysis is treated in this
way, then it will end up being just as mystifying as other varieties of
psychology that masquerade as 'science'. The contribution by de la Rey in
Chapter 13 makes clear what some of the stakes are in relation to political
activism in South Africa. Our contributors have displayed a sensitivity to
language that is as flexible and contradictory as discourse itself. They have

moved backward and forward through the texts drawing attention to rhetorical devices, semantic patterns and ways in which ideological forms are reproduced. Each of the methodological directions signalled in Part Three of the book is tied to a number of theoretical and political agendas, and it is these agendas that bring out what is important in language as a social process.

Even the most extreme journey through postmodern views of language in Collins and Mulder's Chapter 12 carries with it a commitment to change, however 'innocent' it at first seems. Their trip to Utopia breaks with conventional ways of writing psychological reports or accounts of discourse analysis, and this allows them all the more effectively to draw our attention to the ways in which texts construct alternative realities, and the work of 'post-structuralist' writers. Rather than simply *describing* what Derrida says about concepts, they are able to *display* the way a Derridean deconstruction of concepts works. Rather than simply telling us that sexuality is constructed out of dominant discursive forms in particular cultural contexts, they draw us as readers into their 'fictional' text and force us to think with them about the predicament of 'Innocent'. We are then invited to think about which theoretical frames may be useful to make sense of what is going on.

We invite readers to think about whether they want to tell the straight-forward 'realist' tale if they carry out their own discourse analytic studies, or whether they would want to be more playful and, in the process, open up the way psychology as a discipline usually frames issues as if they were simply collections of facts. Although Kelly and Van Vlaenderen's Chapter 11 looks more 'down to earth', the same critical spirit is at work in their unravelling of the way in which participants understand their place in the community health development project. A quite different set of theoretical resources is brought to bear on the various ways in which 'self' and 'other' was constructed in 'modes' of experience. Most of the chapters in this book draw upon the work of Foucault and the broad French post-structuralist tradition, but Kelly and Van Vlaenderen bring in the work of Habermas and the German critical phenomenological school of work to look at dialogue. Conflicts of interpretation are thus opened out in such a way that it is possible to show what consequences there are for the way people can understand their participation.

Psychologists have been drawn into discourse analysis for a variety of reasons. Post-structuralist writing can help us tear out of the strait-jacket of 'scientific' report-writing in psychology, as Collins and Mulder illustrate. The Habermasian tradition shows how people make meaning, and how they must make it in conditions that are not of their own choosing, as Kelly and Van Vlaenderen demonstrate. Terre Blanche's Chapter 10 draws our attention to the ways in which the organization of discourse can help place people in strait-jackets, and the ways in which the meanings they give to their lives are invalidated by professional power. The role of language in the construction of 'psychopathology' is, then, another urgent reason why critical psychologists have been concerned with discourse. But Terre Blanche takes this a step further to force us to reflect on what we are doing as professional 'discourse analysts', and his chapter steps back from discourse analysis to locate it in institutional context. The meta-reflection on the discourse of discourse in his chapter is connected to the project of grounding analysis in the 'conditions of possibility' for texts, in the powers they hold for readers, *and* in the ways in which we try to make sense of those texts and powers from our own positions.

There is a powerful process of 'translation' in discourse analysis, in which an issue that is framed in a certain way in a text is abstracted and repositioned by us, as analysts, in our own text (the psychological report, the journal article, or the book chapter). In South Africa discourse analysis has been taken up and developed in the English language, but English is the first language of a *minority* of the population, and a serious engagement with processes of culture and power demands that there should be an attention to a variety of linguistic resources that people draw upon to make sense of themselves and others. There is a crucial theoretical and methodological issue here to do with how we understand and access the different ways in which social relationships and everyday 'psychology' are constructed in different language systems. The question of 'translation' in discourse in Levett et al.'s Chapter 9 is rooted in positions of power that an analyst enjoys and in the struggle to make meaning, to achieve an intersubjective understanding that might be illuminating and empowering.

To talk of methodological 'innovations' and 'directions' may make it seem as if there are clear ways forward, as if there were technical solutions for what are really complicated political problems. Our contributors raise questions that studies of discourse should address rather than posing answers and closing off possibilities for reinterpreting 'data' or reinterpret-ing the role of discourse analysis in a culture: 'Do we want to treat things that are constructed in language as if they were facts or are they *fictions*?', 'Do we want to arrive at one best account of what is happening or lay open a variety of positions that people adopt?', 'Do we want a method that claims to say all there is to say, or ways of reading that let us say more?', and 'Do we want to translate texts into a language that pretends to be neutral, or acknowledge translation of all kinds as a process suffused with power?'

Identity and subjectivity

Critical discourse work on child abuse, psychiatric labelling and community health is, of course, always already practical and political. We have a strong focus in this book on the *varieties* of power that operate in the politically charged culture that was an apartheid regime and is now 'new' South Africa. The book speaks from a context in which power is *always* an issue to discourse analysts in parts of the world where it is possible to pretend that power is an optional issue that they may choose to study or not, as they wish. Some forms of discourse analysis have wanted to take on board feminism precisely because it attends to the differentiation of gender and sexuality and to the ways in which oppression and resistance are constituted and challenged in the way men and women speak. We represented this aspect of discourse research in Part Two of the book. Feminism is always already sensitive to language, and it helps us to keep in mind the way power operates through 'dividing practices'.

Strebel's Chapter 8, for example, develops an analysis that connects what is ostensibly a medical issue with questions of gender and race. Only by attending to the way that AIDS functions in a specific cultural context and is cross-cut with sexual and cultural privilege is it possible to understand how AIDS 'prevention' might work, and to facilitate reflection on what hinders it. We want to emphasize the way in which cultural context frames the way in which what has now come to be a universal problem is understood. But we also want to make clear in this book the way that the *specificity* of accounts need to be respected. Strebel's contribution is powerful because it locates the talk about a medical problem in *cultural* context, while Foress Bennett's Chapter 7 is powerful because it locates a reading in *personal–political* context. These should be seen as but two sides of the same coin. Personal–political reflections on abuse are, at the same time, reflections within a particular culture. Foress Bennett homes in on a single account, and develops a detailed reading of the testimony of a rape survivor to show how the 'reality' of the event is constructed. Some varieties of discourse analysis that pretend to be 'apolitical' can tempt psychologists to think that a close detailed reading of a text must dispense with wider cultural issues. Foress Bennett's chapter gives the lie to that in its way of reading, which is as detailed as could be *and* thoroughly political.

Identities can also be challenged and subjectivities reworked by discourse analysts who come to a topic with a political and theoretical agenda. Blumberg and Soal in Chapter 6 open up one of the fault-lines in contemporary dividing practices that encourage people to identify as either heterosexual or homosexual. Lesbian and gay identities have been important sites of resistance to hetero-normative classification and regulation of men and women in psychology for many years. What heterosexual dominance also succeeds in doing, though, is reproducing itself as a normal category *and* reproducing the homosexual as the 'other'. Similar strategies of 'othering' are at work in the racial classification systems that many psychologists under apartheid colluded in. Under apartheid, the subject was classified as either 'white', or an 'other'. To be 'black' was to take on an identity that was given by racist classification practices *and* to assert an identity against apartheid. 'New' South Africa now opens the possibility for such an assertion of identity *and* for a challenge to racial dividing practices that say you must be 'this' or 'that'. Blumberg and Soal show how this othering, transgression of boundaries and reinstatement of categories are played out when 'bisexuals' refuse normative categories of heterosexual or homosexual.

We described, in Chapter 1, how discourse not only creates identity categories but also incites subjects within them to reach into themselves and 'confess' the truth of the category. Wilbraham's Chapter 5 takes this idea up with an analysis of the way advice columns constitute certain social relationships and force the subjects of those relationships to feel themselves as deeply and truly wedded to them. While Blumberg and Soal look at how talk about sexuality is regulated as people try to make something different of themselves, Wilbraham traces the contours of the heterosexual relationships that are produced and policed in the texts that people read when they feel troubled. Those networks of discipline and confession that hold heterosexuality in place have to be understood if anything like an adequate analysis of power in a culture like South Africa is to be arrived at.

Power, resistance and transformation

Now we come back to Part One of the book. Discourse analysis in South Africa has so many lessons for researchers into texts in other parts of the world not only because the connection between language and power is so overt, but also because that connection was challenged and troubled during the years of political upheaval that culminated in the destruction of apartheid. That challenging and troubling work continues, of course, and Kottler and Long's Chapter 4 is concerned with one arena where that is happening. Discourse analysis is concerned with the role of interpretation in the closing and opening of gaps between our language and the world, but Kottler and Long show that the process of interpreting and agreeing on what is happening in language and institutional practice is not simple. Their chapter brings the methodological questions we raised above into sharp focus as people try to reflect upon what they do, how they speak and how they may change. Those discourse analysts who believe that the world would be different if we simply spoke about things differently will have a tough time with Kottler and Long's analysis, for they are concerned with the ways in which speaking is intermeshed with institutional power, and how alternative ways of speaking carry big costs.

The discourses of 'transformation' in South Africa reinterpret and reframe challenges to racism oft-times in ways that will legitimate the positions of those in power. Durrheim's Chapter 3 provides a striking analysis of how this is accomplished with reference to talk of violence and 'peace'. Foucault's account of discipline and confession in discourse is often used to highlight the ways in which sex and sexuality become the deep defining markers of identity and subjectivity, but Durrheim shows how Foucauldian concepts can illuminate the way this marking of identity happens in political discourse. The contributors to this book have each, in various ways, struggled against racism and sexual oppression and for transformation and peace in South Africa. What discourse analysis can do is help us to reflect upon the discursive conditions of possibility for that struggle and the ways in which ways of speaking against *and* for peace are part of subtle processes of surveillance and subjectification.

Discourse analysis in this book is part of the critique of apartheid and also a way of understanding what cultural resources we may construct a critical position from. Dixon's Chapter 2 provides a reading of white community responses to 'squatting' by black people which locates discourse in structures and spaces of physical division and regulation. Racists and 'normal' people are having to learn to speak different discourses in the 'new' South Africa, but we can see very clearly from Dixon's account that language functions within specific regimes of knowledge that define how the well-meaning resident understands themself and 'others', and how the 'rights' of individuals can be spoken of in a political context that is still charged with racism. Discourse analysis here is also necessarily an analysis of systems of privilege, and of the way language is used to obscure racism at the same time as it functions to reproduce it.

Discourse analysis in South Africa developed because there was an urgent pressing need to understand what language was *doing* in culture. The theoretical resources that we describe in Chapter 1, and which are elaborated by the contributors, were seized upon because they would be useful to understand and challenge the racist regime of truth that was apartheid and the many other regimes of truth around sex and sexuality that locked people into place under apartheid. These theoretical resources were imported despite the best efforts, it should be said, of radical academics outside South Africa who were determined that the academic boycott should not be broken. The Discourse Analysis workshop in 1994 at the University of Cape Town where the papers that make up this book were presented and discussed was thus one of the first forums for critical psychologists from outside South Africa to meet colleagues from inside the country. Only a few days before that meeting the Psychological Association of South Africa – which had been complicit with the apartheid state – had been formally dissolved, and a new Psychological Society of South Africa founded at a conference at the University of the Western Cape.

Those momentous changes in the structure of academic and profession-al psychology were but a tiny reflection of the debate and turmoil as apartheid crumbled and the dispossessed spoke. There are still deep enduring patterns of legal and economic inequality in this country of 42 million people. Five per cent of the mainly white population controlled 88 per cent of the wealth under apartheid, and 45 per cent of the overwhelmingly black population existed below the agreed minimum living level. The end of apartheid has seen the rapid growth of a black middle class, and the white-controlled multinational companies that have rushed in since the elections have been keen to encourage and co-opt a black professional elite. The stark continuing disparity of wealth and opportunity between white and black as the country become rearticulated with capitalism on a global scale also serves sometimes to obscure the misery of other minority communities, and of women in all groups subject to racism. Through the conference and the discourse workshop there was much discussion of the real conditions within which discourse operates, and this discussion is reflected in the chapters in this book. It would be most peculiar if this were not the case, for South Africa functioned as a society based on brute coercion as well as ideological mystification. The physical organization of space affects and constrains the ways language 'constructs' the social world. This was once at the absurd level of the garage owner in the Eastern Cape who built eight separate toilets for males and females of different 'racial' groups to ensure that any possible mixing was prevented, or it still will be at the level of the black poor in the huge township of Khayalitsha on the outskirts of Cape Town who cannot hope to enter paid work or higher education, let alone debate the niceties of discourse analysis. The progress made since the elections has been slow, hopeful in some areas of education and welfare, but painfully incomplete.

There is understandable exasperation and impatience here with the studied 'relativism' of discourse analysis carried out in the more comfortable parts of the white world. This book is testimony to varieties of discourse work that are critical and committed. In these circumstances, and not only here we hope, the study of discourse should only ever be understood and addressed as being in the context of the reproduction of power or of increasing the possibilities of social change.

Index

Abrahams, D., 111
abuse, 146, 201; child sexual, 125–30,
  132, 135–6, 200; historical, 97;
  sexual, 4, 11–12, 118
accountability, 4
activism, political, 9, 198
Addison, R. B., 163
'addressor', 68
Adorno, Theodor, 28
advertising, 198; ideological, 36–8
advice columns, 65–80, 198, 202
Africa, negative images of, 38
African National Congress (ANC), 34;
  Women's League, 119
'Africanization', 6
Afrikaans, language, 130–1
Afrikaner Resistance Movement, 41
agendas, power of structuring, 51
AIDS, 12, 79, 109, 111–13, 201; action,
  116; cultural agenda, 117; dominant
  discourses, 118; feminist analysis,
  110; prevention, 111; racist view,
  115; sexual stigma, 114
alterity, 163, 165–8
analytic frame, narrative, 104–5
Anderson, B., 37
Angola, 38
Anspach, R. R., 143
apartheid, 3–4, 10, 37–8, 189; aparatus,
  8; culture, 2; discourse, 24;
  dismantling, 5, 9; end of, 204;
  history, 57; ideology, 27; land
  dispossession, 20; language of, 56;
  policies, 195; psychologization, 79;
  regime, 201; sediments, 17; spatial
  organization, 18; state, 39, 142
'attention', practice of, 96

Barry, James, 140
Barthes, Roland, 68
Bassett, M., 110
Beall, J., 194, 196

Becker, M., 110, 117
Ben-Arie, O., 141
Bennett, F. J., 159
Bentham, Jeremy, 181
Bhoomi Sena project, India, 160
Billig, M., 25, 53
bisexuality, 11, 84–7, 89, 94, 202
Blomey, N. K., 23
Boeren, A., 160
'Boerstaat', 17
Botswana, AIDS, 110
Bradley, J., 147
Brinkgreve, C., 66–7
Brown, L. D., 159–60, 163
Browne, A., 127
Brownmiller, Susan, 128
Bulhan, Hussain, 190

Certeau, Michel de, 107
'change agents', 161
change, institutionalized, 44
Christianity, fundamentalist, 13, 180
Christopher, A. J., 20
class, 7
cognitive dissonance, 181
Cohen, J. M., 159
collective action, women's, 118–19
collocations, target words, 147, 149
colonialism(s), 1, 78, 97–8; imagination,
  19; psychological research, 126
communities: disempowered, 165;
  development work, 13; health
  projects, 159, 162, 199–200
confession, 2, 4, 33–5, 66–7, 76–8,
  83–5, 203
'conflict resolution', 35
conscience, knowledge of, 36
consciousness, changing, 112
constructs, spatial, 26
conventional wisdom, hegemonic,
  128–9
Cooper, Saths, 190